HEALTH INSURANCE POLITICS IN JAPAN

A volume in the series

The Culture and Politics of Health Care Work

Edited by Suzanne Gordon and Sioban Nelson

For a list of books in the series, visit our website at cornellpress.cornell.edu.

HEALTH INSURANCE POLITICS IN JAPAN

Policy Development, Government, and the Japan Medical Association

Takakazu Yamagishi

ILR PRESS

AN IMPRINT OF CORNELL UNIVERSITY PRESS   ITHACA AND LONDON

First published 2022 by Cornell University Press

Library of Congress Cataloging-in-Publication Data

Names: Yamagishi, Takakazu, 1972– author.
Title: Health insurance politics in Japan : policy development, government, and the Japan Medical Association / Takakazu Yamagishi.
Description: Ithaca [New York] : Cornell University Press, 2022. | Series: The culture and politics of health care work | Includes bibliographical references and index.
Identifiers: LCCN 2021038895 (print) | LCCN 2021038896 (ebook) | ISBN 9781501763496 (hardcover) | ISBN 9781501763502 (epub) | ISBN 9781501763519 (pdf)
Subjects: LCSH: Nihon Ishikai—Political activity | Medical care—Political aspects—Japan. | Health insurance—Government policy—Japan. | Medical policy—Japan—History—20th century. | Medical policy—Japan—History—21st century.
Classification: LCC RA395.J3 Y34 2022 (print) | LCC RA395.J3 (ebook) | DDC 368.38/200952—dc23
LC record available at https://lccn.loc.gov/2021038895
LC ebook record available at https://lccn.loc.gov/2021038896

For Yuka,
and our two sons, Chikara and Kazushi

Contents

Acknowledgments

When I earned a doctoral degree from Johns Hopkins University, I promised myself that I would publish three books within ten years. The first one, based on my dissertation, is *War and Health Insurance Policy in Japan and the United States*. The second, which discusses the political history of the American health insurance system, is *America no Iryōseido no Seijishi* (A Political History of American Health Care). This Japanese health insurance policy book, my third, fulfills my promise.

It took much longer to write this book than I had expected. But the additional time was not a waste. My mentors, colleagues, and friends inspired me to improve my overall argument and sentences. I truly enjoyed this writing process.

First, I would like to thank my three mentors at Keio University and Johns Hopkins University: Fumiaki Kubo, Adam Sheingate, and Matthew Crenson. Even after I was no longer their student, they continued to teach me how enjoyable academic life is, and they are still inspiring me very much. Words cannot express how much they mean to me. All I can do to repay their kindness is to keep enjoying my research and do the same for my students.

Second, my thanks go to my colleagues at Nanzan University, including Kiyoshi Aoki, Robert Croker, Brad Deacon, Hiroshi Fujimoto, Kazuki Kagohashi, Eriko Hiraiwa, Tōru Hanaki, Masahiro Hoshino, Richard Miles, Satoshi Moriizumi, Mikihiro Moriyama, Tadashi Nakamura, Michiyo Obi, Kōji Ōtake, Midori Shikano, and Tetsuya Yamada. They have made my time at Nanzan happy.

Third, I would like to thank my friends who have inspired me in many ways for this book. They include Katsuhiko Abe, Bob Buker, Kiyomi Buker, Jinlene Chan, Takashi Fujimoto, Kyōji Hara, Atsuko Itō, Nakahiro Iwata, Taku Kambayashi, Miki Katō, Nozomu Kawai, Yasushi Matsuoka, Takeya Matsuzaki, Toshihiro Nakayama, Yōtakō Okamoto, Masataka Ōsawa, Shū Takagi, Setsuko Takase, Mizuho Yagi, and Hirofumi Yamazaki. There were also many government officials who have kindly shared their views with me. The Japan Medical Association has also provided me with its organizational information. I appreciate them very much.

I could not have written this book without institutional support. Nanzan University has given me a sabbatical twice. I owe this book to the university's generous attitude toward research. I would also like to thank former Dean Mamoru Saitō for making my second sabbatical possible and allowing me to complete this book project. My research for this book was also financially supported by the Nanzan University's Pache Research Subsidy I-A-2 and the Japan Society for the Promotion of Science's Grant-in-Aid for Scientific Research.

Part of this book has been presented at Arizona State University, Johns Hopkins University, Nazareth College, and McGill University. I would like to thank Tomoko Shimomura, Erin Chung, Ken Rhee, and Juan Wang for hosting my talks. I also made presentations at academic conferences, such as the International Studies Association, the Social Science History Association, and the Southern Political Science Association. I would like to thank the discussants and audiences for contributing to improving my project.

Earlier versions of portions of this research have been published previously, though they have since been extensively rewritten with new sources. These previous publications include "A Short Biography of Takemi Taro, the President of the Japan Medical Association," *Academia Social Sciences* 1 (January 2011); *War and Health Insurance Policy in Japan and the United States* (Baltimore: Johns Hopkins University Press, 2011); "The Japan Medical Association and Its Political Development," *Academia Social Sciences* 9 (June 2015); and "Health Insurance Politics in the 1940s and 50s: The Japan Medical Association and Policy Development," *Journal of International and Advanced Japanese Studies* 9 (March 2016).

My research assistants, Junko Itō, Sachiko Nishimura and Tomomi Sasaki, helped me to complete the publication process. My students at Nanzan also motivated me to do my best. I particularly thank the students in my special seminar. Their great curiosity and strong will to engage in critical thinking in my class encouraged me to think more deeply about my project.

To publish this book, I was very fortunate that Sioban Nelson, coeditor of the Cornell series the Culture and Politics of Health Care Work, asked questions and gave suggestions that improved the shape of my project. I am also grateful for Suzanne Gordon, the other coeditor of the series. My copy editor, Katy Meigs, was not only patient with my English but also willing to discuss whether anything was lost in translation. All errors and omissions are my own fault.

Lastly, please allow me to mention my family. My mom and dad, Michiyo and Shigeo Yamagishi, always believe in me. They always say to me, "Wherever you are and whatever you do, we are happy if you live happily." My two brothers, Yoshinori and Katsuaki Yamagishi, have also given me warm support.

The biggest thank-you goes to my wife, Yuka, and our two sons, Chikara and Kazushi. Yuka not only supports me emotionally but is also a "special research assistant" for me. Yuka graduated from the University of Maryland to become a pediatric dentist. After that, she became one of the few to pass the special exam to be licensed in Japan as well. She knows how US medicine and Japanese medicine both work in the field. Her experiences helped me polish my analytical lens. My final thanks go to our two sons, Chikara and Kazushi, who live with their mom in Maryland and go to local schools there. They were five and three years old, respectively, when the first book came out. But now it is great to see them old enough to read my drafts and helpfully correct grammatical errors. I am so blessed to have Yuka, Chikara, and Kazushi in my life.

Abbreviations

Chūikyō	Central Social Insurance Medical Council
GHQ	General Headquarters
GJMA	Greater Japan Medical Association
GMHI	Government-Managed Health Insurance
HI	Health Insurance Act
JDA	Japan Dental Association
JHA	Japan Hospital Association
JMA	Japan Medical Association
LDP	Liberal Democratic Party
MHW	Ministry of Health and Welfare
MHLW	Ministry of Health, Labor, and Welfare
MOF	Ministry of Finance
NHI	National Health Insurance Act
PHW	Public Health and Welfare Section
SCAP	Supreme Commander for Allied Powers
SMHI	Society-Managed Health Insurance

Notes on the Text

I use the Japanese spelling of "oo" and "ou" as "ō" and "uu" as "ū." But the names of cities and regions that are commonly known in the English-speaking world are written without diacritical marks—for example, Tokyo (not Toukyou or Tōkyō). According to Japanese custom, I have adopted the order of surname first and given name last for authors of Japanese publications. Otherwise, the order is given name first, then surname. Original Japanese words are inserted in cases in which these words could have other English translations.

HEALTH INSURANCE POLITICS IN JAPAN

INTRODUCTION

To Understand the Health Insurance Policy Development in Japan

In July 1971, Fuji Television Network broadcast a debate between Tarō Takemi, the president of the Japan Medical Association (JMA), and Noboru Saitō, the minister of health and welfare, about negotiating conditions for ending the doctors' strike. Takemi had an overwhelming presence, giving a long lecture on his ideas regarding health care reform. In contrast, Saitō looked like a student of Takemi's. At last, Takemi went on to have a meeting with Prime Minister Eisaku Satō, also televised. In the meeting, one hour and forty minutes long, Satō promised Takemi that the government would reform the health insurance system. These events were widely reported.

Why did the JMA conduct its strike at that time? How could a man from an interest group have enough political power to gain compromises directly from the prime minister? What did this episode mean for the development of health insurance policy of Japan? These questions are important for understanding why Japan has adopted the health insurance system the country has now. This book demonstrates what mechanisms have driven change and changelessness in the development of health insurance policy.

In general, doctors and the government are the two primary actors in health care politics. With their professional education, doctors may be medical scientists. With their special knowledge and experiences, they may be good policymakers because they know what patients need. Doctors also serve as health care providers who directly help patients get well. In addition, doctors are teachers who educate people about their health. With these many roles, doctors claim that they can best handle issues relating to medicine. They contend that they should

1

have the professional autonomy to make decisions about patients, while avoiding interventions from third parties, including the government.

The government has its own claims to expertise in the field of health care. Like doctors, those in government assert that medicine is a science. The government seeks to set standards in medical education and licensing and funds medical research. Paradoxically, the government also intervenes in health care because medicine is not a perfect science and can also be considered a human art. The government must clarify the extent to which it deems human nature as significant in determining the quality of medical treatment. The government also claims the justification to financially assist in caring for those who cannot afford to pay medical costs themselves.

To make the relationship between doctors and the government more difficult, doctors must work to make a living. They are often expected to treat each patient with urgent attention no matter what his or her financial condition is. Pro bono work is almost universally expected of doctors. In Japan, the term *ninjutsu* refers to the tradition that doctors have an obligation to give blessings to people, especially in those in a socially and economically weak position. However, like other workers, doctors have economic interests. They may seek to have better income by increasing their fees, while the government wants to keep health care costs under control. Politicians usually try to avoid tax increases in order to be elected and reelected. Thus, the main theater of battle between doctors and government is public health insurance, which involves government's measures to control health care costs.

Despite health care–related political battles over money, health care politics is also about how scientific knowledge can be used to improve people's health and lives; how individuals, organizations, and the government should behave; and eventually what kind of nation its people would like to make. Health policy reflects and affects how people are born, live, and die; how they interact and join organizations; with what principles and purpose they form the government. For these reasons, health care policy affects not only people's health but also the purpose of the government and the quality of democracy.

Health insurance politics differs among countries. This book focuses on the state of health insurance politics in Japan. Like other advanced countries (except the United States), Japan has a universal health insurance system. However, Japan has its own unique structure and culture, resulting largely from the historical development of health insurance policy and the relationship between doctors and the government. In some other countries, for example, the central government has more power than doctors in shaping health care policy, and in some countries doctors have a stronger national association. In some countries, religion plays a major role in the policy discourse. Some countries developed or expanded their national health insurance coverage later or more slowly. In some countries, the people are more deeply and widely interested in health care policy.

By looking at Japan through a lens of historical institutionalism—with its emphasis on how, through timing and sequence, institutions affect policy preference, strategy, and norms of political actors—we can understand how new health care policies arise and change. This book should give an insight not only to scholars but also to all countries that face health care problems. According to John Campbell and Naoki Ikegami, leading scholars in Japanese health care policy, one of the unique aspects of the Japanese health insurance system is that Japan has developed a commendable "low-cost and egalitarian system" through the "art of balance."[1] But, as this book shows, the Japanese system also has an important defect. Policy development during World War II and the postwar reconstruction prevented health care reform from being discussed except by the government and other limited political actors, and the debate was framed more from the standpoint of the nation's finances than in terms of the people's welfare. This book contributes to the discussion about how Japan adopted its system and how countries might develop health insurance systems suitable for aging societies in an era of globalization.

Before further discussing the development of the Japanese health care system, we need to (1) know how the Japanese health care system compares with the systems of other developed countries; (2) understand the theoretical framework used here for understanding the policy development mechanism; (3) know more about Tarō Takemi, an important figure in Japanese health care history; and (4) have a historical overview of health care policy at the end of the Tokugawa shogunate in order to understand the institutional and political contexts of the Meiji government.

The Japanese Health Care System in Comparison

After the Meiji Restoration in 1868, the new government implemented policies to increase the number of Western-style medical schools, hospitals, and doctors. The government also had to deal with public health problems including the spread of epidemic diseases. The Health Insurance Act of 1922 (Kenkō Hoken Hō) was the first major public health insurance legislation, which covered factory and mining workers in Japan.[2] Public health insurance then expanded from the late 1930s to the 1940s during World War II. The Diet finally passed legislation in 1958 that provided for universal coverage. Since then, many reforms have taken place, and these have not occurred in a political vacuum.

Health insurance is a mechanism that helps people be prepared for future health problems. Along with other factors, the health conditions of the people influence the extent to which the government wishes to intervene in health care financing. Many become frustrated when they observe that those who are not elderly are suffering from serious diseases or dying early, especially if the causes can be prevented. Their frustration is often directed toward the government, particularly after the welfare state developed following World War II. Existing political institutions and policies significantly affect the policy preferences and strategies of political actors and subsequent policy trajectories. The health conditions of the population, geography, and expenditures are all significant variables. International comparison is often used to justify the opinions of stakeholders. When setting policy agendas to respond to identified social problems, policymakers often consider the political implications and study what other countries do about similar problems.

An overview of health insurance programs in the G7 countries (Canada, France, Germany, Italy, Japan, the United Kingdom, and the United States) sets the background for the debate in Japan. Compared with other G7 countries, Japan's life expectancy at birth was shorter during the first half of the 1960s. However, by 1971, Japan's life expectancy at birth had become the longest (figure I.1). In addition, Japan drastically decreased its infant mortality rate during the early 1960s (figure I.2). These improvements were largely the result of expanded health care access, improved maternal and infant care, and rapid economic development.

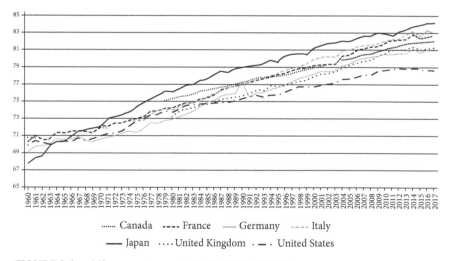

FIGURE I.1.   Life expectancy at birth (1960–2017)

Source: Organisation for Economic Co-operation and Development, "Life Expectancy at Birth," https://data .oecd.org/healthstat/life-expectancy-at-birth.htm, accessed March 15, 2020.

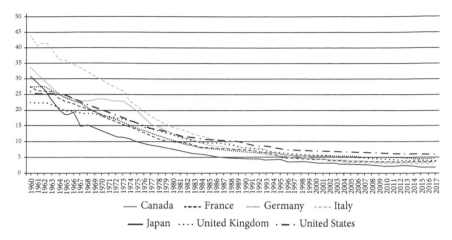

FIGURE I.2.   Infant mortality rates (deaths/1,000 live births, 1960–2017)

Source: Organisation for Economic Co-operation and Development, "Infant Mortality Rates," https://data.oecd
.org/healthstat/infant-mortality-rates.htm, accessed March 15, 2020.

Demography is an important factor in the debate about health care financing because elderly people tend to use more health care services. However, the
elderly generally vote more consistently than younger people, and as stakeholders they have attempted to pressure the government to continue and expand their
policy benefits. At the same time, younger people's financial contributions to
public health care services outbalance the amount of these services that younger
people use, and they wish to avoid being overburdened. When young people outnumber the elderly, health care costs can be fulfilled through smaller contributions from the nonelderly population. The present decreased fertility rate,
however, results in a financial burden on the nonelderly population.

Japan's fertility rate began to significantly decrease, compared with other G7
countries, during the mid-1980s (figure I.3). Women married and gave birth later
than they had previously, and more women were not marrying. To maintain the
same size population, it is necessary to maintain a fertility rate of around two
offspring per couple. In 2005, Japan hit the lowest fertility rate of all G7 countries, at 1.26. After World War II, Japan's population was much younger than
that of other countries. However, over the two decades from 1984 to 2004, Japan became the oldest country (figure I.4). From a political perspective, with this
larger elderly population, it is increasingly difficult for the government to respond
to the elderly's health care needs.

If the price of medical services and drugs is maintained or decreased, it would
be possible to prevent a sharp rise in health care costs while the population is aging. Although in some cases free market mechanisms work to decrease costs, the

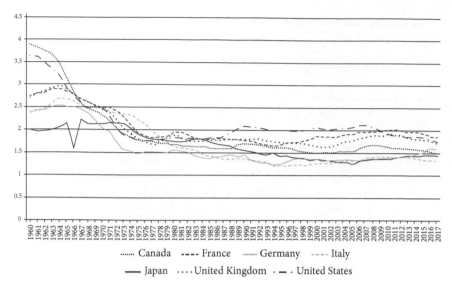

FIGURE I.3. Fertility rates (children per woman, 1960–2017)

*Source: Organisation for Economic Co-operation and Development, "Fertility Rates," https://data.oecd.org/pop
/fertility-rates.htm, accessed March 15, 2020.*

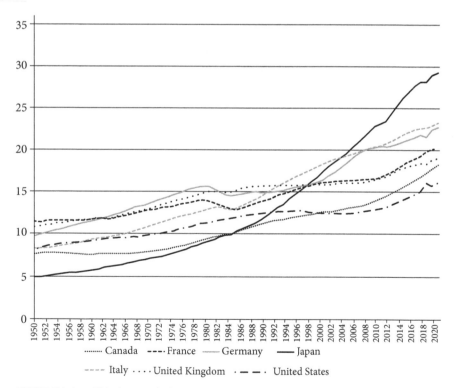

FIGURE I.4. Elderly population (% of population, age 65 and over, 1950–2020)

*Source: Organisation for Economic Co-operation and Development, "Elderly Population," https://data.oecd.org
/pop/elderly-population.htm, accessed February 23, 2021.*

central government usually needs to exercise its power to decrease costs. The government's control includes regulating the price of drugs and fee schedules for medical services. When attempting to reduce health care costs in this way, the government often faces strong opposition from medical associations, pharmacists' associations, and the pharmaceutical industry. The government can also increase taxes or premiums to deal with the rise in health care costs. From a political perspective, however, doing so is difficult, especially for a conservative party.

Total health care expenditures and government health care expenditures can be compared (figures I.5 and I.6). By 1980, Japan was competing with Britain for the bottom ranking in expenditure levels. Japan then increased its expenditures to respond to its fast-aging population. It can be seen that the Japanese government, even with the largest elderly population, succeeded in keeping down costs. These figures, which provide a comparison with other countries, have been useful to stakeholders in Japan in determining what steps are required to achieve their policy goals.

Finally, we can get an overview of the structure of the five different types of health insurance systems of Japan, France, Germany, the United States, and Britain (table I.1). There are four important elements that determine the structure. The first element is the source of financial resources. Britain provides extensive financing for its National Health Service from the general revenue, whereas other countries use a social insurance scheme. There are also differences in the

FIGURE I.5. Total health care spending (% of GDP, 1972–2018)

Source: Organisation for Economic Co-operation and Development, "Health Spending," https://data.oecd.org/healthres/health-spending.htm, accessed February 22, 2021.

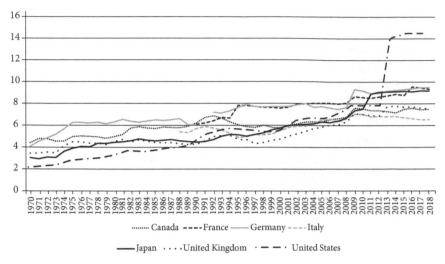

.... Canada ---- France ——— Germany --- Italy

——— Japan · · · · United Kingdom · — · United States

FIGURE I.6. Government health spending (% of GDP, 1970–2018)

Source: Organisation for Economic Co-operation and Development, "Health Spending," https://data.oecd.org /healthres/health-spending.htm, accessed March 15, 2020.

TABLE I.1 Health insurance systems

COUNTRY	RESOURCE	TARGET	OUT–OF–POCKET PAYMENT	FEE SCHEDULE
Japan	Social insurance	Universal (1961)	All 30%	Fee–for–service
France	Social insurance	Universal (1945)	Hospital 20% Outpatient 30% Pharmacy 35%	Fee–for–service
Germany	Social insurance	Universal (join either GVK (public) or PKV (private)) (2009)	Hospital 10 euros Outpatient None Pharmacy 10%	GKV (Capitation) PKV (Fee–for–service)
United States	Social insurance	Nearly universal (compulsory for those over 65, with a disability, or with low income)	Medicare: flat fee Medicaid: varies by states	Fee–for–service
Britain	Tax	Universal (1948)	None	GP (per capita, fee–for–service) Hospital (HRG)

Source: Ministry of Health, Labor, and Welfare, "OECD Kameikoku no Hokeniryōhi no Jyōkyō" (State of OECD countries' health security cost), https://www.mhlw.go.jp/stf/seisakunitsuite/bunya/kenkou_iryou/iryouhoken /iryouhoken11/index.html, accessed March 4, 2020. Data for Japan are from 2014, and for other countries from 2013.

same scheme. For example, while adopting the social insurance scheme, the Japanese government provides heavy subsidies to some public programs. The second element is the extent to which health insurance coverage reaches the population. All of the five countries, except the United States, guarantee universal coverage. The timing of introduction of coverage has varied among countries. A variation is that Germany and the United States allow private health insurance plans to participate in their systems. The third element is how much patients pay out of pocket. This is the financial burden passed on to those who derive benefits. This may seem to contradict the principle of social insurance. The fourth element is the type of fee schedule for doctors. A fee-for-service system provides health insurance payments to doctors separately for each service. A capitation system makes health insurance payments for each insured person.

History Matters

Many English-language works have been published on health care policies in Japan. Campbell and Ikegami describe the key political actors and the system of public health insurance and health care providers and examine how the health care system is well balanced and health care costs controlled.[3] Yoneyuki Sugita focuses on what drove the enactment of the Health Insurance Act of 1922; how the health insurance system quantitively and qualitatively changed from 1937 to 1945; why postwar policy development differed from the Beveridge Plan in Britain; and how the concept of fairness affected the discourse on health insurance policy.[4] Although Sugita tried to examine the political process ideational background for these policy changes, no studies published in English have thus far focused systematically on how Japan historically came to adopt its current health insurance system.

There is considerable Japanese literature on the development of the Japanese health care system. Takeshi Kawakami, in a major work on the development of the medical practitioner system from the Meiji era to the early 1960s, focused primarily on how the government attempted to intervene in the medical-practitioner system.[5] Akira Sugaya focused more on the legal side of the health care system and how health care interest groups developed from the Meiji era to the early 1970s. He concluded that the health insurance system and the health provider system did not develop through a well-coordinated process.[6] Kenji Yoshihara and Masaru Wada, former Ministry of Health and Welfare bureaucrats, provide a detailed description of how the health insurance system developed since the first major legislation in 1922 until the end of the twentieth century.[7] Finally, by covering the premodern period to the 1980s, Kiyosada Sōmae tries to grasp the development of health care politics behind Japan's adopting, maintaining, and changing its health care system. While his book helps one understand the overall political environment that affects health care reforms, the work does not focus much on the details of health insurance politics.[8]

This book hopes to fill the gap these literatures left by examining why the health insurance policies of Japan changed in a certain manner and at a specific time and why political actors acted in a specific way. An analytical lens of historical institutionalism helps one see how history matters to the way policy develops and political actors behave. Historical institutionalism emphasizes what Paul Pierson calls "placing politics in time" by seeing political phenomena not as snapshots but as "moving pictures."[9] In the moving pictures, historical institutionalism pays careful attention to the process through which new policy causes new politics. Drastic policy changes—what are called critical junctures—often accompany external pressures, such as war and economic depression.[10] New policy causes new politics by making new beneficiary groups that support the policy, establishing new rules for stakeholders to follow, and constraining the range of policy alternatives in subsequent periods. This process is called path dependence. Pierson describes it this way: "Over time 'the road not chosen' becomes an increasingly distant, increasingly unreachable alternative."[11]

In the development of Japan's health care system, the Meiji Restoration and World War II were turning points. While health insurance was not born at that time, the Meiji Restoration created the basic institutional arrangement of a health care system. During World War II, to make war mobilization more efficient, the government drastically expanded public health insurance to near-universal coverage and set up its administrative structure. This period became a critical juncture in health insurance policy development. Both turning points share a similarity: doctors did not collectively have much influence. During the Meiji Restoration, the government had almost dominant power to set up a new health care system to catch up with the Western nations, while doctors' associations were still absent. During World War II, the government downplayed and eventually nationalized the JMA and conducted top-down health insurance reforms. The drastic policy changes at these two historical crossroads narrowed the policy options in other periods and shaped political actors' strategies and policy preferences.

The historical development of health insurance policy in Japan also provides comparative and transnational studies scholars with an interesting window into Japan as a comparative case. Japan introduced medical traditions from the Netherlands (in the Edo period), Britain (in the Meiji period and the post–World War II reconstruction period), France (in the Meiji period), Germany (in the Meiji period), and the United States (during the US-led occupation after World

War II). This book demonstrates how those imported ideas were adapted into the existing institutional and political arrangements.

Tarō Takemi and the JMA

Historical institutionalism helps shed light on the development of health care policy in Japan, in part by contextualizing the role that Tarō Takemi played in the development of health care policy. Scholars have struggled to determine his role. Takemi served as the JMA's president from 1957 to 1982, and he made the JMA into a major political player. It is impossible to talk about the political history of health insurance policy without situating the role Takemi played.

The JMA, with Takemi's strong leadership, attracted media attention at the time because of the JMA's determined stance against the government. Scholars such as William Steslicke have investigated how the JMA developed and became an interest group with such power to affect the government's decisions.[12] Taku Nomura has paid special attention to the JMA's relationship with the government. Unlike Steslicke, however, Nomura argues that despite the JMA's surface hostility toward the government, especially bureaucrats, the association often had a cooperative relationship with the government.[13]

As a student of historical institutionalism, I do not engage directly in these debates but instead tackle the question of why the relationship between the government and the JMA appeared the way it did to Steslicke and Nomura. I do so by analyzing the institutional and political contexts Takemi was immersed in during his presidency. Rather than making fundamental reforms to a health insurance system that had been solidified by the time he became the JMA president, what Takemi could do was to gain material benefits within the existing institutional arrangements. In the process of conducting this analysis, I address why Japan's health care has been relatively low-cost even with the great political power of the JMA, which might be expected to have pushed up health care costs.

Medicine in the Pre-Meiji Period

Before addressing the emergence of a new health care system in the early Meiji era, we need an overview of pre-Meiji medicine, given that a health care system does not arise in an institutional vacuum. For a long time, Japanese medicine was an adaptation of Chinese medicine. Japanese medicine emphasized the balance among energy (*ki*), blood (*ketsu*), and body fluid (*sui*), rather than the treatment of the cause of a disease. Herbs and acupuncture were used to cure people with health problems. During the Age of Discovery, in the sixteenth century, Japan first encountered medicine from Spain and Portugal. During the mid-Tokugawa era, Dutch medicine also was introduced and systematically taught. Although the Meiji government conducted sweeping medical reforms, some traditions that had developed during the Tokugawa shogunate (1603–1867) remained.

As in other parts of the world, during the ancient period in Japan prayer and other spiritual activities were often considered the solution to diseases, because health problems were thought to be caused by the presence of gods, demons, or other supernatural entities. The development of increasingly practical medicine, such as the use of herbs, was influenced by practices in Korea and China. When Buddhism was introduced into Japan during the middle of the sixth century from Baekje, a kingdom in southwestern Korea, many priests also moved from the Korean Peninsula to Japan. Many of the priests were intellectuals, and some of them specialized in medicine. The Taihō Code (Taihō Ritsuryō) of 703 created a form of Japanese government administered by legal codes. The legal codes were based on those used by the Tang dynasty in China. Included in the code was medical education, which the Ministry of the Imperial Household took responsibility for overseeing.[14]

Medical positions in the Imperial Court were hereditary. The Tanba family provides an example. Yasuyori Tanba was born in 912. He wrote a thirty-volume medical text called *Ishinpō* and presented it to the Imperial Court in 984. The text was based on many books about medicine written in China during the Sui dynasty (581–618) and Tang dynasty (618–907). Tanba's text was kept in the Imperial Court as a treasure and was never allowed to be removed. The Imperial Court gave Yasuyori the name *Tanba* as a family name for privileged administrative positions, and his descendants continued to serve as doctors in the Imperial Court.[15]

During the Kamakura era (1185–1333), Kanpō, traditional medicine based on Chinese practices, was spread by Buddhist priests from the nobles to the ordinary people.[16] Many priests went to China, and new medical practices and theories were introduced to Japan. Many medical books were written, based on medical textbooks from the Song dynasty (960–1279), Jin dynasty (1115–1234), and Yuan dynasty (1271–1368). The Ming dynasty (1368–1644) particularly had an impact on Japan in the Muromachi era (1336–1573). During the nearly three hundred years of the Ming dynasty, medical books were published and widely read by ordinary people for the first time.[17]

While Japanese medicine was advancing through the importing of theories and practices developed in China, the Japanese suddenly encountered a different kind of medicine when a Portuguese ship drifted ashore on Tanegashima

Island in the southern part of Kyushu in 1543. This incident and the subsequent contact with Portugal brought three important things to Japan: guns, which changed the way battles were fought; Christianity, which influenced the way some people perceived themselves and their society; and European medicine, which showed the Japanese a different method of curing illness.

Luis Almeida of Lisbon was one of the first doctors to bring Western medicine to Japan. He had studied medicine but sailed to India as a merchant. In 1552, he first landed in Japan and met Cosme de Torres, one of the first Christian missionaries, who had arrived in Japan in 1549 with Francis Xavier. In 1555, Almeida decided to give away his wealth, join the Jesuits, and return to Japan. He convinced the feudal lord Sōrin (or Yoshishige) Ōtomo, a Christian convert, to build a hospital, which although primitive was the first in Japan. Hospitals spread to other areas with the missionaries.[18] In 1587, however, the chief adviser to the emperor (*kanpaku*), Hideyoshi Toyotomi, issued the Bateren Tsuihōrei, an edict expelling the Christian missionaries. All the Christian hospitals were closed. Nevertheless, by that time, many Japanese healers had gained knowledge of effective surgical procedures that were not part of the traditional Kanpō. These healers passed if very limited this knowledge down to their pupils.[19]

The Tokugawa shogunate continued to prohibit Christianity and any literature written in foreign languages. In 1636, the shogunate officially banned trade with Western nations. The Dutch were excepted from the ban because their commerce was not usually connected with Christian missionaries. Dutch ships were allowed to land at an artificial island in Nagasaki. In 1720, when the seventh shogun, Yoshimune Tokugawa, allowed the introduction of foreign literature not related to Christianity, written knowledge of Dutch medicine was imported into Japan through the island.[20] Philip Franz von Siebold was stationed in Nagasaki as a doctor to serve the Dutch people there; however, he became famous by teaching Western medicine to the Japanese. Approximately a hundred Dutch doctors had visited Nagasaki by the time Japan ended its isolationist policy.[21]

Traditional Chinese medicine did not quickly die out. Rather, it evolved during this time. Although trade with China was not prohibited under the Tokugawa shogunate's isolationist policy, the Qing dynasty (1636–1912) did not have a big impact on Japan. Medical historian Hiroshi Kosoto points out that in the late seventeenth century—the Genroku era (1688–1704), considered the golden age of the Edo period—Japanese medicine began to develop in its own way. The ordinary people benefited from many medical books that were published with easier terminology and more Japanese interpretations. The long and stable Tokugawa shogunate made it possible for doctors to develop medicine, especially internal medicine, as a result of the lack of wars, as well as to improve doctors' social and economic status.[22]

Traditional medicine started to be called at that time *Kanpō* to distinguish it from Dutch medicine, which was called *Ranpō*.[23] Dutch medicine became an inspiration to innovative doctors. Dissatisfied with the way Kanpō explained the internal body system, Genpaku Sugita, the Obama Domain's official doctor, decided to translate a Dutch medical book titled *Ontleedkundige Tafelen* into Japanese.[24] After an approximately three-year struggle without the use of a Dutch-Japanese dictionary, *Kaitai Shinsho* was published. This book helped ensure the widespread use of Dutch medicine among Japanese doctors.

In 1857, the Tokugawa shogunate began to invest in Western medical education. The shogunate invited J. L. C. Pompe van Meerdervoort, a Dutch military doctor who had trained at the Utrecht Military Medical College, to teach Western medicine in Japan. Ryōjun Matsumoto played an important role in creating the Medical Teaching School (Igaku Denshūjo) for Pompe in Nagasaki.[25] The shogunate and domains sent their delegates to study there. The first graduates included those who became leaders in promoting Western medicine in the Meiji era, including Takanaka (or Shōchū) Satō, Tōyō Sasaki, Jun Iwasa, and Sensai Nagayo.[26]

Furthermore, the Tokugawa shogunate officially accepted Western medicine after an 1858 incident in which the thirteenth shogun, Iesada Tokugawa, suffered from a serious illness. Naosuke Ii, the chief minister (*tairō*) of the shogunate, decided to try any means, in addition to Kanpō medicine, to cure Iesada. Genboku Itō and Seikai Totsuka, who had studied Western medicine under the guidance of Siebold in Nagasaki, were appointed as shogunate physicians, called *okuishi*. Although Iesada was not cured, this marked the first time Western-style medical doctors were assigned this position.[27]

In 1860, the shogunate placed the Otamagaike Vaccination Institute (Otamagaike Shutōsho), which was created by Itō and Shunsai Ōtsuki in 1858, under the shogunate's management to advance the study of Western medicine.[28] Ōtsuki was the first head of the school. In 1861, the school was renamed the School of Western Medical Science (Seiyō Igakusho). The head position was handed to Kōan Ogata, Taizen Satō, Takanaka Satō, and Ryōjun Matsumoto in succession. The school comprised three divisions: teaching, autopsy, and smallpox vaccination. The school's efforts significantly contributed to the promotion of Western medicine during the Meiji era beginning in 1868.[29]

Although the Tokugawa shogunate had an isolationist policy, more and more doctors and ordinary people were exposed to Western medicine because of the Dutch. In particular, after Pompe instituted his program of medical education in Nagasaki, Japanese doctors began to learn and pass on Western medicine in a systematic manner. The shogunate officially admitted the effectiveness of Western medicine and founded the first medical school based on Western medicine. Although Kanpō doctors were still dominant at the end of the Tokugawa shogunate, doctors increasingly influenced by Western medicine helped the new government to initiate the westernization of Japanese medicine as a whole.

WESTERNIZING MEDICINE

Although it is controversial whether the Meiji Restoration was a "revolution" or not, it was an immense step for Japan toward becoming a modern nation. The Meiji Restoration was a reaction to external pressure brought by the Western nations. Commodore Matthew Perry came to Uraga with black ships powered by coal-fired steam engines and demanded that the Tokugawa shogunate open Japan's major five ports to the United States, which meant that Japan would have to end its nearly two-hundred-year isolationist policy. The way the Tokugawa shogunate handled this demand and the following events ignited opposition from domains such as the Satsuma, Chōshū, and Mito. To ease the domestic tension, the Tokugawa shogunate decided to hand over governance authority to the emperor.

The Meiji government's highest priority was to modernize—that is, westernize—the nation. The government implemented policies to abolish the feudal system, strengthen the economy, modernize and expand the military, change the political system, and become more like contemporary Western nations. The government needed to become stronger to rid itself of unequal treaties and prevent colonization by the Western nations. The Meiji government westernized Japan from the top down. It established the Imperial Diet in 1889, won the First Sino-Japanese War in 1895,[1] signed a treaty of military alliance with Britain, and won the Russo-Japanese War in 1905. A democratic movement gradually emerged, but party politics was not much developed, and the elite class— mostly founders of the Meiji government—controlled politics. By the time the Meiji Emperor died in 1912, Japan had become a modern nation and was recognized by many Western nations as an independent power in Asia.

Health care policy became part of the government's westernization plan. The government took the lead in adopting Western medicine as the official standard. Meiji officials had almost a free hand to create a new Japanese health care system. Health care policy became a tool to prevent epidemic catastrophes, to strengthen the military, control social order, and be accountable to the people. The early Meiji period laid out the structural foundation of a Japanese health care system though health insurance did not come in to being yet. This chapter describes the six aspects of health care that the Meiji government took control of: medical education, medical licensing, hospitals and clinics, health care administration, medical associations, and the relationship with doctors and pharmacists. Development in these areas had a major impact on the later health care system, narrowing government options in public health insurance.

Medical Education

As described in the introductory chapter, the Tokugawa shogunate had begun to adopt Western medicine right before it collapsed. The School of Western Medical Science (Seiyō Igakusho) was established in 1860. It was renamed as the School of Medical Science (Igakusho) in 1863. After studying under J. L. C. Pompe van Meerdervoort, Kōan Ogata created seven courses of study: physics, chemistry, physiology, pathology, pharmaceutics, internal medicine, and surgery. Ryōjun Matsumoto set up the order of the curriculum. Doctors of Western medicine were trained in this school. Kenzō Ogawa, medical historian, contends that the 1863 reform was "very important because Western medicine was approved as the standard for Japanese medicine."[2]

The period when the Tokugawa shogunate directly promoted Western medicine, however, was too brief for this standard to spread to the entire nation. The dominant majority among doctors were Kanpō doctors. They were not systematically trained because the shogunate had not intervened much in their practice. Primitive medical-training facilities, which were often connected with temples, existed for training in Kanpō medicine. But, overall, the medical training was limited.[3] Many doctors began to practice after only a brief training under senior doctors without basic formal medical education. In 1873, soon after the end of the shogunate era, a newspaper article noted that four or five out of ten doctors, most of whom practiced Kanpō medicine, were illiterate.[4]

In 1868, Tsunenori Takashina, whose family had served as doctors in the Imperial Household in Kyoto, submitted a petition to the newly created government to make Western medicine the officially approved standard. In 1869, the Meiji government issued the Proclamation of Western Medicine (Seiyō Ijutsu

Sashiyurushi) declaring that Japan adopted Western medicine as the national standard.[5] Westernization of medicine was part of the government's effort for "enriching the nation and building up national defenses" (*fukoku kyōhei*). From its civil war battles with the Tokugawa forces, the government realized that Kanpō was ineffective for curing injured soldiers. It became clear that Western surgical procedures were necessary for a strong military. Masujirō Ōmura, a military surgeon general, claimed that "Japanese medicine has to be westernized. Chinese medicine is useless in military hospitals."[6] Hiroshi Kosoto, medical historian, points out that Kanpō and Western medicine were qualitatively different. He writes, "While Kanpō emphasizes individual body conditions and symptoms, Western medicine is concerned with surgical procedures and public health. The military needed Western medicine to deal with large groups."[7] The elites in the new government were the main figures pressing for developing Western medical education.

Although the government began to actively engage in a policy of medical education to promote Western medicine and improve the quality of doctors, the government was not sure which Western country Japan should emulate. Many Japanese doctors had become familiar with Dutch medicine during the Tokugawa era. Britain, France, and the United States, however, were also possible models because of their contacts with Japan. In 1869, Jun Iwasa and Tomoyasu Sagara were appointed to direct medical education reform. They had full authority in medical affairs.[8]

British medicine initially gained attention because the United States, an English-speaking country, first opened diplomacy with Japan. English as a language was studied by Japanese elites, and it was natural that British medicine gained attention as a model for Japan.[9] British medicine was familiar to many Japanese in the early Meiji era because of William Willis. Willis came to Japan as the British legation's doctor in 1861 and later became a teacher of surgery in the medical faculty of a preceding institution of Tokyo Imperial University. He taught Kensai Ikeda, Tadanori Ishiguro, Tōyō Sasaki, and Jun Iwasa, who became leaders in adopting Western medicine. The British minister to Japan, Harry Smith Parks, also encouraged the Meiji government to adopt British-style medicine.[10] Thus, it once appeared that British medicine would become the model for Japanese medical education.

Iwasa, however, supported adopting the German model. Having researched different types of medicine in major European countries, he concluded, "In Europe, there are no countries better than Germany in medicine." To convince those who supported British medicine, Sagara also claimed, "Britain tends to despise the Japanese. The United States is too new of a country to have developed its medical education. Germany, as a national polity, is a similar country to Japan, although it is less known in Asia."[11] Shungaku Matsudaira, former head of Echizen Domain, headed the administration of education at that time. Iwasa was also from Echizen Domain. This coincidence helped Iwasa persuade the others to accept his preference. The government thus decided that Japanese medicine would be based on the German model. This was not so new to the Japanese, because Dutch medicine was often based on translations of German medical texts.[12]

In 1874, as the first step in formally adopting Western medicine, the government issued the Medical Rules and Regulations (Isei), which importantly included medical education being based on Western medicine. The draft of the Medical Rules and Regulations, with its eighty-five articles, was prepared by Sagara, the first head of the Medical Bureau (Imu Kyoku) of the Ministry of Education (Monbu Shō). In 1874, Sensai Nagayo succeeded Sagara and continued Sagara's work. Nagayo had intensively studied the European medical system. In 1871, he was dispatched as a member of what is known as the Iwakura mission to Europe and the United States. While the main purpose of the mission was to renegotiate the unequal treaties, the delegates also did research on politics, economy, society, and culture. Nagayo researched the legal systems and the administration of medicine. He was greatly inspired by the concept of "public health" or *gesundheitspfege*. He understood this to mean that the government needed to protect the population's general health and that the administrative system needed to be based not only on medical science but also on other academic disciplines. Such concepts did not then exist in East Asia.[13]

The promulgation of the Medical Rules and Regulations was a top-down government policy to westernize medical education and produce doctors who could practice Western medicine. Akira Sugaya states, "The nature of the Medical Rules and Regulations was that Japanese medical traditions were totally neglected while the Western system was transplanted."[14] He also points out its impact: "The Medical Rules and Regulations created a trajectory of development of a private-practitioner system and suggested a clear transformation from the traditional Kanpō to Western medicine."[15]

To take command of medical education, the Meiji government created Tokyo Imperial University's medical faculty in 1877. The School of Medical Science, which the Meiji government inherited from the Tokugawa shogunate, was its predecessor.[16] The new government continued to develop medical education based on Western medicine. In 1871, after Sagara and Iwasa's decision to adopt German medicine, the government invited two German doctors, Benjamin Leopold Müller and Theodor Eduard Hoffmann, to reform Japan's medical education. Meanwhile, the British doctor Willis was fired from his teaching position.[17]

After creating Tokyo Imperial University's medical faculty to take the lead in medical education, the government also needed to create regional medical schools. Under the domain system there were some schools teaching Western medicine, though they were limited in number and quality. Kumamoto Seishunkan and Fukuoka Saiseikan, established in 1756 and 1868, respectively, were examples of these schools. Based on these foundations, the Meiji government attached medical technical schools to regional public hospitals.[18] The number of public medical schools increased from nine in 1876 to forty-seven by 1880.[19]

In 1882, the government issued its Medical School Regulations (Igakkō Kisoku), which stipulated that "excellent" medical schools had to have at least three doctors of medicine (MDs) on their faculties. If they wanted to be considered "good," they had to have at least one. At that time, only Tokyo Imperial University was able to turn out MD graduates. This regulation confirmed Tokyo Imperial University as the dominant power over regional medical schools, creating a clear hierarchy in the world of Japanese medicine—"the pyramidal structure."[20] With Tokyo Imperial University at the top of the pyramid, government had control of medical education.[21]

Medical Licensing

In addition to creating medical schools, the new Meiji government created a licensing system for improving the quality of Western medicine doctors. As many people still practiced medicine without formal education, the government began to consider making national regulations about who should be allowed to practice medicine. Previously, there had been no such national rule. In 1868, soon after the government was established, it issued the Proclamation of Regulations for Medical Science and the Promotion of Medical Science (Igaku Torishimari oyobi Igaku Shōrei ni kansuru Fukoku). This proclamation suggested a policy direction that would result in a national board examination for doctors.[22]

The Medical Rules and Regulations of 1874, moreover, became the foundation for the medical licensing system. Sensai Nagayo, head of the Medical Bureau of the Education Ministry, took the lead.[23] The Medical Rules and Regulations included articles requiring medical licensing exams in the big prefectures of Tokyo, Kyoto, and Osaka. In 1876, the exam was required in all prefectures. In 1879, the government had the first national licensing exam created by the Home Ministry. In 1883, the government created a comprehensive legal structure with the Regulation regarding Medical Licensing (Ishi Menkyo Kisoku) and the Regulation regarding the Medical Licensing Exam (Ijutsu Kaigyō Shiken Kisoku).[24] New doctors were now allowed to practice either by completing a course of formal medical education or by passing the licensing exam.[25]

The Medical Practitioners' Act of 1906 (Ishi Hō) confirmed the policy direction by requiring doctors to complete formal medical education, either university medical school or medical vocational school, in order to practice. The act abolished the path for doctors to practice without formal education, and the licensing system was absorbed into the hierarchy, which had Tokyo Imperial University and the government at the top.[26]

Because of the policy to westernize the practice of medicine in Japan, the number of doctors trained in Western medicine grew rapidly. The Ministry of Education noted that in 1874 doctors trained in Western medicine were only 19 percent of the total number of doctors, while those practicing Kanpō medicine accounted for 81 percent.[27] By 1896, however, doctors of Western medicine increased to 36 percent of the total.[28] By 1925, it was estimated that doctors practicing Western medicine made up 90 percent of all doctors.[29] Kanpō doctors not only lost their traditional status as practitioners of official Japanese medicine but also faced extinction.[30]

Hospitals and Clinics

By the end of the Tokugawa shogunate, there were almost no hospitals run by Kanpō doctors. Kanpō doctors still made house calls and prescribed herbs. A major exception was Koishikikawa Yōjōsho Hospital in Edo. This hospital was created by the Tokugawa shogunate in 1722 after Shōsen Ogawa petitioned to the shogun to create and administer a medical facility for the poor. At that time, rapid migration to Edo was taking place, and the problem of urban poverty had become serious.[31] Koishikikawa Yōjōsho treated the poor with herbs that grew in a farm attached to the hospital. This story confirms that Japan did not develop many religion-based medical facilities as the request was made directly to the shogun.

In 1861, the first Western-style hospital, Nagasaki Yōjōsho, was established by J. L. C. Pompe van Meerdervoort. The spread of cholera in 1858 led him to ask the Tokugawa shogunate to engage more in public hygiene and establish hospitals to accommodate cholera patients.[32] This first hospital was attached to the Medical Teaching School he founded in 1857. It was widely known that the hospital treated people no matter what their social or economic class. The new Meiji government took over the hospital, renaming it the Nagasaki Prefectural Hospital. Students of Pompe van Meerdervoort and Anthonius Franciscus Bauduin, another Dutch doctor, established Western-style hospitals in other regions, and some provinces, especially those in western Japan, created their own hospitals, some of which also provided some medical education.

Hospitals also developed as a result of the civil war. The battles with the Tokugawa forces led the Meiji government to create hospitals for injured soldiers. In 1868, the Imperial Guards Hospitals (Goshinpei Byōin) were established in Kyoto and Osaka for treating injured soldiers. As the war front moved to the east, the government created the Temporal Military Hospital (Kari Gunji Byōin) in Yokohama. In September 1868, it was moved to Tokyo and reorganized as the Great Hospital (Daibyōin). These military hospitals, along with the Tokugawa shogunate's School of Medical Science, became the predecessors of the Tokyo Imperial University medical faculty and hospital.[33]

Besides the military hospitals, the government began to promote public hospitals for civilians. As part of the government's effort to enrich the nation and build up national defenses, it needed to manage public health and prevent epidemics such as the cholera epidemic. To increase the number of Western medicine doctors, many prefectures took over hospitals from the provinces and turned them into prefectural hospitals, which were usually attached to public medical schools. They learned from Nagasaki Prefecture's experience with the hospital that Pompe van Meerdervoort created.[34]

Private hospitals also developed. One of the first private hospitals was Juntendo Hospital. Juntendo Hospital traces its roots back to a private school for Western studies, Wada Juku, established by Taizen Satō in 1838. After Taizen Satō retired, Takanaka Satō succeeded him and opened Juntendo Hospital in 1873. Juntendo became the first private hospital to be allowed to engage in pathological anatomy.[35] Jikeikai Hospital is another example of a private hospital in this period. In 1882, Kanehiro Takagi established Yūshi Kyōritsu Tokyo Hospital to provide medical services for the poor. In 1887, the Empress Shōken became its honorary president, and the hospital was renamed Jikei, meaning "Mercy," at her request.[36]

The Red Cross is another Japanese private hospital. Japan is the only country that extensively developed Red Cross hospitals. Its predecessor, Hakuaisha, was created after a proposal by Privy Council members Tsunetami Sano and Yuzuru Ogi in 1877. Its original purpose was to treat injured soldiers in both the Meiji government and samurai in the rebellious former Satsuma Domain (Seinan War) without discrimination. The idea for equal treatment of all parties had been introduced to the Red Cross by William Willis during the Boshin War between the new government and the Tokugawa forces. In 1886, the Red Cross created a headquarters hospital in Tokyo. In the beginning of the twentieth century, Red Cross hospitals spread across Japan as institutions treating civilians. Many of these were converted from public hospitals. This conversion took place because of a new government policy to stop the increase of public hospitals.[37]

The Meiji government initially led in the improvement of public hospitals because there were no alternatives. Doctors of Western medicine were still a small minority, and private clinics and hospitals were still in a primitive phase of development. The Medical Rules and Regulations of 1874 played an important role in encouraging doctors to open their own clinics. Under the regulations, doctors could open clinics and hospitals with the government's permission. This left room for private hospitals to evolve, but at the beginning, hospitals that had more than ten sickbeds were dominantly public.[38] In 1877, there were seventy-three public hospitals and thirty-five private hospitals: the former accounted for 78 percent of all hospitals.

By 1898, however, the proportion of public hospitals had shrunk to 31 percent. The deflationary policy that Finance Minister Masayoshi Matsukata deployed in 1881 caused this change. His deflationary policy was a reaction to the inflationary policy of the government to finance the Seinan War in 1877, the last civil war during the Meiji era. Matsukata's policy included a provision stating that prefectural authorities could not use local taxes to fund prefectural medical schools. Many public medical schools and attached hospitals were thus sold to the private sector. As a result, private hospitals came to exceed the number of public hospitals in 1888, with many of the surviving public hospitals devoted to specific diseases, such as tuberculosis and mental diseases.[39] Matsukata's decision had a great impact on subsequent health care policy development and on the relationship between the government and doctors.

Clinics, which were defined as medical care facilities with nine or fewer sickbeds, were predominantly private from the beginning. The Medical Rules and Regulations of 1874 stipulated that doctors could open their own clinics anywhere so long as they followed the rules and regulations. The Medical Rules and Regulations also assured that the public authority would be involved whenever patients had unpaid bills. The government played a role in increasing private practitioners and their clinics.[40]

It is important to question why Matsukata chose to decrease budget allocations for public hospitals. In that postwar period, other industries were in a similar situation, and many public companies were privatized. Matsukata considered medical services as commodities like others, because there was no clear distinction between public hospitals and private hospitals and clinics. For one thing, Japanese public hospitals were not started by religious organizations with a mission to provide the poor with medical services. Instead, public hospitals were created by the Meiji government as a strategy to catch up with Western nations. As government institutions, public hospitals had the best medical facilities and doctors. They attracted the wealthy and did not spend much on serving the poor.

"Public" meant not that those were for everyone, particularly for the needy, but merely that they were run by the government. This trend was recognized as a serious problem by the mid-1870s. Sensai Nagayo, then the director of the Hygiene Bureau (Eisei Kyoku) in the Home Ministry, was dissatisfied with the situation and claimed that public hospitals should mainly focus on the treatment of the poor. But his was a minority view in the government.[41] Matsukata's policy in 1881 worked against Nagayo's concerns. The idea of health insurance and other measures emerged within and outside the government as policy options to solve the problem. But the health care provider system that relied largely on private doctors continued to exist and affected the politics of who paid for health care.

Health Care Administration

The Meiji government expanded the administrative capacity to advance westernization of the medical education and licensing system. Furthermore, the deterioration of public health also pushed the government further. As described, the Boshin War against Tokugawa forces led to the creation of Western-style hospitals to treat the injured soldiers. As the battlefield moved from the west to east of Japan, the war also resulted in a large migration of people, and diseases such as smallpox and cholera spread in many regions.[42] The Seinan War in 1877 brought the same problems. The spread of infectious diseases threatened the social order. Moreover, interacting with many foreign ships, products, and people exposed Japanese to new diseases. The rise of social confusion pressured the government to introduce and develop a Western-style administrative structure to deal with these problems.

The very first independent agency to deal with health care administration was the Medical Division (Imu Ka), established in the Ministry of Education in 1872 to deal with public health problems. It was part of the Ministry of Education because medical education was administered through that ministry. The Medical Division also dealt with public health maintenance and control of epidemics.[43] The Medical Division became the Medical Bureau (Imu Kyoku) in 1873.

As the director of the bureau, Nagayo took the lead in promoting Western medicine in Japan. He was born in Ōmura Province (part of Nagasaki Prefecture now) into a family that had been followers of Kanpō. In 1854, he went to Osaka and studied under the guidance of Kōan Ogata at his private school, Tekijuku. Ogata was a doctor, but he also became a well-known "Dutch scholar" (*rangakusha*) who studied broader Western sciences in the Dutch language. He established Tekijuku to teach Western sciences and medicine and attracted many young people, including Yukichi Fukuzawa (the founder of Keio University) and Kensai Ikeda (the first dean of the medical school of Tokyo Imperial University). In 1861, Nagayo went back to Nagasaki to further study Western medicine under Pompe van Meerdervoort. Nagayo became the director of the hospital that Pompe van Meerdervoort established. Then, as described, Nagayo visited Germany and the Netherlands with the Iwakura mission to study medical education and public health administration. In 1873, he returned to Japan, where the directorship of the Medical Bureau was waiting for him.[44]

Nagayo's first big project was to produce the Medical Rules and Regulations of 1874, which was the first comprehensive set of guidelines relating to health care. In 1875, the health care administration, except for medical education, was moved to the Home Ministry. Nagayo headed the newly created Hygiene Bureau (Eisei Kyoku). In 1885, the Hygiene Division and the Medical Division were created within the Hygiene Bureau.[45] As administrative reorganization advanced, research on people's health and the health care system accumulated. Akira Sugaya points out that because the Home Ministry's main task was to maintain social order through policing, the change in ministries relating to public health administration indicates that health care policy was seen by the government as one of its methods of social control.[46] Kiyosada Sōmae also points out that public health administration had to be part of maintaining security because Japan did not have the mature administrative capacity at the local level to control public hygiene.[47]

One of Nagayo's main tasks was to create regulations dealing with the prevention of epidemic diseases. In 1874, he also drew up the Regulation of Smallpox Vaccines (Shutō Kisoku). In 1877, policy relating to cholera was formed to react to the spread of the disease during the Seinan War. In 1880, the Hygiene Bureau issued its Epidemic Disease Prevention Regulations (Densenbyō Yobō Kisoku).[48] The Hygiene Bureau cooperated with public hospital doctors and private practitioners as "collaborators at the front" to deal with the problem.[49]

Health care administration also began to develop in connection with labor policy. In the 1880s, private companies began to grow because of the government's fiscal policy of privatization. For example, the Nagasaki Shipyard was sold to Mitsubishi, and the Tomioka Silk Mill was sold to Mitsui. The government now needed to have regulations to control private working conditions and started to study Western laws relating to labor protections and, more broadly, social policy. In 1881, the Ministry of Agriculture and Commerce (Nōmu Shō) was established, separate from the Home Ministry, to deal with labor issues. Soon, in 1882, the Public Works Bureau (Kōmu Kyoku) of the Ministry of Agriculture and Commerce created its Research Section. The Research Section conducted the first studies of factories, factory workers, and their health conditions. The Research Section actively started to prepare labor protection legislation.

Medical Associations

As the Tokugawa shogunate began to promote Western medicine, doctors who practiced Western medicine gradually increased in number. But at the beginning of the Meiji era, their number was too small to compete with Kanpō doctors. The two types of doctors got along in some situations. As the new government actively promoted Western medicine, however, the two types began to form their own associations to promote their own interests. The movement led to the creation of the first, albeit voluntary, national medical association in 1916. The association was created mainly by private solo practitioners of Western medicine.

Private solo practitioners who practiced Western medicine had to contend with four other groups. The first was Kanpō doctors, who tried to maintain their political power and who were ready to defend their medical system at all costs. The second was doctors in public universities, public hospitals, and the military. These publicly funded doctors had different professional and economic interests than did private practitioners. The third was pharmacists. Doctors traditionally sold their own medicines, and their interests diverged from those of the newly created profession of pharmacists (discussed in detail in the next section). The last was the government. Doctors in general seek to avoid third-party interventions in their relationship with their patients. Practitioners of Western medicine could not contend with all these groups by themselves and come out on top. What Western medical doctors chose to do was to make an alliance with the government to win their battles with the other three groups. This was a natural alliance because the government was the dominant figure to promote Western medicine.

In the late nineteenth century, elite doctors had begun to organize regional medical associations. The first regional medical association, the Medical Society (Igaku Kaisha), was established in 1875 in Tokyo as a voluntary association of prominent doctors, such as Tōan Matsuyama, Tōyō Sasaki, and Tadanori Ishiguro. Public hospital doctors and private solo practitioners joined the society. It was the first association that acted as both an interest group and academic medical society. At that time, the distinction between public doctors and private doctors was not as clear as it was later, because many Western medicine doctors studied under the same teachers, such as Pompe van Meerdervoort, Willis, and Satō (Taizen and Takanaka). These doctors went back and forth between government and private positions. Some Kanpō doctors also joined the regional associations.[50]

The Home Ministry produced the Formation of Private Practitioners' Associations Act (Kaigyōi Kumiai Secchi Hō) in 1883. It stipulated that such regional associations must study and develop medical science, study local diseases, engage in preventing epidemic diseases, and maintain and improve the health of the public. Sugaya explains why the government took this step at this time: "The main purpose was to have private practitioners' associations formed from the top and to have the associations help improve public health."[51]

In responding to the government's initiative, the Tokyo Medical Society (Tokyo Ikai) was formed out of the Medical Society in 1886. Ryōjun Matsumoto, a former student of Pompe van Meerdervoort who had become the surgeon general of the Army, was the first president. Yasushi Hasegawa, a student of Naotaka Satō and later the director of the private medical training school Saisei Gakusha, became vice president.[52] Most members of the Tokyo Medical Society were Western medicine doctors, but prominent Kanpō doctors such as Sōhaku Asada and Ryōan Imamura were also listed as designated committee members.[53] Local medical associations were soon created in other prefectures.[54]

The more that regional-level medical associations appeared and the number of Western medicine doctors increased, the more elite Western medicine doctors began to consider forming their own associations to promote their way of medicine and provide their fellow doctors with financial security. This move was a response to Kanpō doctors' efforts to mobilize to retain the viability of Kanpō medicine. The government's policies regarding medical education and licensing were a serious threat to Kanpō doctors. Although the government did not prohibit the practice of Kanpō medicine, new doctors increased by going through through the medical schools or passing the licensing exam based on Western medicine. It was clear to Kanpō doctors that over time their numbers and political power would diminish.[55]

In 1879, the association Onchisha was formed by leading Kanpō doctors, such as Kokkan Azai and Gyōkō Yamada. Onchisha published many journals, including *Onchiidan*, and established traditional schools such as the Japan-China Medical School (Wakan Igaku Kōshūjo).[56] The association also tried to ally with regional Kanpō organizations to counter the government's initiatives promoting Western medicine. But because their efforts could not drastically change the situation, Onchisha was dissolved in 1887. Kanpō doctors made a final effort to entrench themselves by creating the Imperial Medical Society (Teikoku Ikai) when the new Imperial Diet came into operation in 1890.[57] But the Kanpō doctors' movement led to a countermovement.

In 1893, Western medicine doctors formed the Greater Japan Medical Society (Dainippon Ikai) to advance their attack on Kanpō medicine. The leading figure in its creation was Kanehiro Takagi, a former student of Willis, retired surgeon general of the Navy, and also the founder of Yūshi Kyōritsu Tokyo Hospital. The society's executive directors included Yasushi Hasegawa and Sensai Nagayo. It was created not only to counter Kanpō doctors but also to protect the interests of private solo practitioners. In 1895, by a vote of 105–78, a committee in the lower house of the Imperial Diet declined to enact a bill allowing new Kanpō doctors to be licensed.[58] This failure was a serious blow to Kanpō doctors. The Sino-Japan War that broke out in 1894 became an additional and fatal blow to Kanpō, because Kanpō had originated in the enemy nation. The organized national movement to maintain Kanpō as a legitimate medical system completely died when the Imperial Medical Society was dissolved in 1898 and then longtime leader Azai died in 1903.[59]

Once Kanpō disappeared as a political rival, internal conflicts in the arena of Western medicine began to be visible. There had been hints of these conflicts since the early Meiji era. In 1879, private practitioners in Tokyo formed an organization to oppose the creation of public hospitals and to turn the existing public hospitals into hospitals specifically for the poor.[60] Western medicine doctors were now divided into two groups. The first group was composed of private solo practitioners, many of whom were graduates of private medical schools that trained doctors for shorter periods than the government medical schools. The second group was public, or government, doctors, graduates of the medical school at Tokyo Imperial University.[61] In 1898, professors at Tokyo Imperial University, including Ōgai Mori, formed an association specifically for government-trained doctors, the Meiji Medical Society (Meiji Ikai).[62]

In this historical context, Western medicine doctors in the private sector succeeded in getting the government to amend the Medical Rules and Regulations by inserting a provision stating, "Doctors are allowed to form their own associations. The rules regarding medical associations are decided by the home minister." Although the formation of these medical associations was limited to the regional level, according to William Steslicke, leading figures in the associations were motivated to attract graduates and professors of private medical schools and improve their political status in Japan. Meanwhile, medical associations made it easier for the leading figures to keep a hierarchical order within the medical field and to have control over rank-and-file members.[63] Soon large regional associations of private doctors began to be formed, such as ones in Kanto, Tohoku, Kansai, and Kyushu.[64]

Shibasaburō Kitasato took the lead in forming the Greater Japan Medical Association (GJMA; Dainippon Ishikai) in 1916. Kitasato was known as the father of bacteriology in Japan and became a symbol for private doctors resisting what they saw as the government's unjustified intervention in the practice of medicine. Kitasato at first cooperated with the government in trying to fight epidemics and improve public health. But he broke off his relationship with the government because of very specific circumstances. His personal story and beliefs well qualified him to become the first president of this national organization of private practitioners.

Kitasato was born in 1853 in Higo Province (now Kumamoto Prefecture), the son of a village headman. He studied at Kumamoto Medical School and was particularly influenced by Constant George van Mansveldt, a Dutch physician. In 1875, Kitasato went on to advanced studies at Tokyo Medical School (soon to become Tokyo Imperial University Medical School). After graduation, he gained a position in the Hygiene Bureau of the Home Ministry, where Sensai Nagayo was the director.

In 1885, Kitasato was dispatched by the government to Germany to study at the University of Berlin. Masanori Ogata, who had positions in the Hygiene Laboratory (Eisei Shikensho) of the Home Ministry and at Tokyo Imperial University Medical School, made this arrangement for Kitasato. In Berlin, he was under the guidance of Heinrich Hermann Robert Koch, who became famous as the founder of modern bacteriology. One of Kitasato's major medical findings in Berlin was how to create passive immunity to diphtheria and tetanus. He was the first Japanese to be nominated for the Nobel Prize.[65]

Refusing research positions that were offered to him in Europe, Kitasato returned to Japan with a desire to improve preventive medicine in his home country. However, he was not warmly welcomed by students of bacteriology at Tokyo Imperial University, largely because his research results in Germany differed from Ogata's theories. Kitasato thus decided to establish the Institute for Infectious Diseases (Densenbyō Kenkyūsho) to pursue his own work in locating pathogens and creating vaccines. Believing that infectious disease research should be well coordinated by the government, he agreed to bring his institute under the Home Ministry as the National Institute for Infectious Disease (Kokuritsu Densenbyō Kenkyūsho). He remained as its director. In 1914, however, without consulting with him, the government moved the institute to the Ministry of Education and made it part of Tokyo Imperial University. Kitasato resigned the directorship in protest and created another private research institute, the Kitasato Institute (Kitasato Kenkyūsho, which became the basis of Kitasato University), with the financial support of Yukichi Fukuzawa and Ichizaemon Morimura.[66]

Taichi Kitajima, who worked very closely with Kitasato, suggested a hypothesis regarding the political context behind the incident. He wrote, "The transfer of jurisdiction did not happen in a day. . . . Some professors at the [Tokyo Imperial] university started to panic because they thought that if the National Institute for Infectious Disease were to remain in the hands of Kitasato, private practitioners and hospitals would always look to him for leadership."[67] If Kitajima's argument is correct, the Tokyo Imperial University Medical School professors were worried about losing their long-standing medical leadership position, so they tried to force Kitasato under their institutional umbrella. The result of their anxiety was that Kitasato left the government and became a symbol of leadership for private practitioners.

Two years after this contretemps, in 1916, Kitasato began to serve as president of the GJMA. He had previously been asked to lead this national organization of private practitioners but had declined because he was working for the government at that time. He changed his mind after he resigned as the head of the National Institute for Infectious Disease.[68] Kitasato attracted the association's rank-and-file private practitioners who opposed the dominance of Tokyo Imperial University and the government bureaucracy.[69] Despite Kitasato's wishes, however, the GJMA had been established not as a public institution which would include public doctors but as a voluntary organization. In a sense, Kitasato tried to do to Tokyo Imperial University Medical School what the professors there had tried to do to him. He sought to make his national medical association the legal umbrella organization that doctors in imperial universities and public hospitals would be forced to join, so that the GJMA would become the main actor in making national health care policy. The GJMA's inaugural meeting included a resolution showing the association's strong political motivation. The resolution stated that the goal of GJMA was "to seek the expansion of the political power of medicine. Sending our comrades to the lower house is the only way to reform the administration of health care."[70] Kitasato and other leaders looked for opportunities to make the GJMA increase its authority over the government and its doctors.

Doctors and Pharmacists

One more important motivation mobilized private Western medicine doctors to form the GJMA in 1916: to counter the rising power of pharmacists. At the end of the Tokugawa shogunate, Kanpō doctors were called *kusushi*, which literally meant pharmacists. The doctors charged for their herbal medications but did not seek payment for their clinical diagnoses.[71]

Benjamin Leopold Müller was invited by the Meiji government in 1871 to study the Japanese health care system and make recommendations. He concluded that in order to improve medicine in Japan it would be necessary to develop medical science and pharmacy as separate specialties with separate fees for their services.[72] The government accepted his policy suggestion as part of its overall westernization policy.

The government also had a practical reason for wanting to develop the pharmaceutical profession. By the end of the Tokugawa era, some Western medicines were being imported from the Netherlands, as Western medical practices were gradually spreading. But quantities of these medicines were limited, and costs were high. The Meiji Restoration brought about free trade with foreign countries, and many Western medicines began to be shipped to Japan. Those who did the importing and selling were general merchants and not medical or pharmaceutical professionals. Because the medicines were often of poor quality, the government developed pharmaceutical education to train pharmacists to control the quality of medicines.[73]

The Medical Rules and Regulations of 1874 sought to set a legal foundation for separating the sale of medicines from the provision of medical services. The regulations stipulated that pharmacy was a separate profession from medicine. As in Western countries, pharmacists had to pass a special exam, and doctors were prohibited from compounding medicines for patients.[74] The tradition that doctors sold medications without charging for their clinical diagnoses, nevertheless, remained. Many doctors were still Kanpō doctors, and they would lose their incomes if prevented from selling their herbal preparations. The population was used to the tradition of paying only for medical preparations and not for diagnoses.

The profession of pharmacist was not a popular one. Takeshi Kawakami points out that because those who sold medicines were often general merchants, even after the exam was created these merchants were still allowed to sell medicines as a compromise. In these circumstances, people hesitated to take the exam to become pharmacists. The University of Tokyo (after 1886, Tokyo Imperial University) did not have many students majoring in pharmacy when the Medical Rules and Regulations were adopted. For many years the university had only one or two graduates in pharmacy a year. There were efforts at the local level to found pharmacy schools to produce more pharmacists. Compared with the increase in Western medicine doctors, however, the number of pharmacists did not increase much. In 1890, while the number of doctors was about 38,000, there were only 1,700 pharmacists.[75]

The government nevertheless continued to push for the separation of medical treatment from the sale of medicines. The Regulation of Pharmaceutical Sales and Drug Handling (Yakuhin Eigyō narabi Yakuhin Toriatsukai Kisoku), adopted in March 1889, made concrete provisions for the regulations outlined in the Medical Rules and Regulations. Yasushi Hasegawa and other leaders, mainly solo practitioners, opposed separating the sale of medicines from the provision of medical services. Hasegawa played a leading role in changing the regulation so that the separation of medical treatment and the sale of medicines would be postponed.[76]

Pharmacists took offensive action against the solo practitioners. In 1893, they formed the Japan Pharmacists Association (Nihon Yakuzaishi Kai) and pushed for the compulsory separation of medical treatment from the sale of medicines.[77] In the same year, elite private practitioners, such as Nagayo, Takagi, and Hasegawa, took the lead in forming the Greater Japan Medical Society (Dainippon Ikai) to protect the interests of solo practitioners.[78]

Under pressure from private doctors and pharmacists, and because the number of pharmacists did not increase as much as the government had hoped, the government proposed a compromise. Because the immediate separation of the two professions would cause confusion among people, the government suggested that it would suspend implementation of this separation for a while. But Hasegawa was able to delete the term "for a while" in the final draft. The pharmacists' association was upset about it, but the law stood as written.[79]

The pharmacists continued their political battle. In 1916 a pharmacists' group pushed for legislation to separate the sale of medicines from other medical services. This movement gave another chance for leaders of solo practitioners to mobilize their fellows.[80] They needed to make their national association politically stronger. They soon had an opportunity to do so—but only by cooperating with the government.

Kawakami points out the private doctors' dilemma. They hoped to be allowed to continue with the tradition of selling their own medicines, but when they succeeded, they also kept the tradition that people called all their services, including consulting, medical examination, and diagnosis, the "cost of medicine." Patients did not appreciate, at least by financial reward, intangible services that doctors offered.[81] After this controversy at the turn of the century, this issue was not politicized for a while. But it came back as a very heated debate in the postwar period. Pharmacists found a new ally at that time in the US-led occupation authority (see chapter 4).

A new foundation of medical education, licensing, health care providers, and health care administration was created by the Meiji government, which pushed to westernize Japanese medicine. The Meiji government justified its power to establish these basic health care institutions during a national crisis after the collapse of the long-standing Tokugawa shogunate and in the face of strong Western powers. Medical professionals were mobilized within the institutional and political contexts. Then the idea of health insurance came into politics as industrialization advanced.

2

REACTING TO DETERIORATING HEALTH

By the 1910s, it must have surprised international audiences to see how far Japan had transformed itself in less than half a century since the Meiji Restoration. The nation had achieved westernization of its social, legal, and economic systems. The establishment of the Meiji Constitution in 1889 was particularly important for political development. On the one hand, the constitution stipulated that sovereignty belonged to the emperor, and Japan had a strongly centralized political system. On the other hand, as the first modern constitution in Asia, the Meiji Constitution included progressive aspects, such as the creation of the Imperial Diet with a democratic lower house. People were acknowledged to have a right to some freedom of speech, if not full freedom. With the creation of the new constitution, government officials and politicians recognized that the people's voices needed to be listened to more seriously than during the Tokugawa era.[1]

With the Meiji government's investment in creating state-owned firms and support for private firms, Japanese industry rapidly developed and produced an industrial labor force. More and more people migrated from agricultural areas to urban areas. Many of these new workers suffered from low wages and long working hours, but as individuals they could not improve their conditions. They particularly had a hard time when they became sick or injured. If they did not get well, they were laid off and forced to return to their rural homes. For these reasons, workers started a labor union movement at the turn of the century.

While the westernization of medicine that Meiji government conducted from the top down continued to be solidified, the new health care system could not adequately respond to workers' health problems at the turn of the century. There were no medical service providers who actively attended to the health problems of working-class and poor people. Private doctors opened clinics in urban areas to serve those with higher incomes. These doctors did not have much motivation to provide medical care for low-income people other than honoring the tradition of *ninjutsu* (doctors' obligation to give blessings to people). Public hospitals, which had developed under the umbrella of Tokyo Imperial University, attracted prominent professors and wealthy patients. These doctors did not have a strong incentive to deal with patients with financial difficulties either. To make matters worse, a strong deflationary policy at the end of the century resulted in fewer local public hospitals. There were some grassroots efforts to meet the needs of poor workers with lower-cost health care services. Some of these initiatives came from the private medical area, and some had strong public support. But these measures had only limited impact in meeting workers' health care needs. The combination of the growing labor movement, the formation of party governance, and the introduction of male suffrage resulted in a changed political environment. The government decided it needed to study how Western countries dealt with health care financing.

By the 1910s, the expansion of voting rights had led to an increase in the importance of party politics. In 1918, Takashi Hara became the prime minister and formed the first party-based cabinet. Before that, the Meiji oligarchy (*genkun*) had chosen the prime minister and cabinet members. The Meiji oligarchs and their disciples, many of whom were from Satsuma and Chōshū Domains, were the founders of the Meiji government. Although elections for the lower house had been conducted since 1890, prime ministers and their cabinets were not influenced by election results. The Hara administration (September 1918–November 1921) was the first to clearly depart from this tradition.

The turning point in Japanese political-party development can be attributed largely to a social movement, the so-called rice riots (*kome sōdō*), which began in a fishing village in Toyama Prefecture in 1918. Those who were suffering from rising rice prices engaged in demonstrations against rice merchants who were thought to be raising prices intentionally. The protests resonated with the dissatisfaction of workers in factories and mines, and a few million participated throughout Japan by conducting protests aimed at lowering the rice price. The social turbulence forced Prime Minister Masatake Terauchi to resign and gave Hara an opportunity to form the first party government.[2]

Hara was called "the commoner prime minister" (*heimin saishō*), and his administration was seen as a symbol of evolving democracy in Japan. The period from the 1910s to 1920s, during the reign of the Taishō Emperor, when democracy advanced, is known as the era of Taishō democracy.[3] In 1925, Japan adopted

universal male suffrage. The increase in democracy led to a rising labor movement. Labor strikes increased with support from socialists, who were still operating underground.[4] The government wanted to show its support for democratization
while preventing the democratization movement from going so far as to challenge
the existing political system under the Meiji Constitution.

Facing this dilemma, the government created its first major health insurance
program, the Health Insurance Act of 1922 (Kenkō Hoken Hō) for blue-collar
workers. In 1923, the law also led to the creation of the Japan Medical Association (Nihon Ishikai) and gave it the status of a public corporation. By that time,
Western medicine doctors had increased their numbers, and many had their own
clinics outside the umbrella of Tokyo Imperial University. The Japanese health
care system was based on private solo practitioners. Leading private practitioners mobilized other solo practitioners and their own medical associations to gain
more power as against university professors and public hospital doctors—that
is, the government and its publicly funded doctors. These private practitioners
also fought against the nonconformist private practitioners who challenged the
existing health care system by providing medical services at discount rates.

Importing Policy Ideas from Europe

At the turn of the century, the government realized that more and more people
were working in private firms. The rising labor movement brought the poor conditions in many workplaces to the attention of the government. In 1897,
Tsunetarō Jō, Fusatarō Takano, and Sen Katayama took the lead in forming the
Association for the Promotion of Labor Unions (Rōdō Kumiai Kiseikai). That
year, as part of the association, the ironworkers formed the first modern Japanese labor union with a membership of 1,285.[5] The number of labor unions grew
from nine (1,339 members) in 1903 to fifty-seven (10,938 members) in 1907.[6]
Unions began to go on strike for better working conditions, and labor strikes
rapidly increased after the turn of the century.

The government started to see the labor movement as a real threat to the status quo. In 1900, Prime Minister Aritomo Yamagata played a leading role in
creating the Security Police Act (Chian Keisatsu Hō), which banned strikes and
generally tried to put a brake on the labor movement. In 1910 the government
discovered a plot by socialists and anarchists to assassinate the emperor. This is
known as the High Treason Incident (Taigyaku Jiken) and also as the Kōtoku
Incident (Kōtoku Jiken) after Shūsui Kōtoku, who was considered to be the leader
of the plot. Kōtoku was a well-known figure who cofounded the Common
People's Newspaper (*Heimin Shimbun*). He opposed imperialism and led the

antiwar movement during the Russo-Japanese War. Article 73 of the Criminal Code of the Meiji Constitution stipulated capital punishment for harming or plotting to harm the emperor or his close family members. For violating the law, the government arrested twenty-four people. Twenty-two, including Kōtoku, were sentenced to death.[7]

While the High Treason Incident and the arrests of 1910 resulted in the decline of the socialist movement, the government could not maintain social order only by using a "stick." The government also needed to have a "carrot." Shinpei Gotō, a doctor, bureaucrat, and politician, played a large role in introducing to Japan Western policy ideas that served as such "carrots." In 1890, Gotō went abroad to study in Germany. There he was exposed to political institutions and policies developed by Chancellor Otto von Bismarck. Gotō was inspired by German social policies, including publicly funded health insurance. He observed that Bismarck successfully suppressed the socialist movement through a combination of antisocialist laws and pursuing top-down progressive social policies. Gotō believed that Japan could learn from the German example.[8]

Gotō returned to Japan in 1892 and took over Nagayo's position as director of the Hygiene Bureau of the Home Ministry. Gotō devoted himself to introducing social policies, particularly in hygiene and health, that were based on the German model. In his speech proposing the Workers' Sickness Insurance Act (Shitsubyō no Hoken Hō), he emphasized the necessity of creating a compulsory health insurance program for the nation, stating that "workers' temporary sickness . . . eventually weakens a nation's manpower."[9]

Part of Gotō's plan was soon realized in the creation of mutual aid associations in state-owned firms. The Imperial Railroad Mutual Aid Association (Teikoku Tetsudō Kyūsai Kumiai) was established in 1907 under Gotō's leadership.[10] It was mandatory for the railroad employees to join the association. The benefits offered by the association included compensating workers for medical care needed as a result of work-connected incidents. In 1916 disabilities not connected with work were added to the benefits, and medical costs were paid for up to sixty days. Workers' contribution to the mutual aid association was 3 percent of their wages, with the government matching these contributions with an additional 2 percent of workers' wages. The concept of mutual aid associations spread to other state-owned firms, so that almost all of them had mutual aid associations by the end of World War I.[11] Mutual aid associations also developed in private firms, but state-owned firms took the lead. It is significant that, as in Germany, mutual aid associations were promoted by the government to strengthen government control and national power.

While mutual aid associations in state-owned firms were spreading, the Imperial Diet in 1911 passed the Factory Act (Kōjō Hō), a workers' compensation program for blue-collar workers in designated private industries. The foundation for the legislation was laid when the Ministry of Agriculture and Commerce was created in 1881. The ministry studied conditions in factories and among their workers and proposed measures to regulate working conditions and support workers with other material benefits, including medical services. Labor unions supported the creation of the Factory Act. Elite doctors also supported it. The Greater Japan Medical Society petitioned the government as early as 1897 to produce such a measure. It is important to note that the Factory Act was not intended as an antibusiness measure; more correctly, it was a pro–big business measure. Medium- and small-scale firms opposed the legislation because of possible financial burdens. Big business and heavy industry did not oppose the Factory Act, as they were already hiring more skilled workers and improving working conditions. These large firms tried to use the Factory Act to squeeze out smaller competitors.[12] In a sense, with the Factory Act, the government aided big businesses as they moved to monopolize their industries.

The Factory Act targeted private firms of more than fifteen employees that often required their employees to work long hours under bad conditions, such as in coal mining and textile factories. The law limited working hours to twelve and prohibited late-night work for workers under fifteen and all female workers.[13] Besides improving working conditions, the Factory Act mandated that firms, without any employee contributions, should provide financial compensation to all employees and their surviving family members for work-connected disabilities and death.[14] The Factory Act was important legislation establishing a safety net for workers, but as Takeshi Kawakami points out, the government's case for the legislation was that it would enrich the nation and build up national defenses. Kawakami, *Gendai Nihon Iryōshi*, 286–88.

Nongovernmental Measures

The Factory Act was the first major legislation designed to improve the conditions of workers, but it was obviously not enough. It did not cover those who worked in firms with fewer than fifteen workers or cover sickness and injury that was not work related. The legislation also did not cover agricultural workers, who made up the predominant part of workforce. In the 1910s and 1920s, moreover, health care costs increased because of the development of new technologies such as X-rays that became standard in medical diagnosis, putting greater financial burdens on patients.[15] The government was pressed, especially by private practitioners, to force public hospitals to treat people with financial difficulties. But the government did not do so. To make the situation worse, the government cut back its budget for public hospitals as part of Matsukata's deflationary policy. In response, nongovernment actors began to take the initiative to increase services for the poor.

In urban areas some clinics voluntarily began to offer medical care at a significantly discounted rate. In 1911, the Home Ministry permitted Umeshirō Suzuki and Tokijirō Katō to establish an actual-expense clinic (*jippi shinryōjo*) in Tokyo. The goal of the clinic was to help low-income workers access more affordable medical care. Suzuki graduated from Keio University and worked as a writer for *Jiji Shinpō*, one of the major newspapers created by Yukichi Fukuzawa. Suzuki later worked for Mitsui Bank and Ōji Paper Company. Katō was a doctor who studied at Saisei Gakusha, which had been established by Yasushi Hasegawa. Katō paid his own way to do graduate work in Germany. On returning to Japan, he became involved in providing health care services for the poor. Suzuki and Katō believed that the existing health care system did not adequately meet the needs of low-income workers in urban areas, and thus they formed the actual-expense clinic as a corporate juridical person.[16]

The first actual-expense clinic set doctors' fees for medicines and medical care about one-third lower than the fees set by local medical associations.[17] The government began to support actual-expense clinics by having the Ministry of Communications and Transportation give them low-interest loans.[18] The traditional private solo practitioners and medical associations strongly opposed the clinics and asked the government to stop approving new ones. Municipalities, however, learned from the clinics' success and asked the central government to allow municipalities to create public actual-expense clinics. By 1935, the number of public actual-expense clinics had increased to eighty-five.[19]

A second nongovernmental attempt to provide financial relief in medicine was born in a rural area. Farmers sought to be prepared for possible ill health by creating the Medical Cooperative (Iryō Riyō Kumiai). The number of villages without doctors had increased in the late nineteenth century as doctors moved to industrialized urban areas where there were wealthier patients. In 1928, 38 percent of doctors practiced in urban areas. By 1932, this percentage had risen to 55 percent, and by 1936 to 58 percent.[20] The decreased number of doctors in rural areas can also be attributed to government policies that prevented licensing of new Kanpō doctors. Kanpō doctors tended to practice in rural areas, while Western medicine doctors sought out cities where there was better medical technology and the possibility of higher income. Because new Kanpō doctors were not licensed, the numbers of these doctors decreased over time as they retired. The lack of doctors in rural areas and increasing medical costs led to the creation of farmers' medical cooperatives.[21]

In 1919, a medical cooperative in Shimane Prefecture was the first to provide its members, mainly farmers, with medical care. Some cooperatives built their own medical facilities and invited doctors to work there on a temporary or permanent basis. Medical cooperatives grew in number after the Industrial Cooperative Act of 1922 (Sangyō Kumiai Hō) began to be applied to medical cooperatives. The legislation was modeled on a German act passed in 1900 to support agricultural workers and medium- and small-scale companies that had suffered with the growth of capitalism and the accumulation of wealth in large enterprises. By 1940, 95 percent of farmers belonged to industrial cooperatives.[22]

Christian reformers Inazō Nitobe and Toyohiko Kagawa also took the lead in expanding medical cooperatives. Both Nitobe and Kagawa studied abroad, which influenced their social activism. Nitobe studied economics, history, and political science at Johns Hopkins University in the United States from 1884 to 1887 and at the University of Halle-Wittenberg in Germany from 1887 to 1890. He is internationally famous as the author of *Bushido, the Soul of Japan*. Kagawa studied Christian religion at Princeton University from 1914 to 1916. He devoted himself to helping those who lived in the poorest parts of Kobe. His best-selling autobiography, *Shisen wo Koete* (Facing the death lines), describes his activities in the poor neighborhoods.[23]

In 1932, Nitobe and Kagawa founded the Tokyo Medical Cooperative, which became the foremost medical cooperative. With his experience in the Tokyo Revival Mutual Aid Association after the Great Kanto Earthquake in 1923, Kagawa came to understand the people's need for medical care and decided to create the Tokyo Medical Cooperative. In 1931, the organizing committee met at the Kanda YMCA. According to the articles of the association and other documents, the cooperative was established to decrease the financial burden on the lower and middle classes in medical care. Kagawa was inspired by "sickness funds" in Germany, which developed out of mutual aid cooperatives and were eventually integrated into the government.[24] The number of such medical cooperatives in Japan increased from 4 in 1924 to 22 in 1931 and to 819 in 1936.[25]

The third type of private program originated in private companies. At the end of the nineteenth century, before the development of mutual aid associations in state-owned firms, some private companies had already started to form mutual aid associations of their own to address pressure from their employees and to improve labor relations. Mutual aid associations in Japan were established in a different way from similar "friendly societies" (mutual benefit societies somewhat like cooperatives) in Britain. While labor took the initiative to create voluntary mutual aid associations in Britain, employers took a top-down approach to establish such associations in Japan.

Ani Mining in Akita Prefecture had the first such business-initiated mutual aid association for workers. The idea spread to other companies that had factory workers. The Kanebo Mutual Aid Association (Kanebo Kyōsai Kumiai) was another pioneer. Kanebo was a large textile manufacturer. All employees were required to participate in the mutual aid association and contribute 3 percent of their wages to the fund, while the employer matched the fund by paying at least half of the total of the employee's contribution. Along with providing life insurance and old-age pensions, these mutual aid associations provided hospital and medical care to members at no expense if they received care in assigned facilities.[26]

Sanji Mutō took a strong leadership role in creating the mutual aid association at Kanebo. He was sent by the Mitsui family to reconstruct Kanebo when it was having financial difficulties. He worked to improve not only the manufactured goods and their promotion but also the workplace environment, which he thought would promote the company's image. He reduced working hours and set up an infant nursery. Then, in 1905, after learning about what steel companies did in Germany, he created the mutual aid association, which provided medical care and pension benefits. Many other companies followed the model of Kanebo.[27] The government also encouraged the establishment of private mutual aid associations during World War I, and by 1920 about 600 private mutual aid associations existed in factories and about 170 in mining firms.[28]

An additional private measure was born from a strong initiative by the government and the imperial household for medical services for those with financial difficulties. In 1911, the same year that the first actual-expense clinic was established, the Imperial Rescript for Medical Remedy (Seyaku Kyūryō no Taishō) was issued to set up the social welfare organization Saiseikai Imperial Gift Foundation (Onshi Zaidan Saiseikai), which, with the help of donations from private companies, offered medical services to the indigent and low-income workers, initially for free and later at a low fee.[29] This foundation sought to fill the gap in medical care not provided by hospitals or private solo practitioners. Social policy scholar Takashi Saguchi pointed out the intention of the government in setting up this foundation: "This medical assistance project aimed to shift government responsibility toward private activity as coming from the mercy of the imperial household. While the administrative authority was given to the foundation's national organization, most initiative belonged to the government bureaucrats. Its intention was to strengthen the charity function of the imperial household."[30]

However, these private efforts still left many low-income workers and the poor without sufficient medical services. Seeing increasing numbers of industrial workers who suffered from bad health, the government felt a need to develop a more financially sustainable health care system. What the government tried to do was to integrate some of the emerging private schemes into the first public health insurance program. The government took the initiative to propose a new law to carry this out.

The Health Insurance Act of 1922

After the Meiji Restoration, the government initially focused on medical education and its administration in order to westernize Japanese medicine. At the same time, to prevent the spread of epidemic diseases, the government worked to improve public health and its administration. But, as in other countries, health care costs increased with advances in medical technology, and it became ever more difficult for many people to receive adequate medical care. Existing public hospitals could not meet the need; neither could new public and private schemes. The government turned its attention to public health insurance policy and enacted the Health Insurance Act (HI) in 1922. Preexisting institutions and policies, party politics, and international factors affected the policymaking process that resulted in the HI.

The HI's development was instituted after considerable study and proposals by the government. As described earlier, learning from Germany, Shinpei Gotō was the first major advocate for providing low-income workers with health security. In 1895, Gotō submitted an opinion paper to Prime Minister Hirobumi Itō in which Gotō asserted that the government should take measures to respond to the rising labor movement and to maintain social order. In 1897, he specifically demanded the creation of a public health insurance program for workers. The government, however, concluded that priority should be given to hygiene problems in factories and that it was too early to establish a public health insurance program.[31] Gotō's ideas and proposals, nevertheless, were important steps toward the passage of the HI in 1922.

Pressure for creating a public health insurance program for workers came from the Home Ministry. In June 1916, the Home Ministry established the Research Committee on National Hygiene (Hoken Eisei Chōsakai) to propose measures to improve public health. Tuberculosis among young people was a serious problem and was called a "country-ruining disease" (bōkokubyō).[32] In 1918, the committee urged the government to take quick action: "It is critical to establish a health insurance system not only as social policy but also as a health-and-hygiene policy."[33] Gotō, who served as the home minister from October 1916 to April 1918, supported the results of the committee report. The government was also under pressure from a labor movement radicalized by post–World War I economic and social upheaval. The government, however, needed a political rationale to move forward.[34]

Party politics helped advance adoption of health insurance legislation. The Kenseikai Party, a large opposition party in the Imperial Diet, responded to the proposals of the Research Committee on National Hygiene. In February 1920, the Kenseikai Party introduced a bill in the Diet for public health insurance based on a proposal by Tsubasa Egi, one of the Keiseikai Party leaders. The bill did not pass. The Kenseikai Party reintroduced it in the following two years, but the result was the same.[35]

Japan had almost a two-party system from 1918 to 1932. While the Kenseikai Party (established in 1916 and becoming the Minseitō Party in 1927) mainly represented the urban population. The conservative Seiyūkai Party had support mostly from rural areas. In anticipation of full male suffrage, which eventually became law in 1925, both parties tried to attract new voters. The estimated 9 million working-class votes would be crucial for both parties. After having been the minority party since 1917, the Kenseikai Party now took the lead, with its more progressive policies gaining support from factory workers. Establishing a new health insurance program became part of the party's campaign.[36]

To compete with the Kenseikai Party's plan, the government rushed to use the Labor Division (Rōdō Ka) of the Ministry of Agriculture and Commerce, created in August 1920, as the center for researching health insurance policy. The Labor Division submitted an outline for a national health insurance bill in November 1921 and consulted with the Workers' Insurance Investigation Committee (Rōdōhoken Chōsakai), which did research under the auspices of the Ministry of Agriculture and Commerce.[37] Gen Shimizu, who played a major role in writing the government's health insurance bill, stated that the Seiyūkai Party was not proactive in the first public health insurance program. He wrote, "The government [the Seiyūkai Party] panicked. . . . It rushed to come up with an immediate proposal."[38]

What Britain and Germany were doing also affected the creation of the HI. In 1911, Britain passed the National Insurance Act with strong leadership from David Lloyd George, well known as a radical reformer in the Liberal Party. The legislation's two core elements were the health insurance program and the unemployment insurance program. The programs were funded by contributions from the government, employers, and the workers. The workers chose the approved societies they wished to belong to. The societies administered the programs and collected the contributions, forwarding them to the National Insurance Fund, providing services, and getting reimbursed. Many existing friendly societies and societies run by trade unions were admitted by the government to run the approved societies.[39]

Germany also was a leader in creating social insurance programs. In 1883, Chancellor Bismarck took the lead in creating the Health Insurance Act, which required employers and employees to make contributions to insurance funds. In 1911, Germany introduced the Reich Insurance Code (Reichsversicherungs-ordnung), which placed all of the various existing social insurance plans under the same legal umbrella. Compulsory health insurance was extended not only to factory workers but also to others, such as farmers and foresters.[40]

In addition, the first meeting of the International Labor Organization was held in October 1919 at the Pan Am Union Building in Washington, DC. The ILO was created out of the Paris Peace Conference after World War I. The ILO made proposals for improvements in working hours of industrial workers, maternity protections, protection for female and child workers, and minimum wages for industrial workers. The British and German examples and the establishment of the ILO encouraged other European countries to develop social insurance programs and also affected the policymaking process in Japan.[41]

In March 1922, the Imperial Diet passed the Health Insurance Act with "surprising speed" and without any revisions.[42] The government considered it as a conciliatory policy toward labor unions and as strengthening the nation in international competition. Explaining the aim of the HI in the Imperial Diet, Agriculture and Commerce Minister Tatsuo Yamamoto emphasized that the legislation helped Japan to compete with other countries: "These days we are seeing increasing international economic competition. Because Japan has fewer natural resources and wealth than the Western countries, it is necessary for us to pay more careful attention to labor problems, improving the welfare and lives of our workers to develop industries and improve the nation's wealth."[43]

The HI covered the same people that the Factory Act and the Mining Act (Kōgyō Hō) had covered.[44] The HI was funded half by employers and half by employees. Workers paid no more than 3 percent of their wages for the insurance premium. The government offered up to two yen for each insured worker, which was to be used for administrative costs. The HI program covered all costs for illness, injury, death, and maternity care for workers who earned an annual income of less than 1,200 yen.[45] The program was, nevertheless, unpopular with the enrollees. Under the Factory Act and Mining Act, they had received completely free medical care for work-related illnesses and disabilities. The HI did add non-work-connected health coverage to enrollees' benefits. But now they were forced to make a monetary contribution. In a sense, the health insurance program removed some protections for workers, and labor unions did not actively support it.[46]

The HI had two components, administered by different agencies. The first was Society-Managed Health Insurance (SMHI; Kumiai Kanshō Hoken), which incorporated the mutual aid associations of private firms as the health insurance societies under government supervision.[47] Employers with more than five hundred employees were required to set up health insurance societies to provide health care directly to their workers. Companies with more than three hundred and less than five hundred workers were not mandated to do so but were allowed to establish their own health insurance societies. Under the SMHI program, each insurer had the option to cover families of workers and to have its own clinic.[48] The SMHI program was similar to what Britain and Germany had at the time, although Japanese mutual aid associations were set up more by employers' initiatives, and labor could not participate in the administration of the SMHI program.[49]

Although business gained financial, legal, and other support from the government with the SMHI, Yoneyuki Sugita points out that the government had an incentive to "integrate major corporations into corporatist frameworks" by "imposing legal constraints on the corporations so that the government was able to manage their behavior."[50] That was why Sanji Mutō, who created one of the first private mutual aid associations at Kanebo, opposed forcing private mutual aid associations to be incorporated into the HI. The government justified the compulsory measure by claiming that only a few private mutual aid associations were offering adequate health insurance coverage. But the government also saw the HI as "an initial attempt to devise what would hopefully become a series of labor insurance programs."[51]

The other component of the HI was Government-Managed Health Insurance (GMHI; Seifu Kanshō Hoken). GMHI covered those who worked for smaller firms with more than fifteen employees. In contrast to the SMHI, the government was the sole insurer in this program. This policy scheme did not exist in Britain and Germany. The HI included the GMHI because Japan had not developed mature friendly societies, as Britain had, or trade unions that could administer the program. With the GMHI, the government became not only the large insurer but also the supervisor and fee setter.

The HI also helped the government expand its institutional capacity in health care administration. In response to the passage of the HI, in November 1922 the government created the Social Bureau (Hoken Kyoku) as an extraministerial body to the Home Ministry. Health insurance administration was integrated into the new Social Bureau by moving the policy jurisdiction from the Labor Section in the Ministry of Agriculture and Commerce and other agencies. In June 1923, specifically to prepare for implementing the HI, the Health Insurance Section in the Social Bureau was created.[52] The HI gave the government significant power to supervise the SMHI, to be the insurer of the largest health insurance program, and to decide the budget for health insurance. Private doctors had to accept that the HI brought the government in as a third party in their relationship with patients. But private doctors, at least their leaders, were not necessarily losers in the creation of the HI.

The Birth of the Japan Medical Association

The formation of the Japan Medical Association resulted largely from political battles within the field of medicine.[53] In their contest with Kanpō doctors, Western medicine doctors began to form associations to advance the westernization of Japanese medicine. When that battle was won around the turn of the century, the conflict among Western medicine doctors became salient. By that time, the number of private solo practitioners had increased, and they far outnumbered professors at imperial universities and public medical schools and public hospital doctors. Private solo practitioners made up more than 90 percent of all doctors.[54] These solo practitioners hoped to break away from the tradition in which Tokyo Imperial University was the dominant power. With Kitasato's leadership, they created the Greater Japan Medical Association in 1916 to further strengthen their control over private solo practitioners and their political leverage against public doctors. They concluded that it would be necessary to have legal status for their national organization as a public body and make all doctors, including public doctors, participate in the GJMA. To fight against public doctors, the elite private practitioners sought to approach and work with the government which needed their cooperation to implement its policies on the ground.

They started at the regional level. The Medical Practitioners' Act (Ishi Hō) was amended in 1919 to make the establishment of prefectural-level and municipality-level medical associations mandatory; all doctors, including doctors in the national and other public hospitals, had to belong to these associations. The regional associations gained the status of public incorporation.[55] This was an important victory for the private practitioners. But the next step for the GJMA was for it to become publicly incorporated.

The establishment of the HI gave the GJMA an opportunity to achieve this goal. When Shinpei Gotō had his second appointment as home minister (September 1923–January 1924), he gave the GJMA the status that elite private practitioners wanted. The Medical Practitioners' Act Amendment of 1923 publicly incorporated the GJMA, which was then renamed the Japan Medical Association (Nihon Ishikai).[56] At the first meeting of the JMA, Shibasaburō Kitasato was elected president, and Taichi Kitajima was made chief executive director.[57] Although the new national organization did not yet require mandatory participation, elite private practitioners had achieved their goal of garnering status as a public corporation.

The creation of the JMA was beneficial not only for private doctors but also for the government. The Home Ministry particularly had a stake in having a stronger national organization of private doctors to run the first major public health insurance program. According to writer Yasumasa Ikura, "the government was passive toward the development of national and other public medical institutions. When the HI was to be implemented, private solo practitioners had to be included as part of the government's social policy. The legally incorporated JMA was needed for the government to connect with solo practitioners who were allowed to practice whenever they wanted without any coordination."[58]

Did Kitasato and other leaders only reluctantly accept the HI as an exchange for gaining public corporate status? Public health insurance introduced the government as a third party into doctors' business decisions. Doctors did not like this situation. However, the GJMA had already become involved in the planning for establishing a health insurance system in 1918. In response to the government's research activities on health insurance legislation, the GJMA established its own Investigation Committee on Sickness and Disability Insurance (Shippei oyobi Shōgaihoken Seido Chōsakai). The GJMA invited government officials, such as the head of Social Bureau, to discuss the subject with the association.[59] The JMA accepted the HI mainly for three reasons.

First, the JMA was being threatened by new medical service providers, such as the actual-expense clinics, which the association had no control over. These nonmembers provided medical services at significantly discounted rates and criticized JMA member doctors for being moneymaking businesses. Takashi Saguchi described the actual-expense clinic as "putting medicine as a commodity in the hands of the people. . . . It was a pioneer in the movement for socialized medicine."[60] As competition increased, the JMA concluded that it would be better to cooperate with the government to form a health insurance system than to be seen as only interested in making money. JMA member doctors could also win back patients from rival providers.[61]

Second, coverage by the new public health insurance program appeared to be too small to have a large impact on the incomes of elite solo practitioners.[62] Initially, about 70 percent of doctors participated in the HI, which meant that each doctor had twenty-four enrollees.[63]

Third, the leaders of the JMA hoped to use the HI to expand their influence with other private solo practitioners. To gain this authority they had to acquire institutional legitimacy. Comparison with the JMA's US counterpart is useful. The American Medical Association (AMA) was established in 1847 when the federal government's power was very limited. Thus, the association was proactively engaged in setting up standards for medical schools and a licensing system. The AMA was able to become the legitimate authority on medical practices.[64] The JMA lacked the kind of legal authority the AMA had, and so the JMA relied on the government to provide authority. The JMA's difficult position became apparent, however, when the fee system of the HI was discussed.

The payment mechanism of the HI was determined by a "secret summit conference" between the government and JMA leaders.[65] The resulting mechanism was a combination of capitation and fee-for-service. The JMA was responsible for paying prefectural medical associations according to the number of patient enrollees (*jintō ukeoi shiki*). Doctors were reimbursed based on a fee schedule determined by the JMA. This situation was an opportunity for the national association to have local medical associations under its control. Although the total budget was to be annually negotiated between the JMA and the government, there was a problem for the JMA, because the annual budget would not automatically change with changing economic conditions. Because prefectures got a set amount of the budget, doctors' fees were higher in prefectures with fewer patients.[66] The JMA demanded that the HI set only minimum fees, so that doctors would have the discretion to ask for more from patients, but this request was not accepted by the government.[67]

The payment mechanism also shaped who served as the insurance doctors. The HI plan adopted what is called the principle of collective agreement and free choice (*dantai jiyū sentaku shugi*). This meant that the government and the JMA agreed to provide medical services, JMA members could choose whether or not to accept government health insurance, and patients could choose any doctor from among the JMA doctors who agreed to take insurance payments. This system was a trade-off, as the JMA lost the battle about the fee system. With this system, the JMA could avoid a situation in which the government or SMHI societies might bypass the JMA and directly designate health insurance doctors.[68]

Leading private practitioners agreed to cooperate with the government in creating a health insurance system. It was beneficial for the JMA because it gave the JMA leaders political advantages within the medical field. The JMA succeeded in establishing its status as the representative organization of private practitioners. Not only could the JMA have solo practitioners under its control, but it could also weaken the power of public doctors in medical affairs. Kitasato proudly stated of the JMA, "The approximately thirty thousand members are private practitioners who have direct contact with the people."[69] The JMA also strengthened its position in relation to the private rival organizations, such as the actual-expense clinics, by prohibiting nondoctors from managing clinics and hospitals and refusing to admit them as JMA members.[70]

The JMA's intention to increase its power vis-à-vis the government was less successful. The government, of course, saw what the JMA was trying to do. The JMA was able to get more control over doctors by being the sole professional negotiator with the government. But the government did not guarantee that fees would rise with an increase in the number of enrollees or with inflation. The Medical Practitioners' Act Amendment in 1919, moreover, served as a preemptive attack on the JMA. The legislation included a provision that "if any of the decisions or actions violated existing laws and ordinances or were 'deemed detrimental to the public welfare,' the Home Minister was authorized either to take over control of the association or order it to be dissolved."[71] This was a "political land mine" planted by the government. Kitajima recalled how the government viewed the JMA as an organization. He later wrote, "Government officials made various criticisms. They said that the JMA was always in confusion, that administration offices of regional association were often located in the president's private house, that the JMA's control power over members was weak. We suffered from these criticisms from government officials."[72] While the JMA gained by cooperating with the HI, the association's relationship with the government was not balanced, and the JMA had to accept the potential booby traps set by the government.

The JMA was situated in a difficult context to develop as an autonomous professional group. The government's power remained strong, though democratization advanced. Furthermore, the creation of the HI preceded the formation of the JMA. What the JMA could do was to agree to maximize its benefits within the given institutional setting. The political land mines for the government were detonated when World War II began and expanded. The JMA did not have the capacity to proactively deal with the war.

IMPROVING PEOPLE'S HEALTH FOR WAR

The 1920s were an advantageous time for advocates of democratization in Japan. After the Meiji Restoration, Japan made efforts to create political institutions like the ones of the Western powers. After Takashi Hara formed the first party government and male suffrage was introduced in 1925, political parties seemed to have become the center of political life. Democracy was the new way to operate, and it seemed to be progressing well. There was, however, a parallel movement that increasingly threw a dark shadow over the nation.

With the democratization process advancing, Japan emerged as a rival to Western countries in international politics. Japan also won two large-scale wars: the Sino-Japanese War (1894–95) and the Russo-Japanese War (1904–5). Many Japanese were excited because Japan beat the largest country in Asia (China) and then became the first non-Western country to win a war against a Western country (Russia). World War I then resulted in Japan's obtaining a permanent seat on the Council of the League of Nations and in the shift of concessions in Shandong Province in China from Germany to Japan. Some, especially in the Army, began to pursue economic and political interests in the nearby Manchurian area of northeast China.

In September 1931, seeking opportunities to expand its military activities in northeast China, the Japanese Kwantung Army dynamited the railway track in Mukden and blamed it on China. This event is commonly known as the Mukden Incident. The Japanese Army used this opportunity to invade northeastern China, or Manchuria, and eventually got the entire area under Japanese control. Manchukuo was established there as a puppet state of Japan. Major Western nations criticized the Japanese invasion, and the League of Nations dispatched an inquiry commission, called the Lytton Commission after its leader Victor Alexander George Robert Bulwer-Lytton. The commission concluded in October 1932 that Manchuria should be an autonomous region under China's sovereignty. Of course, the Japanese government disagreed with this decision. Japan chose a path that was more and more isolated from the framework of the League of Nations, which was created after World War I to prevent another international war from taking place. In March 1933, Japan formally announced its withdrawal from the League of Nations. In December 1934 Japan withdrew from the London Naval Treaty, which limited naval shipbuilding by France, Italy, the United Kingdom, the United States, and Japan.

The Mukden Incident and the subsequent establishment of Manchukuo were just the beginning of Japan's war activity. In 1937, the Marco Polo Bridge Incident, a regional military confrontation, quickly resulted in a full-scale battle between China's National Revolutionary Army and Japan's Imperial Army.[1] In December 1941, Japan went on to declare war on the United States and Britain and further expanded the fronts on which the country was engaged in war. Now the Japanese government needed to mobilize all human resources to win the expanded war.

The war lasted for eight years and two months. Mobilization at its peak involved 11.5 percent of the population.[2] This enormous external pressure affected domestic politics and policy in Japan. The war provided a critical juncture for health insurance policy: the government had wider policy options and stronger power to intervene in the health care system.

The nation's health was important in many ways, including the performance of soldiers; the productivity of those working in the war industry; and the health of women as alternative workers, spouses of soldiers, and mothers of future soldiers and workers. Health care policy became part of the national defense. This critical juncture induced involvement in the health care policymaking process by an unusual actor: the military. The military pressured the government to achieve what it had sought, which was the expansion of the health care administrative capacity and the improvement of the people's access to medical services. The wars gave the government justification to make drastic reforms from the top.

On the other hand, this critical juncture also made private actors overall lose the autonomy they had enjoyed during the democratic advances of the 1910s and 1920s. A coup d'état by young officers of the Imperial Japanese Army—what is called the 2-26 Incident—took place in 1936. The victims included two cabinet members, Interior Minister Minoru Saitō and Finance Minister Korekiyo Takahashi. Although the coup d'état was soon suppressed, it triggered further military influence in government interference in society. To prevent further social disorder, the government issued a martial law order. The government banned May Day activities and began to consider dissolving labor unions, which had been active since the economic depression began in 1929. The Japan Federation of Labor (Nihon Rōdō Sōdōmei), which had become conservative, passed a resolution at its annual meeting in October 1937 saying that the organization would cooperate with the government in its war in China. Nevertheless, the federation, too, was eventually dissolved, and its members joined the Imperial Rule Assistance Association (Taiseiyokusankai), a government organization.[3]

Like the labor unions, the Japan Medical Association faced the problem of losing its autonomy. But the institutional and political context was different from the one labor unions faced. The JMA was already working closely with the government. When the Health Insurance Act was passed and implemented, the government cooperated with the Greater Japan Medical Association, later the JMA. The government had not invested enough in the development of public medical service providers, so it had to embrace the medical association. The JMA had its own reason for working with the government. The medical association was hoping to expand its control over all private practitioners and to become the gateway for medical practitioners with whom the government had to negotiate. The government used the opening to absorb the JMA into Japan's war mobilization effort.

As we have seen, the JMA was threatened by nongovernment social movements such as the actual-expense clinics in urban areas and medical cooperatives in rural areas. In 1930, moreover, the proletarian clinic (*musansha shinryōjo*) was founded in Ōsaki, Tokyo. Unlike previous medical movements that criticized the existing system, the proletarian clinic completely opposed the system.[4] Takashi Saguchi describes two routes to socializing medicine. One way is for the government to do so to meet public demand. The other way is when the grassroots does so as a self-defense measure. He calls the former the "socialization of medicine" and the latter the "socialization movement of medicine." He sees them as inseparable paths.[5]

Because of the wartime mobilization situation, the government was strengthening its top-down socialization approach, while at the same time trying to absorb the JMA and other independent movements. The JMA had been working closely with the government and did not really have time to grow as a professional interest group. At the time of the Marco Polo Bridge Incident, the JMA was only twenty-five years old. When the government expanded its war fronts and intensified its war mobilization efforts, the JMA could not resist government demands and was eventually forced to become a state entity. The government passed legislation creating new public health insurance programs and drastically changed the overall health care system. Because of the war, the government could do what it could not have done in peacetime. Although preexisting health care institutions and policies influenced the government's policy choices and speed of action, the war was a critical juncture in the development of Japan's health insurance approach and affected subsequent policy developments.[6]

Creation of the Ministry of Health and Welfare

As Japan became more isolated in international politics after the Mukden Incident, two political forces came to the fore in reforming policy from the top. These were reform-minded bureaucrats and the military. The two groups had different institutional interests and goals. But they shared a belief in the same means for achieving their institutional and ideological goals: they wanted to do away with party politics, correct the flaws of capitalism, centralize the policymaking process, and seek greater public unity under the government. Each group thought it was the one best able to achieve these ends.

The group of government officials were known as the reformist bureaucrats (*kakushin kanryō*). Many of them were in their late thirties and held positions as division or bureau heads. Their young age is important because many of them were promoted to higher positions after the war, and they had a large influence in the postwar policymaking process. They were typically students from Tokyo Imperial University during the 1920s, where they came in contact with Marxist ideas. Some of them leaned toward socialism, while others did not. But, overall, the reformist bureaucrats were interested in how capitalism worked and its flaws. They concluded that a radical reform was needed. Their ambition was to take over the party government and strengthen bureaucratic power to achieve their vision of social justice.[7]

Kiwao Okumura was a well-known theoretician among reformist bureaucrats. He graduated from the Faculty of Law of Tokyo Imperial University in 1925. He studied under the guidance of Shinkichi Uesugi, who was a leading advocate of the nationalist movement and familiar with Marxist theory. Okumura passed the exam for the highest-level civil servant post and chose the Ministry of Communications because he wanted to be in the field where the government had "a strong cultural function" in people's daily lives. He strongly supported the expansion of government power in order to improve "the public interest."[8] Soon after he came back from a research trip to Europe in December 1937, however, Okumura made positive comments on contemporary transformations in Germany and Italy:

In our country these days people are prejudiced against Italy and Germany, thinking they are simply fascist dictatorships. However, the more I have come to understand the totalitarian basis of these countries, the more I can understand its meaning. A nation should not be an aggregation of individuals but should be understood as the supreme moral force. By replacing individualism with totalitarianism, class conflict is abolished, and cooperation is promoted. Seeking only self-interested goals should be abandoned, while contributing to the well-being of the nation and society should be encouraged. Unlimited freedom should be ended, and order established. This is an extremely radical ideology.[9]

Many reformist bureaucrats had an opportunity to experiment with their theories in the field as they were sent to build the state of Manchukuo. The existing political forces did not bother them there because the bureaucrats had the strong support of the Kwantung Army, which had almost supreme authority in Manchuria. These bureaucrats tested strict centralized control of the economy in order to quickly build up the economy and political institutions. Historian Takahisa Furukawa points out, "Generally speaking, from their experiences in Manchuria, they knew that their reforms could be put into practice. Although the implementation process was not necessarily what they had imagined, they concluded that they were successful and that the same reforms should be made in Japan."[10]

Many military officers cooperated with the reformist bureaucrats not only in order to build up a new state in Manchuria but also to conduct reforms in Japan. Those officers were called *seikei shōko* (military officers who engaged in political economy) and were deeply associated with the agendas of the reformist bureaucrats. Like the reformist bureaucrats, the military officers were from the midlevel officer ranks, such as division heads at headquarters or chiefs of staff with dispatched troops. These officers included those who studied at Tokyo Imperial University under war ministers such as Sadaaki Kagesa, Tsukizō Akinaga, and Sumihisa Ikeda. The reform-minded military officers were closely connected with the reformist bureaucrats.[11]

The reform-minded military officers opposed capitalism, wanted to abolish individualistic culture, and wanted to expand government power in the name of serving the public interest. For both ideological and practical reasons, both groups began to pay careful attention to the health of the nation. They saw a deterioration in people's health as a negative result from having a capitalist economy. The reformist bureaucrats sought to intervene in medicine against the private doctors, whom they saw as trying to prevent further rationalization of the medical system. These bureaucrats thought they could help those who could not afford adequate medical care. The reform-minded military officers were concerned with the people's health because the war in China would, at least in these officers' view, require enlisting more healthy recruits. The officers hoped to make the health care system as efficient and effective as possible through their top-down military approach. The bureaucrats and military officers had different motivations, but they shared the same goal of trying to increase their power in the name of serving the public interest. The establishment of the Ministry of Health and Welfare was their first major achievement.

Since the 1910s, institutional capacity regarding health care had gradually expanded. Radical social actions, such as the labor union movement, the Russian Revolution, and the rice riots forced the government to engage in social policies to try to ease tensions. In preparing for the Health Insurance Act of 1922, the Social Bureau (Shakai Kyoku) was created in August 1920. Within the new bureau, the Division of Insurance was created to take over administration of health insurance from the Ministry of Agriculture. In November 1922, the Social Bureau was promoted to become an external ministerial agency in the Home Ministry. Hirokichi Nadao, who became the permanent vice minister of home in 1945, was then a young official in the Hygiene Bureau. He was ordered to move to the newly established Social Bureau. He later described the mood of the new bureau among the officials: "We were the pioneers of the new administration."[12] The new Social Bureau replaced the labor administration and the social administration, whose parts were scattered to many ministries and agencies. The Social Bureau became the central organization of social administration, including health care.[13]

By the mid-1930s, the Army Ministry began to pay serious attention to health care largely because the ministry was shocked by the results of the physical examinations of conscripts: more men failed the exam than in the previous decade.[14] As a solution to this problem, in June 1936, the Army Ministry's Medical Care Bureau submitted an outline for a new ministry, which they called the Ministry of Hygiene (Eisei Shō), to coordinate and strengthen health care administration and take more control over it. Army Minister Hisaichi Terauchi pointed to the success of Germany and Britain in improving the health of their people when explaining why he thought the new ministry was needed. But he understood that the proposal would not be approved easily. He stated, "The government is rather negative about the Army's demand to establish the Ministry of Hygiene as a means for improving health care. . . . The government has had an overall intention of rationalizing and downsizing the bloated bureaucracy. The establishment of the new ministry would go against this intention, and it would be very difficult to make it happen."[15]

To try to convince the government to create the health ministry, Terauchi warned about the deterioration of people's health in a cabinet meeting: "This is dangerous for the nation. We must deal with this problem as an urgent national issue."[16] Four days later, he released a document entitled "Regarding the Establishment of the Ministry of Hygiene." Prime Minister Kōki Hirota decided to expand health care administration. He had the cabinet approve the "Seven Major State Policies," his administration's basic guiding principles, which included the improvement of health care facilities.[17]

Hirota had been appointed prime minister in March 1936 after the 2-26 Incident. He fired many high-ranking military officers in a large-scale reshuffling of personnel. However, he restored the policy by which only active generals and lieutenant generals could be appointed to head the Army and Navy Ministries (Gunbu Daijin Gen'ekibukan Sei). By reviving this policy, which had been abolished in 1913, he hoped to prevent retired officers who were suspected to be involved in the 2-26 Incident from being appointed to these positions. But this also meant that the military gained more influence in the government by acquiring the power to cast a veto and force the entire cabinet to resign. The cabinet had to make decisions unanimously.[18]

The Army Ministry continued to pressure the government to improve health care administration. In May 1937, the ministry presented a more detailed plan for the proposed new ministry. Chikahiko Koizumi, a career Army officer and director of the Army's Medical Bureau, was a central figure in the Army Ministry.[19] When Koizumi became the director of the bureau in 1934, he reformed its administration. He concluded that the health of soldiers depended on how healthy the overall population was. Unlike his predecessors, he frequently addressed questions about public health to the Hygiene Bureau of the Home Ministry.[20] Ichimin Tako, a Home Ministry bureaucrat (who became the president of the lower house in 1941), praised the progressiveness of Koizumi's proposal: "The Army is more responsive (than other government agencies) to social needs relating to social-welfare facilities and health."[21]

When Fumimaro Konoe became prime minister in June 1937, Koizumi aggressively lobbied him to establish the Ministry of Hygiene.[22] As Konoe tried to form his cabinet, moreover, the Army minister proposed creating the new ministry in exchange for supporting Konoe's cabinet. Hirota's decision to have only active military officers as military ministers was significant in this matter. Konoe accepted the deal because he needed to have the Army's cooperation to form his cabinet.[23] Right before the opening of the new ministry in January 11, 1938, a leading newspaper, *Yomiuri Shimbun*, reported:

> The Konoe administration began on June 4 last year. Because the Ministry of Health and Welfare (earlier proposed by the Army Ministry as the Ministry of Hygiene) was decided by his cabinet to be established

on its fifth day, it was considered as the reformist government's first de-
cisive step. But that is not true. The truth is that the military lobbied
the Hirota administration for a health care organization as part of national defense. . . . Therefore, what the Konoe administration did was
just to succeed in what the previous administration tried to do.[24]

Historian Kazutaka Kojima tells a slightly different story than the newspaper does. He points out that Konoe already had his own idea for a welfare state,
and it was different from the idea proposed by the Army Ministry. Immediately
after his administration came into being, Konoe ordered the Planning Agency
(Kikaku Chō) in his cabinet to create a proposal for a new ministry, which he
called the "Konoe plan."[25] Kojima argues that while the Army Ministry focused
on the improvement of people's physical strength, Konoe was thinking more of
social security and social justice.[26] His idea of social security and social justice
was, of course, restricted by the period he was living in. Konoe liked to read philosophy with a Marxist tint. He was close to Home Ministry bureaucrats Ichimin Tako and Kakichi Kawarada, who were thought to play an important role
in writing the final proposal from the Home Ministry.[27] Konoe's idea was within
the framework of the reformist bureaucrats. Compared with the idea of the postwar welfare state, Konoe's plan focused much less on a democratic process for
achieving the proposed new ministry. This difference resulted not only from the
limitations of his own ideas but also from the fact that the military was the main
driving force that could make the proposal a reality.

The Marco Polo Bridge Incident prevented the government from focusing on
domestic policy for a while, and the creation of the new ministry was put on hold.
But soon the government realized that the war could last longer than expected
and that a more centralized administration for mobilizing human resources
would be necessary. At this point the establishment of the new health ministry
regained momentum. In December 1937, as the government reorganization plan
required, the government consulted with the Privy Council (Genrō In), which
gave advice to the emperor, and gained its approval for establishing the new
ministry.

There was a controversy about what to name the new ministry. Konoe's proposal was for it to be called the Ministry of Health and Social Affairs (Hoken
Shakai Shō). Because it included the term *social* (*shakai*), the name was criticized
for appearing to be socialist. Hiroshi Minami, a member of the Privy Council,
researched many works of Chinese classic literature. In *Shu Ching* he found the
term *kōsei*, which meant "security so that the people have an adequate living."
The newly established Ministry of Health and Welfare (MHW; Kōseishō) came
into operation on January 11, 1938.[28]

Army Medical Bureau director Koizumi is considered the founding father of the MHW. He remarked about the new ministry, "Under this emergent war situation, we need to intensify mobilization, and we must immediately improve human resources for the war. . . . I would like to express my high expectation for the new ministry to aggressively advance this goal."[29] The *Yomiuri Shimbun* confirmed what Koizumi said when the newspaper announced that the MHW was established "because we are facing an international crisis and need to make a concerted effort to dramatically improve people's health."[30] Two prominent insiders, Fumihide Okada (vice minister of the MHW, January 1939–April 1940) and Gunji Takei (vice minister of the MHW, November 1941–April 1944), confirmed that the progress of the war pushed the creation of the new ministry. In Okada's words, the MHW "was born out of the war."[31]

The MHW consisted of five bureaus and one independent board for planning and implementing social policies. The five bureaus were the Bureau of Physical Fitness (Tairyoku Kyoku), the Bureau of Hygiene (Eisei Kyoku), the Bureau of Disease Prevention (Yobō Kyoku), the Bureau of Social Affairs (Shakai Kyoku), and the Labor Bureau (Rōdō Kyoku). The Insurance Board (Hoken In) was established as an extraministerial agency.[32] The MHW also had jurisdiction over existing government-sponsored health care agencies, including the National Institute of Public Health, the National Nutrition Research Institute, and the National Leprosarium and Sanatorium.[33]

In addition to the establishment of the MHW, the government centralized the overall administration to gear up for war mobilization. In October 1937, the Planning Agency was promoted to become the Board of Planning (Kikaku In), under the direct supervision of the prime minister.[34] The board's task was to "present proposals to the prime minister with their rationales to improve comprehensive national power both in peacetime and wartime and for the cabinet for to coordinate war mobilization."[35] Masao Taki, Board of Planning's first director, and Kazuo Aoki, the deputy director, were among the group of reformist bureaucrats and reform-minded military officers. While the Imperial General Headquarters (Daihon'ei) was the center for war activities, the new Board of Planning played a central role in planning and implementing domestic policies.[36] The board designed the National Mobilization Act (Kokka Sōdōin Hō), which was established in April 1938 to coordinate material and human resources.

In 1938, Kōgorō Uemura, head of the Industrial Division of the Board of Planning and a well-known reformist bureaucrat, stressed the importance of human resources in war mobilization: "Money and materiel might be borrowed or found, but human resources cannot be supplemented easily, and they are at the center of the war mobilization."[37] Public health insurance became a means for the government to quickly improve people's health. In the same month as the introduction of the National Mobilization Act, major health insurance legislation was passed in the Imperial Diet.

The Creation of Public Health Insurance Programs

As we have seen, the first major health insurance legislation was the Health Insurance Act of 1922. From the beginning, when the HI began to be implemented in 1927, it was an unpopular program. First, doctors complained that the HI fees were insufficient and that the paperwork was very complicated.[38] Second, the insured workers were dissatisfied with the HI because some doctors refused to see insured patients or were reluctant to offer adequate care.[39] Third, large businesses complained that their employees abused the HI, while smaller businesses complained that the HI put more burden on them than on large companies because the same premium load was fixed for all firms that enrolled in Government-Managed Health Insurance.[40] Lastly, those who were very healthy and did not need to use their health insurance tended to be suspicious about the HI.[41]

Coverage under the HI increased only gradually. When the HI began to be implemented, only about 3 percent of the population was covered. To recap: the HI covered workers only in certain industrial sectors and included neither their family members nor agricultural workers, who made up the predominant part of the workforce at that time. The Health Insurance Act Amendment of 1934 expanded the legislation's mandatory coverage from workplaces with more than fifteen employees to ones with more than five employees. The amendment also included workers in the electrical utility and transportation industries. Even with the 1934 amendment, however, the number of enrollees increased to only 4.9 percent of the Japanese population in 1936.[42]

When the war context emerged, the government faced pressure to be involved in health care as part of national defense. The question was how the government would cover the rest of the population. Because of the unpopularity of the HI, private actors were expected to oppose any new legislation for public health insurance. In the case of "total war," however, the government gained stronger political leverage against the JMA and other private actors. Being involved in a total war put the nation in danger of extinction and required mobilizing all resources in society for victory. Japan and other countries saw the nature of war mobilization change with World War I. War activities had to be given highest priority, and civilian needs were subordinated to the requirements of war. At the same time, the idea of universalism became important for the government, because this idea consolidated all the people, no matter which social and economic class they belonged to, behind the goal of winning the war.[43] Countries cannot survive a total war with a divided society.

The concept of total war significantly changed the roles of two organizations in the policymaking process of health insurance: the JMA and the military. In peacetime, the JMA could claim that it was an important actor in the democratic process. In a condition of total war, however, the JMA could be seen as being unpatriotic for lobbying for its own group. Without total war the military had no cause to be involved with health insurance for civilians. But to win the total war, the military was able to push for a more egalitarian health insurance program to improve the health of all Japanese. Reformist bureaucrats took this opportunity to ally with the military and do what they could not do in peacetime.

The deteriorating health of farmers as a result of rapid industrialization began to be noticed in the 1920s. The worldwide depression triggered by the New York stock market crash in October 1929 only made the farmers' situation worse. The spread of epidemic and chronic diseases, especially tuberculosis, devastated the rural population.[44] The Mukden Incident in 1931 boosted the Japanese economy for a short time but did not much improve the economic condition of the rural population. The death rate from tuberculosis decreased slightly but started to increase again in 1933.[45] Expansion of medical cooperatives in rural areas also did not drastically improve this situation. Historian Akira Sugaya has noted that, at that time, it was often the case that farmers could see a doctor only when death certificates were needed.[46]

Because 83 percent of the Army's soldiers were sons of peasants, in 1932, the military became seriously concerned about the anxiety that Japanese soldiers abroad had about their parents' lives back home. The Army started to consider measures to deal with the problem and produced some ways to help farmers financially.[47] In April 1933, moreover, the Social Bureau in the Home Ministry began to study the health conditions of farmers. After about a year, the Social Bureau released a draft for a possible public health insurance program for farmers.[48]

The JMA made efforts to block the Social Bureau's plan. Hitoshi Suzuki, a representative of the JMA, argued in September 1934, "I see that the Health Insurance Act of 1922 has had problems and been ineffective. It will cause further tragedy and danger if we have a large-scale health insurance program."[49] The JMA was frustrated by the administration of the HI, and the association opposed any further state intervention in health care financing. The JMA's argument was not at first criticized for being unpatriotic because the military's role was not yet large enough to allow for characterizing the JMA that way.

Nevertheless, the conflict between the reformist bureaucrats and reform-minded military officers, on one side, and the JMA, on the other, continued. In October 1935, the Home Ministry asked the Social Security Investigation

Committee (Shakaihokenseido Chōsakai) for a more detailed plan for health care for farmers, and the committee soon submitted a report that stated that "health insurance for the rural population is necessary for solving deteriorating social conditions."[50] An event in the mid-1930s also made the Army more impatient to see an expanded health care plan adopted. The Army had dispatched two divisions to Manchuria, and one battalion of about five hundred soldiers turned out to be infected with tuberculosis and had to be sent back to Japan.[51] Soldiers' health, and more broadly the health of the general Japanese population, became even more serious concerns for the Army as the war grew and the Army began to plan to draft conscripts for an extended time.[52] The JMA again campaigned against the committee's proposal. When, in 1936, the Social Bureau proposed its plan to establish a national health insurance program that targeted mainly farmers, the JMA sent telegrams to the bureau charging that "the National Health Insurance Act will kill all of us."[53] An article in a major newspaper reported that medical schools saw a big drop in the number of applicants as a result of the debate regarding the National Health Insurance Act. The applicants were worried about their future under the expanding public health insurance system.[54]

The newly created Ministry of Health and Welfare proposed the National Health Insurance Act (NHI; Kokumin Kenkō Hoken Hō) as its first bill. It was enacted on April 11, 1938, and implemented on July 1, 1938. Kōichi Kido, the first minister of health and welfare, claimed that "the NHI was not directly related to the Mukden Incident." However, he admitted that the NHI did result from "the acute realization of its necessity because of the national emergency."[55] The MHW also commented on the act's passage in the Imperial Diet's upper house: "The MHW made every effort to swiftly expand this policy. But it essentially relies on the self-governing organizations that are based on the spirit of mutual help. It would have been difficult to expand this policy without the people's deep understanding and strong support."[56] Kido and the MHW made such nuanced comments to avoid the impression that the plan was the government's strong top-down initiative. However, an editorial in the *Tokyo Asahi Shimbun* discussed the nature of the NHI:

> In contrast to the Factory Act Amendment (of 1923), which was based on the idea of liberalism, social policies these days are more easily passed because they are needed for the cultivation and protection of human resources in the national emergency. . . . It is hard to overlook that the budget for the policy's implementation was very small. The worry is that the law has a deceptive appearance and is without substance. The NHI and other social policies are such examples, and we have a serious problem.[57]

The JMA had reasons for not opposing the NHI more strongly. To avoid being labeled as unpatriotic, the JMA cooperated with the government. Moreover, solo practitioners themselves were financially struggling. They were suffering not only from the Great Depression but also from competition with the actual-expense clinics and those who provided free medical treatment for the poor.[58] Furthermore, the creation of the Ōsaki Proletarian Clinic in 1930 had led to a movement to create such clinics in other regions.[59] All these alternatives put pressure on the JMA to deal with the people's health. Once again, the JMA cooperated with the government, as the association had when the HI was created. But this time, the JMA was in a more politically defensive position against the government.

The NHI was a weaker program than the HI, mainly for the following two reasons. First, the NHI was less well funded than the HI. Farmers and fishermen were generally poorer, at least in terms of cash income, than industrial workers. Moreover, farmers and fishers did not receive matching contributions from employers. Although the law stipulated that the government would subsidize insurance payments, it could not provide enough assistance. Consequently, NHI beneficiaries were required to make large co-payments, from about a third to half of the cost of services—a provision that did not exist in the HI. Moreover, because the government gave these administrative bodies a great deal of discretion, including control over benefits, some associations provided only minimum medical services to the enrollees.[60] A second reason for the program's weakness was that the NHI set up National Health Insurance associations (Kokumin Kenkō Hoken Kumiai) to run the program, but both the establishment of these associations and participation of qualified members were voluntary.[61] This situation caused adverse selection: sicker, and often poorer, people were more likely to join.

While the HI initially covered only about 2 million people, the NHI had the potential to cover 50 million people. The NHI, with its financial limitations and voluntarism, however, did not expand as the MHW had planned. Because of the necessities of war, as the editorial of the *Tokyo Asahi Shimbun* pointed out, the government was building something that was not as good as it looked.

The NHI was set up this way because it was created not as a result of social demands but from the needs of war. The government had to quickly create a national health insurance program for a much larger population than that covered by the HI. The problem was that government finances were already stressed by rising war expenditures, so that the government had to create a health insurance program as cheaply as possible. The voluntarism and fragmented administration structure were largely the product of the government's financial difficulties, but they became another reason for the JMA to accept the NHI. The JMA realized that it had diminishing negotiating space.

By the time the NHI was created in April 1938, the government understood that it had to mobilize more people for its expanding war fronts. Health and Welfare Minister Kido said in December 1938 that "the war in China has become a long war. We need to produce more measures for the defense of the home front."[62] In January 1939, Seiichi Shindō, director of the Board of Insurance, specifically mentioned the importance of health insurance measures in these circumstances: "Health insurance programs help strengthen our spirit and health for winning the war."[63] Because the NHI mainly targeted those in rural areas, the government also planned programs for workers not covered by HI.

The first legislation in 1939 was Seamen's Insurance (Sen'in Hoken Hō).[64] Because Japan is an island country, private seamen were critical for the war activities and the economy of the home front. Hisatada Hirose, vice minister of the MHW from January 1938 to January 1939 and the minister from January 1939 to August 1939, argued for the bill: "Because seamen play a large role in national defense, it is crucial to provide security for the seamen."[65] In addition to being better subsidized by the government than other health insurance programs, it was also a comprehensive social security program including also old-age pensions and life insurance.[66]

The second program in 1939 was White-Collar Workers' Health Insurance (Shokuin Kenkō Hoken Hō). The White-Collar Workers' Health Insurance Act passed after only one month of discussion. Hirose argued in the Diet that the White-Collar Workers' Health Insurance program should be established "for strengthening human resources for the battlefield and activities on the home front in this national emergency."[67] In contrast to the generous benefits of the Seamen's Insurance program, the White-Collar Workers' Health Insurance program reflected the government's financial problems.

The White-Collar Workers' Health Insurance program included a plan to give the government more power in keeping down health care costs. Unlike the HI, which did not require any co-payments, the White-Collar Workers' Health Insurance program required a co-payment by enrollees of 20 percent of the cost of care. The program also set a new fee schedule, with fee-for-service compensation based on a government point system (kinrō teigaku shiki), whereas the HI relied on the combination of capitation and fee-for-service (jintō ukeoi shiki). With the new system, the government set the fee per official point at 20 sen (1/5 yen) and created a fee schedule based on how many points each medical service had. This fee-schedule change, according to historian Takeshi Kawakami, allowed the government to avoid troublesome negotiating with the JMA and keep down the cost of medical services.[68]

It is important to note here that the fee-for-service system replaced the old system and by doing so gave the government more power, as the government could set the fees. This fee system was adopted for all programs after the war, when the system became the focus of the battle between the government and the JMA.

Radical Expansion of the Government's Power

In July 1940, Prime Minister Konoe advocated the creation of what was known as the Greater East Asia Co-Prosperity Sphere (Daitōakyōeiken) with Japan at the head. This was the philosophical idea that Japan would liberate Asian regions from European imperialism, and these areas would develop together under Japan's leadership. This concept supported Japanese expansion into Asian regions outside China. This idea gained strong support from the government, particularly the Army, which sought to secure natural resources in Southeast Asia. In September 1940, Japan signed the Tripartite Pact with Italy and Germany and thus became part of a military coalition. Now required to be prepared for a devastating war with the Allied Powers, the government had complete justification to be involved in health care, as it was necessary for victory. With the increasing military budget, however, the government needed to make its health care system as economically efficient as possible. The government undertook drastic reforms from the top.

After the MHW was established and the NHI began to be implemented, the Diet started discussing fundamental reform of the entire medical system and medical regulations. In July 1938, the government set up the Medical Care and Pharmaceutical Research Council (Iyakuseido Chōsakai), to be headed by the minister of health and welfare.[69] One of the main purposes of the council was to prepare a proposal for improving the medical provider system that had up until then been based largely on private practitioners. The council submitted a report in October 1940 that recommended the government gain greater control over private practitioners. The report suggested reorganizing the JMA so that all doctors would be required to join the new JMA. The president of the new JMA would be appointed by the government. The report also included proposals for building public hospitals and clinics in areas that had no doctors, authorizing the government to designate insurance doctors, and expanding the coverage of health insurance.[70] These suggestions of the council became the basis for the drastic reforms of 1942.

Koizumi, a longtime advocate for a larger role for government in health care, became minister of health and welfare in July 1941, a position he held until July 1944. He took the lead in bringing to fruition the council's recommendations. He introduced the slogan, "Healthy soldiers, healthy people" (*kenmin kenpei*), which suggested that a strong military relied on having a healthy population.[71] He believed that the existing medical provider system needed to be overhauled. In his first interview with medical reporters when he became minister, he demonstrated his confrontational attitude toward private practitioners.[72] Koizumi had a powerful justification for radical reform: everything would be for winning the war and realizing the Greater East Asia Co-Prosperity Sphere.

The government had to deal not only with the quality of Japan's population but also with the quantity. Before the war, the government was planning to reduce the country's population because Japan was limited in natural resources. By 1940, however, the government reversed this policy because of the human resource needs of the war. The government found that not only tuberculosis but also a high mortality rate lowered Japan's life expectancy to ten years shorter than major Western countries from 1926 to 1930. The birthrate also had declined from 36.2 per 1,000 in 1920 to 27.2 per 1,000 in 1938. In January 1941, the cabinet prepared the Outline for the Establishment of Population Policy (Jinkō Seisaku Kakuritsu Yōkō) as part of its proposal for improvement of the health education system and the expansion of health insurance. A policy entitled "Give birth for the nation!" (umeyo huyaseyo) was implemented in order to increase the size of the population.[73] A cabinet meeting in January 1941 proposed a policy for increasing the population from the current 72 million to 100 million by 1960.[74]

The government increased the facilities and capacity of health centers (hokensho). In 1937, the Health Center Act was established to improve the network of health centers. Nine new centers were created in 1938, 30 in 1939, 6 in 1940, and 53 in 1941. The number reached 770 by 1944. The regulation to implement the Health Center Act stipulated that each center must have three public health nurses (hokenfu). Women were mobilized to work as public health nurses, and their occupation status was improved. There were many different kinds of names for those who engaged in guiding the local residents about their health problems. In July 1941, the government unified them as public health nurses and set standards, such as age and education requirements.[75] While women might well have derived benefits from the newly introduced checkup programs and nutrition programs as well as a record system for expectant and nursing mothers and their babies, the investment in health centers and public health nurses resulted from the government's concerns for improving the Japanese people's health for the war.[76]

The combination of the report of the Social Security Investigation Committee, the new population policy, Koizumi's strong leadership, and the changing war situation led to the enactment of the National Medical Care Act (Kokumin

Iryō Hō) in February 1942. This was only a few months after Japan's attack on Pearl Harbor. The first article of the act stated, "This law aims at improving the people's health by reforming the medical system."[77] The act changed and integrated the regulations on medical care, including the Medical Practitioners' Act and the Medical Rules and Regulations. The National Medical Care Act reflected the recommendations of the Medical Care and Pharmaceutical Research Council, such as creating new public hospitals and clinics, regulating private hospital construction, and reorganizing the JMA as a state entity. Meanwhile, public health nurses, along with nurses and midwives, for the first time had the legal status of medical personnel, joining doctors, dentists, and pharmacists.[78]

The National Medical Care Act also allowed for the establishment of the government-owned Japan Medical Corporation (Kokumin Iryō Dan). With a budget of 100 million yen, the corporation was set up to purchase private hospitals and clinics, run them as public facilities, and educate medical professionals in them. The Japan Medical Corporation was established in April 1942 with Ryōkichi Inada as the president. Inada was a professor at Tokyo Imperial University, and his vice president, Shin'ichiro Takasugi, was the Navy's surgeon general. The JMA had no representatives in the corporation's executive body.[79] Koizumi showed strong leadership by establishing this huge extradepartmental organization in order to achieve his plans to improve the people's health for the war.[80]

While engaged in restructuring the medical provider system, the government also expanded its power over public health insurance by amending the HI and the NHI. Koizumi again demonstrated his strong leadership. He helped to get the Army Ministry and the MHW to join together in supporting expansion of health insurance coverage. In January 1942, Akira Hirai, head of the Insurance Bureau of the MHW, stated, "We have no goals other than winning the war. . . . Healthy soldiers go to the front to beat the United States and Great Britain; healthy people keep up efficient munitions production."[81]

The HI was amended in February 1942 to incorporate the White-Collar Health Insurance program. The merger changed the politics of the HI. The HI adopted co-payments and the government-controlled fee-for-service payment system of the White-Collar Workers' Health Insurance program. The JMA lost its status as sole negotiator with the government for the budget of the HI.[82] To make things worse for the JMA, the amendment included a provision that doctors could not refuse to accept national health insurance.[83] The amendment passed because "the necessity of strengthening war mobilization led the government to expand the national health insurance system to have 'healthy soldiers, healthy people.'"[84]

The NHI was also amended in February 1942. The NHI was a voluntary program. When the NHI was established, the MHW had a ten-year plan for its gradual expansion. The first three years saw the number of enrollees exceeding what had been planned. But the government needed to push harder to meet war demands. The NHI was amended in May 1942 to make national health insurance associations mandatory, to require almost all people not covered by other health insurance programs to participate in the NHI, and to make it mandatory for doctors to accept health insurance.[85] In October 1941, Koizumi, who had actively supported universal health insurance, declared that Japan must have national health insurance associations in all municipalities within three years. He proposed a new slogan—"All people should have health insurance" (*kokumin kaihoken*)—to go along with the existing wartime slogan "All people are soldiers" (*kokumin kaihei*).[86] In 1942, the government had to budget for 10 million new enrollees. The Imperial Rule Assistance Association, which was created in October 1940 with the strong leadership of Prime Minister Konoe to integrate all political parties into a single party, initiated a coordinating body to create the NHI associations.[87] By the time Japan surrendered in September 1945, national health insurance associations existed in an estimated 95 percent of all Japanese municipalities.[88]

In February 1943, the government standardized the health insurance fee for the HI, the NHI, and Seamen's Insurance. The MHW became responsible for deciding the common medical fees of these programs with nonbinding advice from the JMA, the Japan Dental Association, and the Japan Pharmaceutical Association.[89] In June 1944, the government further strengthened its power to set fees by creating the Committee on Health Insurance Medical Fees (Shakaihoken Shinryōhōshū Santei Iinkai) in the MHW. This committee was composed of eleven members from the JMA, the JDA, and the JPA; eleven from public hospitals, the NHI associations, and others; and eleven from government agencies. This new fee-setting process reconfirmed that the JMA had lost its position as sole negotiator with the government. Akira Sugaya points out that the balanced membership allocation was nominal at the time: the government had control of this committee.[90] The committee could not have been established at this time and with this structure had it not been for the devastating war: the committee was a child of the government's war activity. The Committee on Health Insurance Medical Fees left an important legacy to those engaged in postwar health insurance policy development. Kenji Shimazaki writes, "The few years before WWII ended made the foundation of the health insurance administration up to now."[91]

Under the government's leadership, by 1944 national health insurance programs covered 41 million people, about 70 percent of the population. The rise in national health insurance coverage amazed an officer in the US-led occupation authority in Japan: "There were no other examples in the world like the rapid increase of national health insurance in wartime."[92] The hasty top-down building of the quasi-universal health care system, however, resulted in fragile institutions. In many cases, municipality heads set up their NHI associations through arbitrary decisions, without discussion and cooperation of the members. While the quantity of those insured increased, the quality of care deteriorated.[93] Overall, the national health insurance movement in this period was not set up to insure people against illness or accident but to maintain human resources for the military at low cost. When the war was over, many NHI associations stopped functioning altogether.

Moreover, the Japan Medical Corporation could not reorganize the medical provider system as much as Koizumi and the reformist MHW bureaucrats had hoped. The corporation planned to build a hierarchical medical provider system with two central hospitals (500 beds), one each in the east and west of Japan; one prefectural general hospital (250 beds) in each prefecture; and smaller hospitals at the municipality level. Clinics and other health facilities were at the bottom of the pyramid. The devastation of the war and financial limitations resulted in the corporation achieving only about 30 percent of its goals in quantitative expansion and almost no progress in qualitative change.[94] It was more difficult to change the medical provider system that grew up largely with private practitioners than to expand health insurance coverage for uninsured people.

Another difficult task for the government was the separation of medical treatment from the sale of medicines, which had been pending since the political compromise at the turn of the century that allowed doctors to keep selling medicine. The pharmaceutical policy had been based on the Regulation of Pharmacist Business and Drug Handling of 1898 and other regulations. But the expanding war led to shortages of medicines, and the regulations had to be integrated. The Medical Care and Pharmaceutical Research Council set up the Special Committee on the Pharmaceutical System. The Special Committee proposed promoting the status of pharmacists legally and financially. In January 1943, the government passed the Pharmaceutical Affairs Act (Yakuji Hō). The issue of the separation of medical services and the selling of medicine was still not included. The government had to avoid unnecessary conflict between doctors and pharmacists. What was most important for the government was to "get medical and pharmaceutical practices under control."[95]

Nationalization of the JMA

Shibasaburō Kitasato had been known as the symbolic father of the JMA since its establishment. He had a great deal of respect from private doctors. At that time, many of the presidents of local medical associations were prefectural assembly members, mayors, and other noted people. Nevertheless, they faithfully followed Kitasato's directions. Even though he left his government position after the fight over his research institute, he had deep connections with politicians and bureaucrats, including Giichi Tanaka, who served as prime minister from April 1927 to July 1929.[96] But Kitasato died in June 1931, two months before the Mukden Incident. Kitajima, the former chief executive director and longtime right arm of Kitasato, was elected as the new president of the JMA. Kitajima did not have as much power against the government and respect among the JMA elites as Kitasato had enjoyed. The devastating war made Kitajima's situation worse.

As JMA president, Kitajima experienced increasing pressure from the government to make the JMA cooperate more and more with the country's war mobilization effort. State capacity increased with the newly created MHW. Public health insurance expanded with the NHI, the White-Collar Workers' Health Insurance program, and Seamen's Insurance. After 1942, the government dramatically gained power over health insurance and medical providers through the National Medical Care Act, the Japan Medical Corporation, and the amendments to the HI and the NHI. The government could legitimately intervene in health care during a national crisis. As things progressed, the JMA was publicly attacked as unpatriotic. In 1939, an editorial in the *Tokyo Asahi Shimbun* stated, "The reform of the medical system requires the regeneration of liberal principles and professional ethics. Medicine belongs not to doctors but to the public. Doctors should work for the nation as quasi-public servants."[97] The JMA had received this kind of criticism even before the war, but the association could counter that it represented the interests of private practitioners and that it was an important part of the democratic governing process. As the war intensified, however, the JMA gradually lost its legitimacy to resist the government's intervention. In June 1941, Koizumi called for reforming the JMA in an interview with medical reporters: "Of course, the reform is urgent. We are in a new era. We must change the old system. Reform! Right now! The JMA must immediately reform itself to adjust to the new era! Otherwise, the government will impose reform on the JMA."[98] The JMA could not fight against what Koizumi called "a new era."

The JMA found itself absorbed more and more in the government's war mobilization activities. After Japan opened its war against the United States in December 1941, the government issued the Ordinance for the Conscription of Medical Personnel (Iryōkankeisha Chōyōrei) to prepare private doctors for "when the nation is under air raids, when designated factories need emergency medical care, when epidemic diseases spread, and when medical providers drastically decrease in some regions."[99] Doctors who remained in the homeland rather than at the battlefield were to be forced to work in military industry factories, in villages without doctors, or for other public organizations.[100]

The JMA was not entirely against this movement. In 1940 there was a national celebration for the 2,600th anniversary of the ascension to the throne of the first emperor of Japan, Jimmu. There were many exhibitions and sports events to celebrate. The occasion was of course used by the government to affirm the current regime and the war. The JMA responded with a movement called *idō seishin sakkō undo*, which asserted that doctors and medicine should serve the public, but this time emphasizing particularly their service to the emperor.[101] In September 1941, moreover, the JMA preemptively made its own reorganization plan, reorganizing the JMA into the Imperial Medical Association (Teikoku Ishikai) to demonstrate its cooperative stance toward the government's war mobilization. The plan was submitted to the director of the Bureau of Hygiene. Then the JMA formed the Division of Cooperation with the Imperial Rule Assistance Association (Taiseiyokusan Kyōryoku Bu) and made a detailed reorganization plan. The Tokyo Division was formed, and Toshihiko Nakayama and Korekiyo Obata took the lead as its manager and vice manager (both became JMA presidents after the war).[102] In November 1941, senior members of the JMA, such as Aihiko Satō, Haruo Hayashi, and Yasaburō Taniguchi, went further by amalgamating the JMA with the Imperial Rule Assistance Association.[103]

In August 1942, the government issued the Ordinance for the Japan Medical Association and the Japanese Dental Association (Ishikai oyobi Shikaishikai Rei) to clarify provisions about the medical and dental associations in the National Medical Care Act. Article 40 of the act stated, "The minister of health and welfare has authority over the JMA, and the minister of health and welfare and prefectural governors have authority over the prefectural medical associations to order to improve medical care and health-guidance systems."[104] The ordinance also stipulated that the JMA should be reorganized as a new association that all doctors would be compelled to join. In addition, the president of the reorganized JMA was now to be chosen by the government.[105] Kitajima stated in the last general assembly of the JMA, with Health and Welfare Minister Koizumi and Director of Hygiene Bureau Hirokichi Nadao in attendance, "The National Medical Care Act is bringing a big change to our medical system. But it aims only at strengthening the JMA and clarifying its mission to contribute more to war mobilization policy."[106] Kitajima had told Koizumi that he could not accept working only for military needs, yet he could not resist the government's power.[107] The *Yomiuri Shimbun* summed up the general public's opinion of the matter: "[The JMA had to] eliminate the spirit of its traditional liberal guild organization and cooperate with the Japan Medical Corporation."[108]

The new Japan Medical Association began operation with the permission of the MHW in January 1943. As the ordinance indicated that the new JMA should closely cooperate with the Japan Medical Corporation, Inada, the president of the Japan Medical Corporation, was appointed president of the JMA.[109] Now the JMA was not a representative group of solo practitioners but a state organization that also forced hospital doctors to join and whose members collectively worked for the government. To advance organizational integration, the government soon tried to merge the JMA into the Japan Medical Corporation. Although this merger did not happen because of confusion at the end of the war, the JMA had completely lost its autonomy with the reorganization of 1943. As Kazuo Miwa, doctor and writer, puts it, when JMA president Kitajima was forced to resign, "the liberal tradition of Yukichi Fukuzawa, Shibasaburō Kitasato, and Taichi Kitajima died out."[110]

During the war, the JMA saw that the government intervened more and more in health care and restrained what doctors and the JMA could do. The new institutional and policy developments were justified as contributing to victory in the war. Under this political pressure, the JMA gave up the status of an independent professional group. The end of the war, however, did not bring the lost Fukuzawa-Kitasato-Kitajima liberal tradition back to the JMA. In the period of postwar reconstruction, the JMA was in an institutionally and politically weak position as a result of the wartime legacy and a new political enemy, the US-led occupation authority.

REFORMING HEALTH CARE WITH THE UNITED STATES

World War II was a critical juncture in the institutional and political development of Japan's health insurance policy. Many full-time employees enrolled in the Health Insurance program, either in Government-Managed Health Insurance or Society-Managed Health Insurance, depending on the size of their employers. Those who did not have employers were expected to join the National Health Insurance program. The government had more political leverage in the policymaking process because the government had the legitimacy to intervene in health care and to justify stricter regulation by asserting that Japan was in a national crisis. In contrast, the autonomy of private actors, such as the Japan Medical Association, shrank. During this period the government drastically expanded administrative capacity and public health insurance coverage. The government asserted the power to set fee schedules and turned the JMA into a government organization.

Historical institutionalism tells us that the wartime legacy of health insurance policy should greatly impact the policy trajectory after the war by constraining policy options to be taken. This process is called path dependence. While path dependence had an effect in the postwar reconstruction, however, this period was more complicated than historical institutionalism would assume. Japan lost the war with devastating results and was under the US-led occupation. More than 2 million people had lost their lives. Many large cities had been bombed and destroyed, and life-saving infrastructure, including hospitals, had been severely damaged. Immediate action was needed to deal with the situation. In a sense, the national crisis moment continued. However, the ultimate decision maker was no longer the Japanese government but instead the US-led occupation authority.

After the war, the General Headquarters (GHQ) of the occupation authority was set up in Tokyo to administer Japan. Although other Allied nations played minor roles in the military occupation of Japan, final authority belonged to the United States. General Douglas MacArthur, as supreme commander for the Allied Powers (SCAP), headed GHQ.[1] His top priority policy was demilitarization and democratization through abolishing many wartime laws and organizations. Health care reform was not initially seen as an important part of the project, but GHQ soon began to pay attention to the need for such reform. Crawford Sams, a military doctor and director of the Public Health and Welfare Section (PHW) of SCAP, created initiatives and was, de facto, the person who made final decisions in this area.

The occupation period lasted about six and a half years, from September 1945 to April 1952. There was a wider array of health policy options with new policy ideas coming from the ex-enemy country, which had a different historical background and had experienced a different course of health policy development from Japan's. Many actors within GHQ and from the United States tried to influence reforms. Japanese actors also tried to influence reforms within the institutional framework set by GHQ. Interestingly, the political battle ended up solidifying the institutional and political developments that had taken place during the war. In terms of historical institutionalism, the postwar reconstruction period could have been another critical juncture, but postwar reconstruction instead played a role in consolidating the institutional arrangements for health care that Japan had developed during the war.[2]

General Headquarters and the Ministry of Health and Welfare

General MacArthur arrived at Atsugi Naval Air Base on August 30, 1945, only fifteen days after the government released the emperor's announcement of Japan's surrender. The photo of the very American MacArthur getting off the military aircraft, wearing a pair of sunglasses and smoking a corncob pipe, shocked many Japanese, who feared that a drastic political and social change would take place in their country.

One of the most important decisions the United States made before the occupation began was to retain the emperor in order to promote social stability. Although the emperor's status was changed to being the "symbol of the state and of the unity of the people," in the words of the May 1947 Constitution of Japan, as Minister of State for the Enactment of the New Constitution Tokujirō Kanamori has explained, the Japanese polity continued as "a nation with an emperor as the center of the people's admiration."[3] Another decision was to adopt indirect governance, in which the Japanese government continued to exist, as a means to support new GHQ policies.[4] As part of GHQ's demilitarization and democratization policy, in addition to those who were executed as the result of the Tokyo Trial, many politicians and military officers who were considered to have been deeply engaged in the conduct of the war were removed from their roles. The middle-ranking bureaucrats working for the Ministry of Health and Welfare, however, almost all remained.[5] These bureaucrats had allied with the military during the war to reform social policy, but now they tried to ally with GHQ.

GHQ sought to reform the bureaucracy but did not try to weaken its power. T. J. Pempel describes the overall characteristics of GHQ's bureaucratic reform: "Although the bureaucracy was indirectly affected by political changes in other areas, few direct attacks on the political powers of the Japanese national bureaucracy were attempted during the U.S. Occupation. . . . Bureaucratic 'reform' was interpreted almost exclusively in terms of improving the efficacy of Japanese administration."[6] This policy stance was welcomed by the bureaucrats who had tried to rationalize the administration and exclude influences from party politics.[7]

Organizationally, the occupation combined military and civil functions under the broad authority of MacArthur at GHQ. There were fourteen social staff sections under him; roughly divided along functional lines that mirrored the structure of Japanese government ministries, these sections drafted and transmitted specific directives to be implemented by their Japanese counterparts.[8] In the case of public health, which included the coordination of medical care, refugee relief, and the operation of social programs such as health insurance, responsibility fell to Sams and the Public Health and Welfare Section.[9] As in other staff sections, civilian officials in the PHW, rather than military officers, carried out most of the tasks. Many of the civilian administrators had significant experience with New Deal agencies in the United States.[10] These administrators were motivated to make progressive reforms and needed a Japanese counterpart organization to help planning and implement the new policies.

Health insurance reform was not much discussed in the United States when planning for the occupation took place.[11] In November 1945, soon after the occupation started, the US military Joint Chiefs of Staff (JCS) issued its "Basic Directive for Post-Surrender Military Government in Japan Proper" (JCS-1380), which set forth specific goals for the economic, political, and social reconstruction of Japan. These reforms included a massive redistribution of farmland, drafting a new constitution, and breaking up Japan's industrial and financial conglomerate corporations (*zaibatsu*). But no reform plan for the Japanese health insurance system was included.[12] At the beginning of the occupation, the occupation authority was involved only in what was directly connected with demilitarization and democratization, what was needed to secure minimum social order, or what was directly related to the safety and welfare of US military personnel.[13]

As one of its top priorities, GHQ had to deal with the repatriation of about 6.6 million Japanese people outside of the home country, including servicemen and civilians. In October 1945, GHQ sent an emergency order to the Japanese government to decide on the responsible administrative agency to carry out this effort. It was decided that the MHW would be given the responsibility. About 6 million people returned to Japan in the first three years. Because many of them were poor, the government began to assist them financially. But because this assistance was against GHQ's demilitarization and democratization policy of terminating benefits for military veterans, GHQ ordered an end to this financial help.[14]

For the same demilitarization reason, GHQ directed the Japanese government to transfer the administration of hospitals for military officers and veterans from the military to the MHW. Under this policy, 146 military facilities with 71,933 beds were turned into national hospitals and sanatoriums, now open to ordinary people. With the increasing number of former soldiers returning home, the government had to find other options for assisting them. At this point, social security programs, including general health insurance that did not specifically target veterans, started to gain attention.[15]

Another urgent task facing GHQ was dealing with epidemic diseases. When the war ended, many people were lacking the necessities of life as the infrastructure, including hospitals and clinics, was destroyed in many cities. Many people were living with bad sanitary conditions. To make it worse, many people who were returning from abroad brought epidemic diseases, which quickly spread. These diseases included cholera, smallpox, and typhus. In September 1945, GHQ sent a memorandum to the Japanese government asking it to research the situation with regard to epidemic diseases and to deal with them. The Japanese government succeeded in getting epidemics under control by 1946. Particularly, policy toward typhus gained the public's attention. This disease was spread by lice. GHQ was deeply concerned with the curtailment of lice, fleas, flies, and other possible sources of disease. GHQ introduced the insecticide DDT (dichlorodiphenyltrichloroethane) to Japan. It was symbolic of GHQ's new public health measure that many Japanese children were sprayed on their heads with DDT powder.[16]

To implement these policies and others, including regulations relating to marijuana, sexually transmitted diseases, and food quality, GHQ empowered the MHW by expanding its administrative capacity. In May 1946, GHQ directed that the administration of public health and medical care should be increased in size and headed by technical officers (*gikan*)—that is, people trained in the medical field. In response, in November, the Japanese government replaced the Hygiene Bureau with three new bureaus: the Public Health Bureau (Kōshū Hoken Kyoku), the Medical Bureau (Imu Kyoku), and the Prevention Bureau (Yobō Kyoku), headed by technical officers. GHQ also directed the establishment of branches of these hygiene bureaus at the prefectural level.[17]

As a result of GHQ's initiatives, the term *kōshūeisei* (public health) began to be widely used. The term was also included in the new Constitution of Japan.[18] The US concept of public health was more to have the government and grassroots voluntary organizations work to protect the health of the people as a human right. This concept, however, created a problem in adopting the US directive into the Japanese institutional, political, and cultural context. Because GHQ's public health policies were made and implemented from the top down, they empowered the MHW while sidelining nongovernment actors. It can be argued that GHQ just did not have much time for deliberation given the social turmoil in which it was reorganizing the Japanese government, but GHQ's top-down stance in this area can also be attributed to Crawford Sams.

Sams served in the US Army Medical Corps, eventually being promoted to the rank of brigadier general in 1948 while serving in Japan. After service in North Africa, Europe, and the Philippines, he was transferred to Japan to head the PHW.[19] Like MacArthur, Sams was trained in the military; he was used to a hierarchical and authoritarian decision-making process while he believed in US liberalism and had a strong allergy to communism.[20] The reforms that Sams actually undertook in Japan were not what his contemporary conservatives would have approved of in the United States. Although Sams later recalled that "there were many communists in the PH&W," he supported measures developed by his progressive section officers, such as the Daily Life Security Act (Seikatsu Hogo Hō) in 1946, the Unemployment Insurance Act (Shitugyō Hoken Hō) in 1947, and the Child Welfare Act (Jidō Fukushi Hō) in 1948. His later words demonstrate his rationale: "I hope to have influenced the thinking of many peoples in the underdeveloped countries so that they can know that, literally their lives are worth saving and that this very essence of our concept of democracy is more desirable than the promises of the dictatorships of the welfare or socialist state, where the individual is nothing and the welfare of the state is of primary importance." What he was doing in Japan was "helping to rebuild a destroyed nation and to establish health and welfare programs which, on a nation-wide basis, are among the most modern in the world today."[21] From his viewpoint, Japanese social policy was out of date and in need of modernization. He allied with the MHW to modernize social policy.

Ideas for Radical Health Insurance Reforms

As described earlier, abolition of veterans' benefits caused the government and GHQ to have to look for other ways to improve social policies. As early as December 1945, the Labor Advisory Committee attached to the Economics and Scientific Section reviewed Japanese social policies and made policy recommendations to the PHW. The twelve members who made up the committee brought with them expertise in labor relations, social insurance, and wage policy development from their work in New Deal agencies such as the National Labor Relations Board, the Social Security Board, and the War Manpower Commission. The chair of the Labor Advisory Committee, for example, was Paul L. Stanchfield, who formerly served in the Office for War Mobilization and the War Production Board.[22] These committee members had been working as government officials and expanding their roles in dealing with the Great Depression and war mobilization.[23]

In contrast to the viewpoint of Sams, who saw Japan as having backward institutions, what the Labor Advisory Committee discovered was Japan's nearly universal, if fragmented, health insurance system. The committee found that the system compared favorably to those of other Western nations, especially with "the broad coverage of the National Health Insurance program . . . in providing health security for farmers and self-employed persons."[24] The Labor Advisory Committee suggested further reforms, however, stating in the committee's interim report of April 1946 that "a comprehensive reform of social insurance can and should be undertaken."[25] In particular, the report noted that with the PHW's separate programs for industrial wage earners, farmers, and the self-employed, the section should consider "the feasibility of consolidating some or all of these programs into a unified, comprehensive social insurance system."[26]

The committee had the British system in mind. The committee's members believed that the British model should be adopted in Japan and that doctors' compensation should be based not on a fee-for-service scheme but on the British capitation model, by which doctors are compensated by the number of patients they see. In Britain, William Beveridge, highly regarded economist and Liberal politician, was leading a campaign for progressive and comprehensive social insurance reform. In 1942, he released what is known as the Beveridge Report, which included advocating free universal health care funded by central government taxation. The White Paper on National Health Service of 1944 confirmed his idea. After the Labor Party won the election in 1945, the National Health Service bill was introduced in the British House of Commons.[27] In describing Japanese views on social security reform, the Labor Advisory Committee noted that "the influence of foreign thinking, particularly of the British

'Beveridge Report,' is clearly discernible."[28] Yoneyuki Sugita writes, "Allegedly, outside of Great Britain, no other country was more influenced by the Beveridge Report than Japan."[29]

Synchronizing with the Japanese, who had a great sympathy with what was going on in Britain, reform-minded GHQ officials tried to get support from their fellow progressive officials in the United States. When the PHW had a chance to expand its administration in April 1946, the section reached out to the US Social Security Administration in recruiting for the position of bureau chief as well as for the other top officials. Meanwhile, Sams requested that the Social Security Administration send a mission to study the social security system of Japan. The letter of invitation sent by Sams was passed on to longtime Social Security Administration commissioner Arthur J. Altmeyer. The letter stated the mission's goal as "arousing Japanese interest in social security problems, encouraging early action by [the] Diet and emphasizing [the] need for [an] integrated program properly geared to Japan's needs and economic conditions."[30] The subsequently launched Social Security mission was led by William Wandel, a Social Security board officer.

Wandel's group arrived in Japan in August 1947. The mission included Burnet Davis, who worked for the US Public Health Service. He was the son of Michael Davis, chair of the Committee for the Nation's Health, the chief group lobbying on behalf of President Harry S. Truman's proposed health care reform plan. Burnet Davis was familiar with the ongoing reforms in Britain. He had just returned from a mission to London, where he was attached to the British Ministry of Health during the drafting of the National Health Service bill.[31]

The Social Security mission was expected to prepare a detailed proposal for comprehensive reform of Japan's health insurance system by integrating the various health insurance programs into a single national program. According to a PHW memorandum, the mission "will consult . . . for [the] purpose of drafting a National Health Bill which will incorporate a unified National Health Insurance Program with a National Medical Care Program."[32] As Wandel wrote in June 1947 to Isidore S. Falk, his former colleague at the Social Security Administration, "Health insurance is the major field of social security in Japan. . . . Permanent revision requires amalgamating National Health Insurance with Health Insurance, on a compulsory basis."[33]

Meanwhile, in Japan, the MHW continued to be responsible for health insurance. In March 1946, the MHW established its own Social Insurance Investigation Committee (Shakaihoshō Seido Chōsakai) to conduct a wholesale review of the social security system, including health insurance.[34] The committee, comprising ministry officials and a number of reform-minded Japanese scholars with social policy expertise, issued a report in December 1946 that called for the integration of the multiple health insurance programs into a single national program.[35] In particular, the committee proposed that Health Insurance and National Health Insurance should be merged into a single residence-based health insurance program.[36] In October 1947 the committee issued its "Outline for the Social Security System" (Shakaihoshō Seido Yōkō), which called for "not a patchwork but a progressive, comprehensive social security system."[37]

The members of the Social Insurance Investigation Committee coordinated closely with PHW officials. Toshio Tatara, a social work and social research scholar, points out that "the relationship between PH&W, SCAP and the Ministry of [Health and] Welfare was particularly a good one, and there were many direct contacts between the personnel of both organizations."[38] In June 1947, the members of the Research Committee and officials in the PHW and the MHW regularly began to meet to discuss the future of the Japanese social security system.[39] Reformers in the MHW and PHW shared an admiration for British policy developments during and after World War II. According to Makoto Suetaka, a member of the committee, "The Beveridge plan was the model for the committee's plan. . . . Its principal spirit was that in the new liberal society, Japan's social security system had to guarantee basic living conditions by protecting people from poverty."[40] Their grand plan, because it resembled that of the Beveridge Report, was called the "Japanese Beveridge plan."[41]

Meanwhile, Social Insurance Investigation Committee members were motivated by other social security measures, such as the Labor Standards Act (Rōdō Kijun Hō) and the Unemployment Insurance Act, enacted in April and December 1947, which gave hope of moving toward establishing a comprehensive social security system in Japan. The new Constitution of Japan also encouraged reformers, with Article 25 stipulating that "all people have the right to maintain the minimum standards of wholesome and cultured living. In all spheres of life, the state shall use its endeavors for the promotion and extension of social welfare, and of public health."[42] Article 25 clearly stated the government's responsibility to provide a safety net for the people. This article of the constitution provided the theoretical basis for reformers who believed in the government's responsibility to provide for social welfare.

Not all Japanese were as enthusiastic as the MHW and the Social Insurance Investigation Committee which were planning to introduce a British-style national health insurance system in Japan. The Ministry of Finance (MOF) early on expressed concern about the cost of this reform. As the *Asahi Shimbun* described it, because the grand plan envisioned a huge increase in governmental subsidies, "some see the proposal of the Social Insurance Investigation Committee as a dream, one that the realist officials in the MOF are reluctant to endorse."[43] So long as GHQ remained enthusiastic about reform, however, the

MOF's concerns were peripheral to most social policy debates. For example, SCAP forced the MOF to accept a fifteen-fold increase in its budget allocation for the MHW in 1946 to cover the anticipated costs of the new Daily Life Security Act.[44] But as the occupation went on, international and political contexts, along with the constraints of preexisting health care institutions, began to present obstacles for the reformist officials and scholars in Japan and GHQ.

A Patchwork of Reforms

Radical reform of health insurance appeared to be gaining support in Japan and in the United States by 1947. But the momentum soon waned. GHQ stopped strongly advocating fundamental health insurance reform. There were two main reasons for this change. The first was that there was opposition to the British model from conservatives in the United States, and the US influence was too big to ignore. The second was that GHQ adopted a deflationary policy, known as the Dodge Line. As a result, what GHQ finally did was to patch the existing health insurance system that had developed during World War II.

This result came about because what the PHW officials were trying to do was politicized and strongly opposed by the American Medical Association (AMA) and its conservative allies in the United States. The powerful AMA conducted a devastating campaign to kill the Wagner-Murray Dingell bill, which reflected Truman's national health care agenda. The Social Security mission also became a target of the AMA. Forest A. Harness (R-Indiana), head of the House Subcommittee on Government Publicity and Propaganda, took the lead in attacking the mission in Congress. When Harness found that the Social Security mission was going to Japan, he sent a cable to General MacArthur on August 20, 1947, claiming that there was "evidence of a general program to implant compulsory health insurance in various states and foreign nations."[45] Harness concluded that "the real purpose of the mission is not to assist Japan in working out her basic problems in health and welfare, but to force upon that country a compulsory system of socialized medicine."[46]

The AMA joined Harness's campaign. AMA president George Lull sent a letter to Sams expressing his strong opposition to the Social Security mission and the promotion of "socialized medicine" in Japan.[47] In the following weeks, MacArthur received letters from concerned doctors around the United States, urging that he "not support or abet the socialistic and undemocratic proposal of the Social Security mission to Japan which has as its purpose the 'putting over' of compulsory sickness insurance on this vanquished nation."[48] MacArthur replied to these doctors by assuring them that "there is no slightest concept at this headquarters of any socialized medicine in Japan."[49] In September 1947 the *Journal of the American Medical Association* reported that "the War Department disclosed that General MacArthur had denied allegations by Representative Harness of Indiana, chairman of a House Expenditures subcommittee studying propaganda."[50]

When the Social Security mission completed its work in December 1947, MacArthur sent a copy of its report both to Harness and to the president of the AMA.[51] The mission did not embrace an integrated and compulsory health insurance program as recommended by the Japanese government or reformist members of the occupation authority. Instead, the report asserted that "under this economic situation, Japan should adopt gradual steps toward universal health insurance coverage for the people." The report proposed that the HI and the NHI remain as two core components in the health insurance system without clearly recommending their integration. This was a shift from the policy stance that the occupation government had taken previously.[52]

To further assuage the AMA's concerns, Sams invited its representatives to "visit Japan, and judge for themselves the situation here."[53] In August 1948, members of the AMA arrived in Japan.[54] After their mission ended, the AMA mission report sent to Sams in October 1948 reiterated their organization's concerns about concentrating too much authority over health care in the hands of the MHW. Members of the mission warned that such a concentration of authority over medicine could lead to the return of a totalitarian government in Japan. To avert this threat, the AMA mission report recommended that the occupation promote a health insurance system that more closely resembled the one found in the United States, with employment-based private insurance coupled with means-tested public programs for the poor.[55] Sams attended the AMA's convention to assure them that total nationalization of medicine would not take place in Japan.[56]

In December 1948, GHQ's economic policy change further discouraged the movement to adopt the British model. The US Department of State and Department of Defense directed the occupation authority to follow "Nine Disciplines for Economic Stabilization" for Japan, which proposed a fixed currency exchange rate, a balanced budget, reduction of governmental subsidies, and a strengthened taxation system.[57] In February 1949, Joseph Dodge arrived in Japan to promote the disciplines, particularly the deflation policy. The occupation authority proceeded to impose draconian cuts in public spending, a tight money policy, and balanced-budget requirements on the Japanese government. The deflation policy made it more difficult for the government to increase expenditures on social security measures.[58]

With GHQ losing momentum to implement radical reforms, reforms to cobble together the wartime policies went ahead. The main purpose of these reforms was to make the health insurance programs financially more sustainable.

Among the various existing programs, the NHI had the worst financial problems. Unlike the HI, which had contributions from employers, the NHI was financed by contributions from the enrollees and a minimal government subsidy to cover administrative costs. In the postwar economic crisis, many enrollees could not pay the premium. Others did not pay it because they believed that their contribution did not financially benefit them and that medical services with the NHI were inferior in quality. In 1946, about 40 percent of the NHI associations did not function as they were supposed to.[59]

The way that the NHI had been expanded by the government for the purpose of aiding the war effort affected people's perception of it. Many of the NHI associations were created without deliberation at the grassroots. Now that the war was over, people asked why they would still need the NHI. What the government did to repair it was mostly to improve its financing, not seriously considering to benefit people's lives and the community.

In June 1948, the Diet easily passed an NHI amendment, shifting basic administrative responsibility from NHI associations to municipalities. Residents' participation had been made compulsory when local representatives had decided to create the NHI.[60] Thus, once a national health insurance association was established in a municipality by its legislature, its residents had to participate in the program. Yonekichi Kojima, an official in the MHW, contended that the compulsory nature of the NHI was not antidemocratic but necessary to avoid healthy people opting out of joining.[61] A further NHI amendment in 1951 allowed municipalities to collect the premiums for more administrative efficiency.[62] Although the government subsidy covered 100 percent of administrative costs, the heavy financial burden imposed on the insured remained.[63]

The HI also had financial problems. GHQ's deflationary policy after 1949 reduced the budgets of all the national health insurance programs. Previously, because the fee schedule did not keep up with inflation, many doctors refused to accept health insurance, and people considered that health insurance was for the poor. With the deflationary policy, however, relatively wealthy people started to use health insurance, and health insurance payments rapidly increased.[64] This development affected the finances of the HI by increasing the premiums from 3.6 percent of wages in 1947, to 4.0 percent in 1948, and to 5.5 percent in 1949 for workers in small companies that were covered under Government-Managed Health Insurance. These increases were not enough to balance HI's budget, and in 1949 the program had a deficit of 3.1 billion yen.[65]

In another reform undertaken to piece together parts of the wartime policies, the government centralized the decision-making process for setting fee schedules. In June 1944 the government had created the Health Insurance Medical Fee Council. After the war ended, the fee-setting power was returned to the

JMA. But in 1947, the government took this power back again by creating the Social Insurance Medical Fee Council (Shakaihoken Shinryōhōshū Santei Kyōgikai). Then, in 1950, the council was reorganized as the Central Social Insurance Medical Council (Shakaihoken Iryō Kyōgikai, called Chūikyō). The minister of Health and Welfare consulted the new council, which discussed the fee schedules for all national health insurance programs with input from the council members representing medical providers, insurers, insureds, and the public interest (usually academicians). The minister was expected to decide the fee schedules based on reports of the council. In addition, whenever new medicines and medical technologies were introduced, the minister was supposed to consult the council about changing the fee schedule.[66] The main purpose of the council, in the government's view, was to keep down national health insurance costs as part of the overall government budget.

GHQ's clear change of policy priorities in late 1948 put the integration of national health insurance programs aside in favor of creating a patchwork of top-down reforms for policies that had developed under wartime pressures. The MHW and GHQ were now allied in pursuing this policy as part of the fiscal austerity plan. In contrast, the JMA could not actively engage in these reforms.

The Enfeebled Japan Medical Association

The occupation authority introduced rigorous policies to demilitarize and democratize Japan. Although the Home Ministry was abolished because of its central role in the war mobilization, this change did not much affect the MHW. The MHW gained legitimacy to intervene in health care, as health insurance programs that had developed during the war were patched together to be financially more sustainable. Meanwhile, GHQ actively played a role in changing the nature of the Japan Medical Association, which had been turned into a state organization during the war. As GHQ had done with *zaibatsu* (big business conglomerates) as part of its overall demilitarization and democratization policy, GHQ dissolved the state JMA and made it into a democratic and voluntary organization. But GHQ did not actively include the new JMA in policymaking processes. Rather, GHQ treated the JMA's new leaders as obstacles to the occupation's goals. The reorganized, democratic, and voluntary JMA became marginalized.

In November 1945, GHQ directed the democratization of the regional and national medical associations. In February 1946, Toshihiko Nakayama was elected as the first denationalized JMA president. The JMA planned to reorganize itself, as GHQ made the MHW abolish the National Medical Care Act of

1942. GHQ insisted that the creation of and participation in the new JMA had to be voluntary. JMA leaders, however, were worried that many doctors would choose not to join the new JMA. In August 1947, the old JMA established a committee, led by Tōru Sakakibara and Junzō Kurosawa, to set up this new national organization. When the new JMA was established, it was assumed that these two would be elected as president and vice president. But just one day before the election, GHQ sent a directive that the new leadership should not include anyone who had served as a board member in the nationalized JMA during the war.[67]

The first meeting of the House of Delegates of the new JMA was held on August 30, 1947. The delegates decided to postpone the election of officers, declaring that "to make clear the meaning of the newborn JMA, we need to clean up the feudal residue and make the JMA democratic both in name and reality."[68] The newly created JMA would have to be "established based on the free will and self-awareness of doctors" and "dedicated to promote medical ethics, to improve and propagate medical knowledge and techniques, and to advance public health as a means of improving the welfare of society."[69]

But to Sams, the JMA was an obsolete organization, even as reorganized. The most serious challenge he made to the new JMA was to demand the separation of medical treatment and the sale of medicines. It was reported that Sams said it was "a surprise" to him that Japanese doctors sold medicines.[70] He believed that Japanese doctors cared only about selling medicines and did not pay attention to the advancement of medical science and technology. The JMA opposed Sams because taking away doctors' ability to sell medicine without overhauling the existing fee system would be a financial disaster for doctors. In 1950, Takeo Tamiya was elected president of the JMA, indicating the JMA's strong will to resist GHQ pressure to stop doctors from selling medicines.[71] In response to Tamiya's opposition, GHQ sent a memo to the Health and Welfare Minister Jōji Hayashi expressing GHQ's lack of confidence in the new JMA executives: "It is difficult to trust the JMA executive board because they send incorrect information to the members."[72] After only three months as JMA president, Tamiya was forced to resign (an episode discussed in more detail in chapter 5).[73]

GHQ continued to forbid the new JMA from returning to a central role in health politics. Instead, GHQ empowered the Japanese government. Article 25 of the Constitution of Japan, articulating the government's responsibility for "the promotion and extension of social welfare, and of public health," ironically helped to create an environment in which the government and the GHQ worked together to oppose the JMA's representation of private interests working for public health. Private doctors in a sense had been working under, with, and for the government. Now, after the war, the JMA struggled to find its identity and to contribute to a democratized Japan. GHQ also sought to establish political forces as possible counters to the JMA. GHQ engaged in fostering the national association of nurses. Before the war ended, the Japan Midwives Association (Nihon Sanba Kai), the Imperial Nurses Association (Teikoku Kangofu Kyōkai), and the Japan Public Health Nurses Association (Nihon Hoken Kyōkai) coexisted. GHQ helped them merge into the Japan Association of Midwives, Nurses, Public Health Nurses in November 1946.[74] Furthermore, as discussed more in chapter 5, GHQ also tried to mobilize the pharmacists to counter the JMA. William Steslicke points out that the period when the JMA was an underdog was critical for its power: "The Welfare Ministry [MHW] with SCAP support had been 'first to the post,' and the JMA and Japan Dental Association were forced to come from behind and to fight defensive battles."[75]

Preparing for the Post-Occupation Period

While undertaking patchwork reforms and reorganizing the JMA, the government also promoted discussion of long-term goals for the social security system. This discussion was initiated by the Social Security mission report. In response to the report, the Japanese government established the Advisory Council on Social Security (Shakaihoshō Seido Shingikai) in December 1948, which replaced the Social Insurance Investigation Council. The new council played a central role in proposing social security reforms. As requested in the Social Security mission report, the council was given the same rank as the cabinet and had to be consulted by the prime minister and related ministers when making fundamental changes regarding social security.[76]

The Advisory Council on Social Security had forty members, including Diet members, government officials, insurer representatives, medical professionals, and scholars. In the first meeting, Vice Chairman Jōji Hayashi stated the mission of the Advisory Council: "Freedom from want is the fundamental goal of free men in the world. It is said that how healthy a nation depends on how much it achieves this goal. To restart as a nation with a deep culture and peaceful mind, Japan needs to establish a system of social security."[77] Hyōe Ōuchi, the first president of the council, said, "To make Japan a viable country, it is necessary to guarantee true social security for its individuals."[78]

After about six months of discussions, in November 1949, the Advisory Council released a memorandum with its suggestions for the overall direction of Japan's social security reform. The memo stated: "Social security is a fundamental right guaranteed by the Constitution. The system provides for people on a basis of equality, with economic compensation for old-age, permanent and temporary disabilities, unemployment, sickness, death, and childbirth. It eliminates people's anxiety and maintains the social order, and it achieves the ideal of democracy."[79]

In October 1950, the Advisory Council gave its "Recommendation with Respect to a Social Security System" (Shakaihoshōseido ni Kansuru Kankoku) to Prime Minister Shigeru Yoshida. In the area of health insurance, the council stressed that the various employment-based programs should be consolidated and the benefits improved. Universal health care should be achieved by making the rest of the population enroll in the NHI. To fund the NHI, the council suggested increasing government expenditures to cover part of the nonadministrative costs. The council also recommended that public medical facilities should be expanded with improved relationships with existing private solo practitioners. Lastly, the council recommended that the administrative authority should be empowered by establishing a ministry that would exclusively deal with social security.[80]

GHQ opposed the recommendations of the Advisory Council on Social Security in regard to establishing universal national health insurance. In considering the financial situation of Japan, the PHW stated, "Compulsory national health insurance is not acceptable under SCAP policy."[81] In the process of drafting the response, moreover, GHQ sent to the government the following judgment on universal health insurance: "It is socialistic, and it is also not feasible given Japan's financial situation."[82] This was another sign of GHQ's retreat from the goals of the occupation authority before 1948.

Its own organizational problems prevented the Advisory Council on Social Security from disputing the occupation officials and realizing its radical proposals. The council members had various backgrounds and conflicting interests, but the council's recommendation had to be unanimous. Tokuo Kojima, who was administrative secretary of the council, lamented, "In Great Britain, Beveridge himself had full responsibility to propose his plan. In contrast, it is understandable from the beginning that the council, which included different interests, would face difficulties in making a policy proposal."[83] Although this was probably not the intention of the Social Security mission that had suggested the creation of the Advisory Council on Social Security, creating the Advisory Council as such a "democratic" organization prevented it from taking radical action to change the health insurance system.

Unlike the Beveridge Report, which was written by Beveridge alone, the "Recommendation with Respect to a Social Security System" could only suggest a broad goal, such as the introduction of universal health care, without clearly proposing when and how to achieve the goal. The recommendation, however, definitely meant more than nothing. Former MHW officials Kenji Yoshihara and Masaru Wada write, "The recommendation provided to the people not only a definition of social security but also what it should be in the future in a period when people were thinking of social security as an extension of the police and firefighting."[84] Tokuo Kojima has said, "The year 1950 should be celebrated as the embryonic phase of social security."[85] Because the recommendation of the Advisory Council did not guarantee an action by the government, however, many of the proposals were postponed or just ignored.

The problem of too many participants was not the only reason for the dark fate of the recommendation. Wartime policy development had radically increased the government's power to intervene in health care. The government had expanded health insurance but had done so mainly to use human resources as efficiently as possible. Although the military was now out of the policymaking process, MHW officials cooperated with GHQ to decrease the JMA's power and maintain the existing health insurance structure at a low cost. The fragmented health insurance system divided the beneficiary groups. Beneficiaries of the HI, for example, did not have a strong incentive to improve the NHI. Japan intensified the movement to introduce universal health care after GHQ left in April 1952. But the road toward universal health care, much like the path taken during the postwar reconstruction, was constructed of patchwork reforms.

ACHIEVING UNIVERSAL HEALTH INSURANCE

The two crisis moments—World War II and the US-led occupation—that Japan had experienced created and improved the foundation of the country's health insurance system from the top down. The Ministry of Health and Welfare held power by allying with the military during the war and with the occupation officers during the postwar reconstruction. When the occupation forces were ready to leave Japan, the political actors involved in health insurance policy, including the Japan Medical Association, sought to expand their influence in the policymaking process. But they did so within the framework of existing institutional arrangements. In the decade of the 1950s, path dependence narrowed the policy options for stakeholders.

Two types of positive feedback mechanisms produce path dependence. The first type may be described as learning or adaptation effects. The oft-cited example of such effects is the adoption of the typewriter keyboard. Whether it is the most efficient keyboard for typing or not, the early adoption of the prevailing keyboard by major typewriter manufacturers produced a situation in which people became accustomed to the layout. The widespread use of this keyboard made it more expensive to switch to a possibly better alternative because of the demands of equipment replacement and worker retraining.[1] In politics, learning effects are found when citizens' expectations conform to existing policies, including their normative judgments, or when bureaucrats follow standard operating procedures to identify problems and determine solutions. Peter Hall and Rosemary Taylor argue that historical institutionalism tends to "see individuals as satisfiers, rather than utility maximizers."[2] As in the case of typewriter keyboards, such institutional adaptations may lead to change becoming economically and politically too expensive or undesirable.

The second type of positive feedback mechanism that produces path dependence can be described as the effect of political configurations. Policies have distributional consequences for different groups in society. In addition, policies create groups with an interest in the status quo, such as program beneficiaries and bureaucratic agencies in the case of social policies. Like learning effects, political configurations may make policy or institutional changes unlikely. Unlike learning effects, however, change becomes unlikely because of vested interests that aim to defend the status quo. Moreover, according to Pierson, because legal force is behind political institutions and policies, policy feedback mechanisms, described later in this chapter, are more rigid than economic activities in producing change.[3] These positive feedback mechanisms affected the government, the Japan Medical Association, and other stakeholders during the postwar reconstruction period.

As the feedback mechanisms of path dependence occurred, serious challenges to existing institutions were discouraged because of opposition by the beneficiaries of the existing policy structure. Political actors tried to maximize their interests in accord with institutional and political constraints by adjusting their policy preferences and strategies. Tarō Takemi, JMA president from 1957 to 1982, was a masterful tactician who brought visibility to the JMA and made it politically powerful. But it was hard for the JMA to fully come back to the policy-making process because its influence had been taken away for a while. Therefore, Takemi's entry on the scene came too late to have a large influence on the road toward universal health insurance.

The path dependence effect was further strengthened by party politics. After the war, many parties were formed, and many also disappeared. On the side of the conservative forces, two groups fought over leadership in the early 1950s: one group was led by Shigeru Yoshida and the other by Ichirō Hatoyama. What made them different was largely their views on foreign policy. Yoshida's policy was more "realistic": he favored strengthening US-Japan relations, minimizing the defense budget, and focusing on Japan's economic development. Hatoyama, in contrast, claimed that Japan needed to be more independent of the United States and have a new constitution that would allow it to have its own military, which was prohibited by the existing peace constitution.[4] While the two groups in the conservative front struggled to attain leadership, the progressive front conducted a preemptive attack by merging into one party.

The Socialist Party of Japan (Nihon Shakaitō), once formed, had its own administration in 1947–48 under Tetsu Katayama, but it soon ended because of internal conflict.[5] In 1951, the party was dissolved and split into two parties (both self-named Nihon Shakaitō). Mosaburō Suzuki took the lead in the left socialist group known as the Leftist Socialist Party, and Inajirō Asanuma became the leader of the right socialist group known as the Rightist Socialist Party. Advocating a nonarmed neutrality, the former gained popularity among the youth. The latter had difficulty in establishing party unity and sending a clear message to the people. In January 1955, the election for the lower house led to both socialist parties combined winning 156 seats (out of 467), the highest number of socialists in the Diet's history. In October, the two groups reunified with the aim of seeking to take the majority in the Diet.

To counter this movement among the progressives, the two conservative parties were urged to merge. Although some major politicians, such as Shigeru Yoshida and Kenzō Matsumura, opposed this strategy, many supported the formation of a unified conservative party, and thus the Liberal Democratic Party (LDP) was born in November 1955.[6] Socialists supported nonarmed neutrality and the expansion of the welfare state, including health care. Considering the socialists' rising popularity, the LDP adopted a position supporting both a welfare state and aggressive economic development, while opposing nonarmed neutrality.

It was conservative forces and bureaucrats who created and solidified the health insurance system during the war and the US-led occupation. It was also conservative forces, now merged into the LDP, and bureaucrats who sought to achieve the universal coverage. They tried to push for the universal health insurance while seeking to maintain existing institutions on which these actors had had a large influence. They were in a better position to navigate the existing institutional arrangements than the JMA because the conservative forces and bureaucrats had created these arrangements, while the JMA had been left out of the policymaking process during the war and the occupation.

Furthermore, the LDP came into existence at a fortunate time because the 1950s saw rapid economic development, which helped the conservative forces that had prioritized the economic growth with strong ties to big business. The Korean War (June 1950–July 1953) helped boost the Japanese economy because Japan sold the United States goods required for military use.[7] By 1955, most of the economic indicators, such as the gross domestic product (GDP), industrial production, agricultural production, and personal consumption were back to prewar (pre-1937) levels. In 1956, the White Paper on the Economy proclaimed, "Postwar reconstruction is now over."[8] Economic development allowed the LDP the luxury of distributing financial rewards to stakeholders in health insurance policy, including the JMA, while keeping support from business.

The JMA's Slow Recovery and the Government

In the early 1950s, JMA presidents tried to have an impact on health insurance policy, but they could not do much to counter the government, which had been intensifying its control over health care. Taku Nomura, doctor and writer, called this period in the JMA's history "the time of absolute bewilderment and state of inertia."[9] The JMA's first two presidents—Akira Takahashi and Takeo Tamiya, who were well-known Tokyo University professors—attempted in vain to transform the association into a more prestigious and powerful organization.[10] By the time Yasaburō Taniguchi, a professor at Kumamoto Medical Vocational School (later Kumamoto University Medical School), became the president in 1950, the financial condition of doctors had deteriorated so much that the JMA was impelled to take action.[11]

Doctors suffered after the war because the national health insurance fee did not increase on a par with the rapid postwar inflation. Itaru Narita, who served as an executive board member of the JMA, stated, "Before 1949, very few among the poor had health insurance. Most medical treatment was at one's own expense."[12] Takahashi's 1948 comment supports this observation. He stated, "People are not happy with health insurance, and they become frustrated in dealing with it. This is a sad fact."[13] Not only JMA members but also government officials admitted that the national health insurance fee for doctors was very low. Taketo Tomonō, head of the Health Insurance Section in the MHW and later the governor of Chiba, said, "There may be a better way of saying this, but health care services paid for by health insurance can be considered as charity from the doctors' perspective. It may be considered minimum health service, but doctors realize that they have a responsibility to provide their services."[14]

As doctors suffered financially, they directed their criticism at the Central Social Insurance Medical Council (hereafter Chūikyō), which had not increased doctors' fees in many years. The council decided on the national fee schedule, which applied to all national health insurance programs, based on the advice of six medical provider representatives, six insurer representatives, six employers and insured representatives, and six public-interest representatives.[15] Many doctors believed that the council overall hesitated to increase fees because the MHW backed the Federation of Health Insurance Societies (Kenkō Hoken Kumiai Rengōkai), which advocated lower health care costs. The federation was a beneficiary group of the HI program—more specifically, of the Society-Managed Health Insurance program. The federation was formed from the health insurance societies of large companies: it represented the interests of the SMHI program and employers. Employers and labor unions in the big companies both wanted to lower their contributions. They shared the government's goal of keeping down medical costs. The government connection was strengthened by the practice of *amakudari*, in which retired MHW officials were appointed to positions in private entities such as the Federation of Health Insurance Societies.[16]

In 1950, Iwao Yasuda, the head of the Social Bureau, described the government's attitude in this period: "The budget for Japan's social security has to be settled in a financially difficult time. . . . We have to carefully consider making the social security system as economical and efficient as possible."[17] This was how the government viewed the necessity of low health insurance fees at that time. In April 1950, the JMA began to resist this situation and passed a resolution asking for a fee raise by increasing the unit price per official point from 10 yen to 18.17 yen. The unit price had not been changed since 1948. The JMA threatened that if the change was not approved, the association would call for doctors to withdraw from health insurance practice.[18]

Labor unions this time concluded that the benefits of national health insurance were too limited and dissented from the employers' view on this issue. The JMA cooperated with labor unions for the first time in its history. In November 1951, the JMA and the labor unions cohosted the Mass Meeting for Strengthening Social Security Health Care (Shakaihoken Iryō Kyōka Kokumin Taikai). The General Council of Trade Unions of Japan (Sōhyō), the Japanese Confederation of Labor Unions (Nihon Rōdōkumiai Sōdōmei), the National Peasant Union (Zenkoku Nōmin Kumiai), and thirteen other organizations joined the meeting. They demanded tax breaks for doctors who engaged in health insurance practices and a financial contribution from the government to increase national health insurance fees.[19] The General Council of Trade Unions of Japan had a satellite office in the JMA's headquarters building. The phrase "labor-medicine cooperation" (*rōi teikei*) became popular at this time.[20]

The collaborative pressure from the JMA and labor unions forced the government to propose raising the unit price per point, but it was much less than what the JMA requested, between a 10.5- and 12.5-yen increase depending on the region. The JMA was not happy about the government's proposal; neither were the health insurance societies. Employers fought this decision because the fee increase led to their having to make a higher financial contribution to the SMHI program. Health and Welfare Minister Ryūgo Hashimoto nevertheless posted an edict for the fee increase in December 1952.[21]

Regional medical associations in the Kanto/Koshin'etsu region passed a resolution in January 1952 stating that "they would accept the government proposal only if all executive board members of JMA resigned from their positions."[22] The regional associations thought that JMA president Taniguchi was weak-kneed when facing the government. Taniguchi himself was cautious about the JMA taking such an aggressive action as calling for doctors to withdraw from health insurance practice. One of his concerns was that such an action would ignite public antipathy toward doctors. He was also concerned that JMA members might not be cooperative enough to carry out such an ordered action. Many rank-and-file members and some regional medical associations concluded that Taniguchi was just too weak to be president.[23]

Taniguchi resigned, and Takeo Tamiya was unanimously elected as the new president in February 1952. This was the second time he served as president of the JMA, after he had earlier resigned over a confrontation with GHQ as to whether doctors would be allowed to sell medicines. Takemi became one of the two vice presidents, an important step to his becoming president later.[24] In April 1952, many JMA members envisaging the upcoming end of the occupation hoped that their representative organization would soon become more active in the policymaking process.

Tamiya aggressively tried to change government policy. As Sams had promised when he advocated a clearer separation of medical treatment and the sale of medicines, an Extraordinary Council on Health Insurance (Rinji Iryōhoken Shingikai) was established in June 1952 to discuss a new fee system. In the council's third meeting, the JMA proactively submitted a paper titled "The Three Principles of Health and Social Insurance." These three goals were (1) to secure doctors' firm position in the health insurance system, (2) to improve health insurance coverage and the fee rate, and (3) to improve and integrate the multiple health insurance programs and administer them in a democratic way.[25] Because Takemi proposed these principles, Kazuo Imai began to call them "Takemi's three principles."[26]

The JMA also began to look for more ways to improve doctors' financial situation. Takemi was the personal physician of Prime Minister Yoshida. When Takemi visited the prime minister's house to give him a check-up in December 1951, the physician mentioned to Yoshida and finance minister Hayato Ikeda that the unit price per point had remained the same since 1948. Considering the still weak economy and financial concerns at the time, Ikeda did not follow up by proposing to raise doctors' fees. Instead, the finance minister offered preferential tax treatment for doctors that would allow them to retain 72 percent of their income as "necessary business expenses."[27]

The Extraordinary Council on Health Insurance resolved to push for this preferential tax treatment for doctors. The Federation of Health Insurance Societies, which usually opposed the JMA on the issue of health insurance fees, joined to support the move, because the preferential tax treatment was an alternative to fee increases. This support shows that the health insurance system and health insurance fee system were not in great shape. The proposed tax break was merely a political band-aid for frustrated doctors from a government that had nothing else to offer. The LDP and the Leftist and Rightist Socialist Parties co-sponsored and passed an act that changed how doctors were taxed. The act had an important supplemental resolution: "Because this law is a temporary measure until the rationalization of the national health insurance fee is realized, the government is expected to enforce it immediately."[28] The government then began a serious discussion on rationalization of the new fee system to replace the preferential tax treatment, but it was difficult for the government to get the JMA on board.

The preferential tax treatment for doctors started out as a temporary measure, but it ended up continuing for twenty-six years. It brought financial benefit to doctors, but it haunted the JMA because the public perceived the tax break as a favor from the government to the JMA. The negative public image helped the government's side in later fights with the JMA about proposed fee increases by suggesting the possibility that the government could end the tax break. Jirō Arioka, an *Asahi Shimbun* journalist, points out that the tax break was not the result of unreasonable demands by the JMA: "This measure was later under attack as unfair tax treatment [by forces including the Federation of Health Insurance Societies]; we need to recall that the JMA and the Federation of Health Insurance Societies jointly wrote the policy draft."[29]

GHQ eventually left Japan in April 1952, but health insurance politics did not change much. The government had had the all-powerful GHQ's support for about seven years. During this time, the government had solidified the foundation of the health insurance system and maintained its power over health insurance programs and doctors. Although the JMA continued in the 1950s to push for higher fees, reform of the fee schedule system, and restructuring of the health insurance system (integration of programs), it was not until the late 1950s, when the association lost a major battle with the government, that the JMA adopted a different political organizational strategy under President Takemi.[30]

Battles over *Iyaku Bungyō*

One of the greatest medical legacies of the GHQ was the revival of the issue of the separation of medical treatment and the sale of medicines (*iyaku bungyō*). This was an old issue, pending since the Regulation of Pharmacist Business and Drug Handling of 1898. At that time, doctors won the government's favor to postpone the compulsory separation infinitely. Pharmacists continued to fight back, and they had an opportunity to win a big victory after the war. This time, pharmacists had GHQ, the ultimate authority in Japan, as their ally.

Sams saw the sale of drugs by doctors as indicative of the backwardness of Japanese medicine and sought to abolish the practice. In the United States, there was a clearer separation between these activities. Seeing Japanese doctors make money from selling medicine, he commented, "[Japanese] doctors sell medicine. Dentists sell gold. They are nothing more than merchants."[31] Sams pushed his agenda to end the practice by inviting a mission from the American Pharmaceutical Association in July 1949 and having it issue a report supporting his views. The Japan Pharmaceutical Association was on GHQ's side in pushing to achieve what the association called an "agenda of seventy years' standing."[32]

In March 1951, the Extraordinary Investigating Committee on the Pharmaceutical System (Rinji Iyakuseido Chōsakai) held six meetings and voted 19–11 to introduce legislation in the Diet to separate medical treatment and the selling of medicine. The JMA insisted that before establishing a compulsory separation, Japan needed to drastically revise its national health insurance fee system to clearly separate medical services and drugs, with more appreciation for the former. The JMA was afraid the new legislation would merely separate the two practices without improving the fee schedule for doctors. The JMA was unable, however, to win enough votes for this proposal.[33]

The decision of the Investigating Committee was in accord with the request made by Sams. The decision was not, however, the end of the battle between doctors and pharmacists or between doctors and the government. As Hideo Yoshida, who attended the Investigating Committee as a neutral member and labor union representative, put it, the council's "conclusion supported the pharmacists' position, but it did not end the history of conflict between doctors and pharmacists, nor did it send the goddess of peace."[34] To make things worse for many pharmacists, their strong supporter Sams resigned from his position in April 1951 when General MacArthur was removed by President Truman. The bill to separate medical treatment and the selling of medicine was passed in the Diet in June 1951, but the heated debate led to the bill's including conditions that promised further political battles between doctors and pharmacists. The eventual law said that policy implementation would not take place until January 1955, when a new advisory council would make decisions on its implementation.[35]

In November 1954, the JMA held its National Doctors Convention (Zenkoku Ishi Taikai). Opposition to the separation of medical treatment and the sale of medicines was one of the top agenda items. The JMA's pressure had made the Diet add several amendments that acted as loopholes. Separation of medical treatment and the sale of medicines could be waived if the patient or his or her attendants requested medicine from the doctor.[36] Patients were used to having medicine sold in clinics and hospitals; therefore, they preferred to get it that way without understanding what the separation of medical treatment and the sale of medicines would mean to them and to the health insurance system. According to William Steslicke, "the intent of the law was completely subverted" by these amendments.[37] Takemi, not yet JMA president at the time, explained the rationale of the JMA's opposition: "The separation should not be done over a short period of time. . . . What makes it especially difficult is that many drug stores behave like street vendors. If we move quickly to introduce the separation, I am afraid it will not serve the people well."[38]

Health Insurance Act Amendment of 1957

With the separation of medical treatment and the sale of medicines a topic of heated debate, discussion about a new national health insurance fee system (*shin iryōhi taikei*) began in earnest. The initial goal was to increase the fee for medical services so that the financial condition of doctors would not suffer after they were prohibited from selling medicines. Although the JMA supported increasing fees for medical treatment, what the association wanted was to take the initiative in the debate about the separation of medical treatment and the sale of medicines and about the new fee system. At the same time, the government tried to use this opportunity to get more control over the health care system to further reduce health care costs.

In the mid-1950s, the government faced an urgent health insurance issue, with the finances of the Government-Managed Health Insurance program in bad shape. The situation improved temporarily during the Korean War, but the program soon became financially strapped again. The deficit was largely attributed to the increase of the unit price per official point in 1951. The deficit rose to 4 billion yen in 1954 and 6 billion yen in 1955.[39] In the beginning of 1955, Chūjirō Kimura, the administrative vice minister of health and welfare, noted, "This won't be a peaceful year. Health insurance, one of the core components of social security, faces a 'massive' deficit. Our nation is going through the worst crisis in the history of health insurance."[40] Budgeting for creating the National Defense Forces and its administrative agency at the time added to the government's financial difficulties in dealing with the GMHI deficit problem. The government needed to keep health care costs down.[41]

In response, in April 1955, a seven-member committee was created in the MHW to study how the health insurance system should be changed to resolve the deficit problem.[42] The committee comprised Kazuo Imai (general director, Federation of Clerical Work Mutual Aid Associations), Shūzō Inaba (general director, National Economy Research Institute), Bunji Kondō (professor, Osaka

City University), Gen Shimizu (president, Seamen's Insurance Association), Chōtarō Takahashi (president, Hitotsubashi University), Kenjō Nakamura (director, Japan Development Bank), and Tomitarō Hirata (professor, Waseda University). Imai stated that the committee, although it had been set up by the MHW, was not under the ministry's control: "We tried to get away from the influence of the MHW and as outsiders to create our own white paper."[43]

The JMA did not have a representative on the committee, and so the association went into panic mode. When the price of antibiotics was reduced by the government in August 1955, regional associations saw this move as showing the government's strong intention to establish the new national health insurance fee system from the top down. The associations criticized the JMA leaders. At the same time, JMA president Junzō Kurosawa was seen by rank-and-file members as too weak to resist the expected government-initiated new fee system. In September, the JMA held an extraordinary House of Delegates meeting where the association approved the resignation of President Kurosawa and other executive members. In October, Korekiyo Obata was elected president.[44]

Obata, as the president of the Tokyo Medical Association, had demonstrated that he could take a strong stand against the government. Insisting on higher fees and objecting to the separation of medical treatment and the sale of medicines, in September 1954, the Tokyo Medical Association conducted a one-day "holiday" campaign despite the government's threat to suspend the organization. Obata, greeting the gathering of the Tokyo Medical Association, remarked, "Today, it is scandalous to hold this kind of gathering. . . . It is time now to carry a big stick."[45]

Obata, however, could not stop the seven-member committee when, in the same month in 1955, the committee submitted a report to the minister that included a new fee system and tighter regulations on doctors who accepted health insurance payments. The report justified stronger government control over doctors based on their having a "public" role.[46] The JMA opposed the report for its aim of increasing government control.

One of JMA's most serious concerns about the committee's proposal was what was called "the double-designation system" (nijūshitei seido). To practice with national health insurance, traditionally, doctors had to be registered. In addition to the registration of doctors, this new system required the registration of medical facilities such as clinics and hospitals. The government's rationale was to regulate communist-inspired doctors who conducted health insurance fraud. The government also claimed that this new requirement would help in dealing with situations in which administrative staff and technicians, rather than doctors, committed fraud.[47] To solo practitioners who were also clinic owners, however, the double-designation system appeared as double supervision. The JMA opposed it as a sign of the government's tightening control over doctors.

Takemi later recalled the controversy: "The MHW came up with the double-designation system as a cheap measure to tie doctors' hands and feet. It was a case of bad administration."[48] Shinjirō Koyama, deputy head of the Bureau of Insurance, said that "this measure was to prevent doctors from having a hostile attitude toward the government when the universal health insurance system would be introduced."[49] The measure would give the government more power to control hospitals and doctors. Ready to fight the proposal on the fee system and the designation system, Obata shared his concerns in his New Year's greeting to JMA members in 1956: "We doctors are surrounded by enemies as far as social security is concerned."[50] Despite Obata's assertiveness, however, JMA's political power was not much improved.

The proposed Health Insurance Act Amendment, which included most of the seven-member committee's proposals, was first introduced in the Diet in February 1956 and was reintroduced in December 1956. The JMA held an extraordinary House of Delegates meeting and passed a resolution totally opposing the bill. Frustrated particularly by the double-designation system, additionally, the regional associations demanded that the JMA should take more aggressive action, such as resigning from health insurance practice in protest. Obata thought it would not be possible to get the government to withdraw the bill and that it would be possible only to add amendments to it.[51] He was cautious about the strategy of resigning from health insurance practice, which many delegates wanted to pursue. He said, "I am not sure if 'resignation' will give the public a positive feeling. Considering the pros and cons, I believe that the JMA should not mention the term in an imprudent manner."[52] His strategy was not appreciated by most of the JMA members.

Despite the JMA's opposition, the government passed the Health Insurance Act Amendment in the lower house in March 1957 without major revisions. This was a clear victory for the government.[53] The MHW worked hard to get Diet members behind the bill. Tatsuo Ozawa, head of the Health Insurance Division of the MHW, recalled, "We paid extra attention to Diet members, not only of the majority party but also of the minority parties. Each time they went home, we saw them off at train stations, such as the Tokyo Station and Ueno Station. We were always around the Diet. Frequently, we also met with JMA leaders."[54]

The passage of the bill was a big disappointment for many JMA members. Right after the bill was passed in the lower house, the JMA again held an extraordinary House of Delegates meeting. Many delegates condemned the way the JMA leaders handled the situation. Their comments included this one: "When

I wanted to petition the Diet members, I was told that the JMA leaders had already approved the government proposal."[55] The delegates asked for a no-confidence vote on the JMA leadership, which passed 82 to 51. Obata immediately submitted his resignation. Many rank-and-file members believed that Obata should have been more aggressive in threatening the resignation of the JMA's doctors from health insurance practice.[56]

The day after Obata resigned, the JMA, along with the Japan Dental Association, hosted a rally they called "Absolute Opposition to the Health Insurance Worsening Amendment" (Kenpo Kaiaku Zettaihantai Zenkoku Ishi Shikaishi Sōkekki Taikai). At the rally they demanded immediate withdrawal of the amendment act. They also requested the government to subsidize 20 percent of medical benefits for the NHI—the existing system guaranteed only administrative costs—and to increase national health insurance fees. Their efforts were in vain. The upper house passed the amendment, with only a minor modification, on March 31. The JMA's frustration led to Tarō Takemi's ascension to the presidency of the organization.

Takemi Takes Charge

Tarō Takemi was a unique doctor and a unique president of the JMA. He was raised by a father who had gone to the United States to study in 1887, just about twenty years after the isolationist Tokugawa shogunate ended, and by a mother who had obtained the best possible education for women at that time, having studied at Ochanomizu High School and Tokyo Joshi Kotō Shihan Gakkō. Takemi often said, "I respect my parents above all."[57]

When he was fourteen, Takemi suffered from a kidney disease and had to stay in a hospital for about two years. His family was told that he might not recover. However, he did recover from the ailment. The period of hospitalization gave him time to read many books, including the writings of Yukichi Fukuzawa, a liberal thinker and the founder of Keio University. Takemi decided to transfer to Keio Futsūbu School. His book collection also included Charles Darwin's *On the Origins of Species*. Takemi was captivated by the mystery of life and became interested in pursuing medical education at Keio University.[58]

Takemi was seriously interested not only in medicine but also in other fields of study. One of Takemi's later friends recalled that Takemi had "an ability to think flexibly by adopting other people's opinions. When faced with problems relating to philosophy, economy, and law, he asked specialists in these fields and learned more about these fields directly from them."[59] At Keio, Takemi did not study medicine as an isolated area of study but in relation to other academic disciplines. This approach later led to occasions on which he was not understood by many people, including JMA members.

When Takemi was a second-year student at Keio, he got to do research in Makoto Koizumi's laboratory. Koizumi, a parasitologist, was not only a professor for whom Takemi had great respect but also a person through whom Takemi gained opportunities to get to know the famous intellectuals of the time. Koizumi was a good friend of Shigeo Iwanami. Iwanami was the founder of Iwanami Shoten, an influential publisher. Through Iwanami, Takemi became acquainted with the progressive "Iwanami-faction scholars" (*Iwanami-kei gakusha*), such as Kitarō Nishida, Yoshishige Abe, Tetsurō Watsuji, and Toyotaka Komiya. At Keio, Takemi had the opportunity to deepen and widen his knowledge.

After graduating from medical school, like many other graduates, Takemi first worked at Keio as a member of the hospital staff, as this was important for his future career. It was also important that he not be assertive in the laboratory. Since factionalism in medical academia was very strong in Japan, not listening carefully to older graduates and mentors was seen as treasonous.[60] Takemi did not like this environment.

He worked in the laboratory alongside Chūjirō Nishino, a leading internal medicine scholar. According to Takemi, Nishino diagnosed patients not based on scientific medical knowledge but on his instinct and experience. To Takemi, Nishino was like a "fortune-teller."[61] Takemi decided to resign from his position, which was considered suicidal in terms of his career.[62]

Takemi, however, was prudent. After he resigned from his position at Keio, he was able to join the Institute of Physical and Chemical Research (Rikagaku Kenkyūsho, known as Riken), which was established in 1917 as the first large-scale national science research institute. Takemi was acquainted with Yoshio Nishina, who was a physicist studying theoretical physics, nuclear physics, and cosmic rays at the institute. When Takemi told Nishina that he was thinking of leaving Keio, Nishina invited Takemi to work for him, saying, "Medicine might not be a science. But what you say is scientific."[63]

Although Takemi worked for no pay at the Institute of Physical and Chemical Research, he was happy there. Doctor and writer Kazuo Miwa writes that "Takemi adapted himself well to the environment of the Institute of Physical and Chemical Research. The institute provided an environment where mentors and disciples could discuss things freely; it included scholars from various academic disciplines, and it provided a unique space for them to cohabit under the same roof."[64] This interdisciplinary and untraditional environment allowed Takemi to approach medicine from a wider perspective than he found at Keio.

After World War II, the US-led occupation authority closed the Institute of Physical and Chemical Research. For Takemi, who had left his position at Keio hospital, there was no way to go back to work in a medical school.[65] He decided to open his own clinic. He had patients from his time at Keio and from the institute's own clinic, which he had headed. Iwanami helped Takemi open his clinic in Ginza, Tokyo, in summer 1948.[66]

Takemi ran his clinic according to his own standards. He instructed his receptionist: "The following should have priority for consultation: those who are in severe pain and suffering; those who serve as ministers of state; those older than eighty; and wartime servicemen." A famous story goes that when Fumimaro Konoe, the retired prime minister, came to see Takemi, Konoe was made to wait with other patients. Takemi did not take patients with national health insurance, nor did he sell medicines in his office. All he accepted was "gratitude" and whatever patients offered.[67]

Ginza was close to both the economic and the political center of Japan. Takemi's clinic attracted many influential and wealthy people. It became a meeting place for Iwanami-faction scholars and, later, for politicians. Takemi had many politicians as his patients because he knew an influential politician at that time, Nobuaki Makino. Makino was the son of Toshinobu Ōkubo, who played a leading role in the Meiji Restoration. Makino trusted Takemi, who was about thirty years younger, not only as a doctor but also as a friend.[68] Takemi's connection to Makino was strengthened by Takemi's marriage to Makino's granddaughter in 1941. Through this marriage, Takemi developed kinship with Shigeru Yoshida (see figure 5.1).[69]

Takemi became involved in important national political negotiations because of his connection with Makino. Prime Minister Kijūrō Shidehara needed to convince Yoshida to become the next prime minister. Shidehara chose Takemi to convince Makino, who had a large influence on Yoshida. When Yoshida was choosing his first cabinet, moreover, he was accompanied by Takemi for a week and used Takemi as a messenger to the cabinet member candidates. This episode led some people to call Takemi a "kingmaker."[70] These experiences gave him a chance to see how things work in politics. Other doctors also began to realize that Takemi was a unique medical doctor in being very close to the center of political power.[71]

In 1950, this reputation helped Takemi become a prominent figure in the JMA. Takemi became the JMA's vice president when Takeo Tamiya was president. Takemi had become known for his kinship and close ties to Prime Minister Yoshida. When Tamiya was asked to become the JMA president, his only condition was to have Takemi as his vice president. Although some were concerned about Takemi's reputation for being independent, Tamiya had a high regard for Takemi's political connections. Two Tokyo Imperial University medical school professors, Tsurayuki Sasa and Kōsaku Kakinuma, played a role in convincing

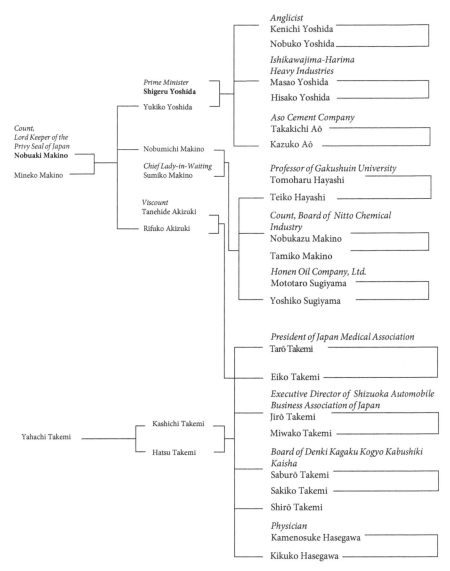

FIGURE 5.1. The family tree of Tarō Takemi. Names in boldface appear in the text. Note: This family tree is based on Ikura Yasumasa, Shindan Takemi Taro (Judging Tarō Takemi) (Tokyo: Sōshisha Shuppan, 1979), 109.

Takemi to take the position of vice president.[72] At the time, Japan was still under the US-led occupation, and Tamiya needed someone who had personal connections to Yoshida and who could do tough negotiating with GHQ.[73]

After GHQ left and Yoshida resigned in December 1954, some speculated that Takemi lost his status in the JMA. However, Takemi was elected president of the JMA in April 1957, with 104 votes out of 152.[74] Many were surprised by his victory; his opponent, the president of the Tokyo Medical Association, Zenshirō Matsuda, was expected to win the election.[75] In order to fight back effectively against the government's efforts to control the health insurance system, the JMA needed a president who could break through the long-term stalemate. From December 1955 to January 1956, when the HI Amendment Act was being discussed, many JMA members became even more radical.[76] *Shakaihoken Shunpō*, an influential magazine of social welfare policy, described the reasons for Takemi's election: "Takemi served as the vice president from 1952 to 1953, proposed the three principles of health insurance in the Extraordinary Council on Health Insurance, which was established in June 1952, and started the debate on the national health insurance fee. His comeback demonstrates that he was supported by the JMA members who felt that no progress had been made in these areas."[77] *Shunpō* also pointed out that Takemi tried to reach out to hospital-owner doctors by including San'eki Kanzaki, a member of the Japan Hospital Association (JHA), as an executive board member—which became a problem for Takemi later.[78]

Obata had not been able to effectively deal with the pressure from the JMA members. It was probably not Obata himself but the traditions of the JMA that prevented the organization from aggressively engaging in politics. The JMA was not a lobbying organization in a modern sense. Shigeru Tanaka reminisced: "I opened my clinic when I was twenty-five years old, and the next year, 1951, I joined the JMA. It was like a salon where gentlemen gathered. As a young man, I was taught many things not only about medicine and but also about life."[79] The JMA as an organization was not well prepared to influence the health insurance policymaking process. The JMA needed to change the nature of its leadership and organization. Takemi undertook to transform the JMA. He was still young, fifty-three years old, and had many years to serve as the president if he wished.

Because of his aggressive attitude toward the government, particularly the MHW, Takemi was known as "belligerent Tarō" (*kenka Tarō*).[80] His bombastic and provocative personality was well known to JMA members. He had run for president three times in the past but never gained enough votes in these earlier elections. Shūichi Hido, a delegate from Niigata who knew Takemi well, argues that he came up short in those elections because of his strong personality. The election in 1957 was different: the same personality helped him get elected.[81] Hido described Takemi's leadership: "To compare the organization to a baseball team,

Takemi was manager and pitcher at the same time. He was also a cleanup hitter."[82] His style of leadership as simultaneous manager and player was different from the traditional salon-style leadership of previous JMA presidents.

Steslicke writes of Takemi's impact on the development of the JMA, "It was not until after the election of Tarō Takemi as president in April 1957 . . . that the JMA began to attract widespread attention and condemnation as an *atsuryoku dantai* (pressure group). It is only since Takemi's election and forceful leadership, moreover, that the JMA [became] of key importance in medical care administration and politics."[83] Hajime Mizuno also notes, "It was Takemi, who, for the first time, brought up policy ideas themselves and began to fight [against the government]."[84]

Takemi was convinced that the bureaucrats had distorted the health care system in Japan.[85] His inaugural speech demonstrated his strong intention to challenge the government. He said, "When we see the present condition of social insurance, I think there are many contradictions and many items that need reform. The health insurance reform proposal, which we have recently fought against, was out of step with the necessary process of science and democracy. We need to reverse this course, which is leading to a police-like authoritarian administration."[86]

Takemi believed that doctors, not government bureaucrats, should play the leading role in the health care policymaking process. He wrote, "Currently, medicine is practiced not for people's welfare but for bureaucratic power. Under this circumstance, people's welfare and doctors' knowledge are meaningless. It is unforgivable that technical officers who know nothing about clinical medicine instructs have no respect for veteran doctors in the field."[87]

Takemi disliked bureaucrats having so much power over the administration of the GMHI program and supervision of the entire health insurance system. In addition, he was particularly hostile toward the SMHI, the big companies' health insurance program. He believed that the program was mostly a tool for employers to keep their employees loyal. Having younger and healthier enrollees than other insurance programs, many SMHI associations had better finances and often had their own facilities, such as exclusive hot spring resorts. Takemi wrote that the SMHI program "symbolized the egoism of anti-social security."[88]

To demonstrate to other JMA leaders that he would be a strong president who could resist bureaucratic power, right after he became president, Takemi told the other leaders not to appease MHW officials by continuing the accustomed ritual in which the newly elected JMA president and other leaders paid a respectful visit to the minister of health and welfare. Takemi's message demonstrated his strong political leverage and confrontational attitude toward the MHW, which was what many JMA members wanted.[89]

Takemi was not against dealing with all political powers. He was suspicious of bureaucrats, and he criticized many LDP politicians, including the ministers of health and welfare. He liked, however, to deal with powerful LDP politicians whom he could trust in order to gain compromises from the government. Thus, the bureaucrats were bypassed, which was not the regular practice of the JMA with the MHW bureaucrats. The MHW therefore forcefully resisted Takemi's challenges.

Takemi's First Battles

It can be said that Takemi was elected to recover from what I would call the JMA's twenty lost years. He confronted the MHW bureaucrats who had gained power during the war and the postwar reconstruction. Takemi also broke away from the short-lived labor-medicine cooperation. He believed that socialism was a synonym for fascism.[90] Thus, he had to face opposition on many fronts. But this oppositional stance was what his supporters wanted. With his personal connections and his strategy, Takemi achieved success soon after he won the election.

One of the first major achievements of the Takemi presidency concerned the Health Insurance Act Amendment of 1957. It had been passed in the Diet, but the government and ministerial ordinances for its implementation were yet to be issued. This authority belonged to the minister of health and welfare, who was Hiroshi Kanda at that time. Takemi dealt directly with Kanda with the help of Takemi's personal connections, University of Tokyo professors Hajime Kaneko and Teruhisa Ishii. Takemi was able to block the double-designation system. Since the compromise with Kanda was made around four in the morning after a fifteen-hour negotiation, Takemi called this "collective bargaining at dawn" (*akatsuki no dankō*).[91] Arioka argues that this victory played a role in strengthening Takemi's presidency in its early period.[92]

Takemi continued to aggressively oppose the MHW.[93] He criticized government officials for using the Extraordinary Council on Health Insurance to introduce a fee system that greatly reduced national health insurance fees. The Extraordinary Council, created after the preferential tax treatment was passed, was supposed to make changes in the fee system to reflect this preferential treatment. Takemi withdrew the JMA representatives from the Extraordinary Council, and it stopped meeting.[94]

In July 1957, when Kenzō Horiki became the new minister of health and welfare, he—along with LDP secretary-general Seijirō Kawashima and the chair of the Special Committee on Social Security, Ryūgo Hashimoto—visited the JMA headquarters to pay respects to Takemi because Horiki was afraid of losing the cooperation of the JMA. Previous ministers had never done so. As we have seen, new JMA presidents formerly paid such a visit to the head of the MHW. This change demonstrated to JMA members that Takemi had been successful in getting the upper hand in negotiating with the government.[95]

Even with his aggressive personality and strong leverage in the political network, Takemi could not easily overcome the JMA's stagnation. He knew that it would be extremely difficult to reverse the course of institutional and political development. Part of his inaugural address affirmed this understanding when he said, "We have a responsibility to offer the necessary technological and social cooperation for creating a universal health insurance system."[96] Looking back later, Takemi said, "It was inevitable that Japan would adopt a universal health insurance system. . . . The universal health insurance system that the MHW was planning, I believed, involved too much intervention from the government in doctors' professional freedom. I tried to get a handle on such intervention."[97]

Takemi could only try to maximize the JMA's interests within the institutional environment that existed. His desperate attitude also reflected the strong power of bureaucrats in the policymaking process. MHW officials took steps to achieve universal health care while retaining their control over it. They were fortunate to have Horiki as their minister. Although he seemed polite to Takemi at the beginning of his term, Horiki later went on the offensive to implement his agenda, including the introduction of the new national health insurance fee system. Takemi knew he had to demonstrate the JMA's power against the government.

A new national health insurance fee system began to be discussed in the early 1950s. It was deeply connected to the issue of the separation of medical treatment and the sale of medicines. The government and the JMA agreed that the existing fee schedule assumed that all doctors made a large part of incomes by selling medicine. That assumption was the reason the fee schedule did not fairly cover doctors' other medical services. The new national health insurance fee system was supposed to appropriately price doctors' medical services to make it easier for them to stop selling medicine.

It was not a good time, at least for the JMA, to discuss the new national health insurance fee system. Health insurance finances had deteriorated in the mid-1950s. The government, along with the Federation of Health Insurance Societies, tried to reduce health care costs. The JMA strongly opposed the introduction of the new fee system, which the association saw as not much improving, and possibly worsening, the overall financial condition of its members. Takemi pushed hard for an increase in the existing fee schedule.

Horiki tried to reduce the JMA's pressure by making a surprise proposal. He introduced a fee system with two fee schedules. The two fee schedules were called No. 1 (kō hyō) and No. 2 (otsu hyō). The No. 1 fee schedule was designed to more clearly separate medical treatment from the selling of medicine. The schedule fixed ten yen as the unit price per official point in a payment-by-case scheme. The No. 2 fee schedule was based on the existing fee schedule. Clinics and hospitals could choose whichever system suited them. The MHW insisted that the No. 1 fee schedule would allow doctors to earn the same level of income or more.

Takemi strongly opposed this plan. He thought that the No. 1 fee schedule was a gateway for the ongoing bureaucratic attempt to control and nationalize medicine because of the way its case payment scheme worked. Takemi stated, "For example, in some cases, urine examination and blood pressure examination are included in the price. Doctors who receive payment without doing the blood examination are better off. There is no medical ethics here."[98] Takemi also opposed the move to lock in the price per point at ten yen, as locking in this price would make it difficult to increase fees to keep pace with inflation. Many JMA members still believed it would be impossible to make a living if they lost the revenue that they traditionally received from selling medicines.[99]

The JMA also saw the new fee schedule as a political tactic to divide the medical community. With two fee schedules, The No. 1 mainly for hospitals and the No. 2 for clinics, doctors would be separated into two categories. An increasing number of doctors had transformed their clinics into hospitals, and many others were hired by hospitals. While the JMA was trying to maintain its membership, the government was trying to divide doctors into two groups and weaken the JMA's political power in the field. Takemi called the government's proposal a "maneuver to divide the medical world."[100]

In protest, the JMA made flyers with messages such as "Protect the people from the atomic and hydrogen bomb launched by the insurance bureaucrats" and "You will have peace of mind if you get rid of the insurance bureaucrats and the insurers' boss" (which was the Federation of Health Insurance Societies).[101] According to one account, five hundred thousand protest flyers were distributed all over the country. This action by Takemi gained media attention, and he began to be treated like a celebrity.[102]

While the JMA continued its opposition, the government had luck with Chūikyō. In October, San'eki Kanzaki, one of the council members recommended by the JMA, expressed his support for the new fee schedules. While he was an executive board member of the JMA, he was also vice president of the Japan Hospital Association, which was a public hospital–based organization. The JHA leadership had been frustrated by the JMA, which supported fee schedules favorable to clinics, and by Takemi, who always had a confrontational attitude toward the government.

Takemi was furious about Kanzaki's betrayal and pressed him to resign from Chūikyō. Health and Welfare Minister Horiki also made up his mind to fight.

On October 18, under pressure, Kanzaki submitted his resignation as an executive member of JMA and also as a Chūikyō member. Horiki met with Kanzaki and JHA president Hirotoshi Hashimoto and said, "The Central Social Insurance Medical Council needs you [Kanzaki] because you represent the JHA. Considering the role of the council, it would be ridiculous not to have you. Since you still have the rest of your term, I would like to ask you not to resign."[103] Kanzaki agreed to stay in Chūikyō.

Kanzaki later recalled this incident and claimed that the JMA should have been more cooperative in discussing the new fee system. He wrote, "I thought that it would be more democratic if a general plan was proposed and then to deliberate on it in a cooperative way. . . . The MHW should not oppose major revisions only by being too concerned about its organizational honor. . . . I have repeatedly said this. The Central Social Insurance Medical Council is not a place for fighting and having splits."[104] He also wrote, "The JMA seems to believe that the JHA is its lower branch. But they have an equal relationship."[105] Kanzaki's comments demonstrate both the difficult relationship with the MHW and the JHA leaders' frustration with the JMA and its president, Takemi.

The argument about Kanzaki was also about whether JMA members had organizational autonomy in Chūikyō. The JMA claimed that its members should be expected to work for their organization. Masami Takada, the head of the Insurance Bureau, asserted that once a member was appointed, that person no longer represented the interests of his or her organization. Furthermore, the deputy head of the Insurance Bureau, Shinjirō Koyama, stated, "Organizations were selected to recommend council members, but it was not a collective negotiation. The council should reflect the opinions of as many as possible, and, hence, members from medical service providers should have representatives from hospital associations."[106]

The LDP initially sided with the MHW. The LDP tried to convince Takemi to cooperate with the MHW, but these efforts were in vain. Yasaburō Taniguchi, a former JMA president and now a member of the upper house, tried to calm Takemi down. Takemi paid no attention. Ryōgorō Katō, a physician and former minister of justice, also tried to put pressure on Takemi. Katō said, "It would be harmful [for the JMA] if you take a rebellious attitude against the LDP." Takemi, however, replied, "What a silly comment for an old-fashioned obstetrician to make! Those who depend too much on worthless political parties cannot be called politicians."[107] Takemi stopped the JMA from recommending members to Chūikyō. Chūikyō met once in June 1959 without a JMA representative, but after that it became inactive.[108] This political battle continued, and it resulted in a reorganization of Chūikyō.

Horiki pushed for the new fee system and tried to issue a government notification to enforce the system. With pressure from the JMA, however, the LDP leaned more toward not forcing the new fee system if the JMA opposed it. This stopped Horiki from issuing the notification.[109] Horiki's fight with Takemi ended when Prime Minister Nobusuke Kishi formed a new cabinet in June 1958. Ryūgo Hashimoto, a longtime friend of Takemi's, became the new minister of health and welfare. Hashimoto asked Takemi to accept the introduction of the two fee schedules and set the unit price per official point at ten yen while making three important compromises.[110] One was to postpone the implementation of the fee system by a year. Another was to raise the fee by 8.5 percent. The last was to promise to merge the two fee schedules in the near future.

Takemi also got Hashimoto to agree to the general principle of the fee schedule so that the price per point would not be fixed permanently but would be flexible with economic indicators.[111] Takemi asked for one-on-one direct negotiations with Hashimoto, during which Takemi received assurance on this point. After the deal, Hashimoto called in the administrative vice minister, Shigeo Tanabe, and the Insurance Bureau head, Masami Takada, and explained the compromise to them.[112] Takada strongly objected to Hashimoto's deal and furiously said, "Minister, you just agreed to an outrageous compromise. It will delay the MHW's plans for the next ten years."[113] This is another example of how Takemi, because of his connections, was able to bypass the bureaucrats and deal directly with influential LDP politicians.

Miwa states that Takemi's decision "protected his friend [Ryūgo Hashimoto], who often brought his son [Ryūtarō Hashimoto, who later became minister of health and welfare and prime minister] to Takemi's house, and also strengthened his power in the JMA." Miwa also writes that "Takemi might also have been moved by Hashimoto's honest pleas. This decision [to have the two fee schedules] was a source of trouble in the future."[114] At that time, winning a compromise from Hashimoto helped Takemi continue on as the "fighting JMA president."[115]

Most of JMA's rank-and-file members were happy as long as Takemi showed his strong fighting spirit against the government and helped them gain some material benefits.[116] Getting material benefits in the short term was more appealing than spending a long time trying to get fundamental reform, whose outcome the members could not imagine. Arioka mentions that Takemi's experience as vice president under the second Tamiya presidency taught him that to lead the JMA he should not explicitly argue for his "correct" principled views. What he learned was to represent what solo practitioners needed, so that he could lead the association.[117] Miwa points out that Takemi's showy activities were aimed at demonstrating to the JMA members that he was confronting the government so that he could have a stable presidency for many years, as Shibasaburō Kitasato and Taichi Kitajima had done.[118]

Takemi often said that he did not want to be the leader of a bunch of "greedy village heads" (*yokubari sonchō*).[119] To him, the JMA was full of private solo practitioners who did not care much about the improvement of medical science and ethics, and more broadly the health insurance system. He described his dilemma: "The JMA stands between the bureaucrats and greedy doctors."[120] Unlike other interest groups, the JMA was expected to play a unique public role, directly serving the health of the Japanese. Like other interest groups, the JMA also had to keep the members happy by giving them material benefits. It is hard to blame doctors for taking this approach when they had lost autonomy and respect as a professional interest group during the war and the following reconstruction period. Takemi could have played a role in changing the organization's overall character, but he chose not to because he had many fronts he needed to fight on, and he could not afford to lose the support of the JMA membership.

What he chose to do in order to build a foundation for a long-term presidency was to take an aggressive attitude toward bureaucrats, provide doctors with material benefits that he won by making compromises with influential LDP politicians, and make the JMA appear to be a powerful interest group under his strong leadership. Along with his favorite vice presidents, he won reelection in 1958 against Taniguchi, who had tried to convince Takemi to be more cooperative toward the government. The *Japan Medical Association Journal* describes this election as "a turning point in which the JMA would be totally changed, lose its autonomy, and come under MHW control forever."[121]

Takemi succeeded in expanding his support base. In his first election in 1957, he understood that he was in a lucky situation because of the division in the Tokyo Medical Association. Now he had a clearer mandate. But what awaited him were more battles against the government, including struggles over introducing a universal health insurance system, merging the two fee schedules, and making fundamental reforms. Although Takemi won some political battles in his first term, he could not much change the existing institutional arrangements, in which the MHW had firm control. As the introduction of universal health insurance neared, Takemi needed a boost to counter the MHW and further solidify his political base within the JMA. That happened in 1961.

CONSOLIDATING UNIVERSAL HEALTH INSURANCE

In March 1958, the Diet passed a law requiring that all municipalities provide national health insurance within three years. As discussed in the previous chapter, the establishment of universal health insurance was a result of policy path dependence. Still, there were political battles over policymaking. Before the law passed, stakeholders fought over how to cover the uninsured, which would affect their political leverage in the new system. The political battle continued even after the law was passed, as many related issues, including the new fee system and fee-setting mechanism, still needed to be settled. But it is important to distinguish whether political battles were about making adjustments to policies or about challenging their substance.

Japanese politics underwent a change in this period. The Liberal Democratic Party continued to be in power, but it faced challenges and had to transform its policy priorities. Its most difficult challenge was revision of the Security Treaty between the United States and Japan. Prime Minister Nobusuke Kishi tried to modify the treaty and strengthen Japan's position vis-à-vis the United States. He confronted strong opposition from a movement that wanted to abolish the treaty itself. The antitreaty protest marches were the largest mass demonstrations in modern Japan. The revision of the treaty was finally realized in June 1960, but Kishi decided to step down to take responsibility for the social turmoil. The Socialist Party of Japan, the largest minority party, could not much take advantage of this troubled period, largely because the LDP had achieved rapid economic development and expansion of social welfare provisions.[1]

Hayato Ikeda of the LDP was elected as the next prime minister in July 1960. His slogan was: "Generosity [*kanyō*] and patience [*nintai*]." Many people hoped that Ikeda would bring in a change more responsive to the population, after the long period of social and political turbulence during Kishi's politically inept tenure. Ikeda emphasized economic growth with his income doubling plan, which aimed to double the GDP within ten years from 1961. The postwar reconstruction period was clearly over. Japan was entering a time of fast economic development. The rapid growth from 1958 to 1961 is known as the "Iwato economic boom,"[2] one of the largest in Japanese history. The Tokyo Olympics of 1964 also improved the economic situation. After a short economic downturn, another long economic boom, known as the "Izanagi economic boom,"[3] took place from 1965 to 1970. The economy was now the government's top policy priority. The Ikeda administration also stressed the importance of having a solid social welfare program to reduce economic disparities. The 1960s, with an enlarged economic pie for Japan, was a great decade for the government to both invest in economic growth and expand social welfare.[4] The battle between the government and the JMA continued in this changing economic and political environment.

The JMA, with Tarō Takemi as its president, tried to take advantage of the LDP's difficulties in the early 1960s and was determined to gain concessions from the government for its members. While the government often changed its minister of health and welfare, Takemi remained as the JMA president, which gave him some advantage. With his strong connections with influential politicians in the LDP, he was able to maneuver in the robust bureaucracy. In 1961, Takemi conducted a controversial campaign in which he threatened that JMA members would withdraw from health insurance practice. As a result, he won compromises from LDP politicians regarding fee increases and representation on the fee-setting committee.

The political battle heated up in this period because it could lead to a gradual institutional change in which the JMA could gain more power. Takemi did his best to win some skirmishes, which helped him to go on being reelected as the JMA president. However, he could not change much given the robust nature of the government institutions. With Takemi's aggressive performance, the JMA appeared to be on the offensive, while the government looked defensive, but the institutional arrangements of health insurance remained almost intact. What the government and the JMA did in the 1960s with the economic boom and expansion of health insurance benefits was, in political scientist Paul Pierson's words, mostly for "political credit claiming."[5] The political battle was not much about the substance of the health insurance system.

The Law Requiring Universal Health Insurance Coverage

The manner and timing of Japan's introduction of universal coverage shows the institutional, political, and historical context that Takemi and other political actors faced. As discussed, the issue of universal coverage, which had been a priority of the occupation authority at first, was put aside in the later period when the United States went in a more conservative direction. This policy change was known as "reversing course."[6] Universal health insurance regained attention when the Advisory Council on Social Security reaffirmed that the introduction of a universal health insurance system would be necessary for Japan. The stagnation of National Health Insurance programs after the amendment of 1948 made policymakers realize the necessity of a stronger measure. Masayoshi Yamamoto, director of the National Health Insurance Section of the Ministry of Health and Welfare, wrote in 1950, "After the NHI was amended in 1948, many municipalities joined NHI in the first year, but by the middle of the second year, we could see that the NHI had hit its ceiling. . . . We sense that people are considering legislation to make it mandatory for all municipalities."[7] Meanwhile, the JMA did not actively participate in the policy debate because the association had been forcibly restructured and was weak during most of the reconstruction period.

A side effect of the deficit problem of the Health Insurance program was to push the government to make universal health insurance a higher policy priority in the early 1950s. Suffering from the stagnated postwar economy, the population generally started to use HI, which had previously been considered by many merely as a welfare program. In 1951, the unit price per point for doctors' fees was raised as inflation continued. In this situation, the Government-Managed Health Insurance (one of the two pillars of HI), which included workers in small companies, faced financial difficulty. The government, as the insurer of the program, needed to subsidize the GMHI.

The government's action brought up criticism from some that tax money was being spent on the workers' health insurance program, while not providing for many uninsured people. Hideo Inbe, director of the National Health Insurance Section (and later director of the Social Security Agency), commented retrospectively on the relationship between the problems of the HI and the uninsured: "Not only scholars but also newspaper editorial writers and LDP politicians began to believe the logic behind the unfairness of the subsidy. Therefore, public opinion in favor of helping the uninsured became very strong when discussing the government subsidy of the HI."[8]

In March 1954, the Advisory Council on Social Security released a statement on the situation: "With advances in medical science and medical care, medical costs have continued to increase. But people's incomes have not been able to catch up with the cost increases. It is hard to ask people to make financial contributions to national health insurance, but we still have 30 million uninsured people."[9] In July 1955, the government set up the Special Committee on Medical Security (Iryō Hoshō Tokubetsu Iinkai) in the Advisory Council on Social Security to plan policies to achieve universal coverage. The details of the universal health insurance plan were presented in the Diet when the HI's deficit problem was under debate. In December 1955, the MHW concluded that it would be better to achieve universal coverage by making it mandatory for all municipalities to establish the NHI.[10]

This decision was not automatic. Many of the uninsured were employees who worked for small companies with fewer than five employees, which the HI program did not cover. While the MHW leaned toward the idea that the NHI would be expanded to cover them, the Advisory Council on Social Security and the JMA insisted that a new employment-based program be established for these uninsured, what was called the Class 2 Health Insurance Program (Dainishu Kenkō Hoken).[11] This conflict illuminates the different visions of the health insurance system at that time. The Advisory Council and the JMA supported integrating multiple programs into two categories: employees in the Society-Managed Health Insurance, Government-Managed Health Insurance, and other programs would be placed into one new employment-based program; and others would be placed into the NHI. Putting the employees who worked for small companies into the NHI, which was residence-based insurance, would make the distinction between the two programs blur. The MHW supported more status quo, fearing that creation of yet another employment-based and financially weak program would lead to integration of the two programs and weaken the MHW's political power. The GMHI was the important source of power for the government to control the health insurance system. This political battle ended in favor of the MHW.[12]

In November 1956, the Advisory Council on Social Security presented its Recommendation on a Medical Security System (Iryō Hoshō Seido ni Kansuru Kankoku), which emphasized, "along with education, equal opportunity of health care has to be treated as one of the highest policy priorities."[13] The council recommended that Japan should achieve a universal health insurance system by fiscal year 1961. Kazuo Imai, an Advisory Council member, reminisced about the historical significance of the recommendation: "It [the recommendation] became a trigger to introducing the universal health insurance system. It was a historic document."[14] In 1957, furthermore, Prime Minister Kishi announced a policy of "health insurance for the whole nation" and established the Promotion Headquarters for Universal Health Care.[15] The way was paved for universal health care.

Hirokuni Dazai, executive director of the Advisory Council and an MHW official at that time, recalled his reaction to the Advisory Council Recommendation: "The recommendation included the five-year financial plan for 1961, but I did not personally think universal health insurance would be realized by 1961."[16] Inbe also stated that many MHW bureaucrats believed it would be very difficult to achieve universal coverage by that date.[17] Their statements suggest that the movement to introduce universal health insurance had more political momentum than bureaucratic faith at the time.[18]

The comments of these bureaucrats also show that they did not believe Japan was ready for universal health coverage. Takemi also retrospectively pointed out this issue: "Japan's universal health insurance was mismanaged by the conservative party [the LDP]. Because Japan did not prepare enough, it was obvious that we would be mired in a mess. Catch-phrase politics without sufficient scientific research was the end result of this situation."[19]

While the MHW had a lukewarm attitude toward the immediate introduction of universal coverage, the All-Japan Federation of National Health Insurance Organizations (Zenkoku Kokumin Kenkō Hoken Chūōkai), which was composed of municipality-level NHI associations, was a leading advocate of immediate universal coverage.[20] The Japan Association of City Mayors (Zenkoku Shichōkai) and other local organizations, such as town and village associations, also actively supported universal coverage. The expansion of government-subsidized national health insurance appealed to mayors and their constituencies. These organizations also tried to get subsidies to create NHI hospitals in their districts.[21]

Problems with the Daily Life Security Act of 1947 also encouraged the hesitant MHW to engage in health insurance reform. The act provided aid for medical treatment for low-income people. In early 1950, more and more people fell under the act's coverage, and the program's budgetary needs rapidly increased. Iwao Yasuda, head of the Social Bureau, said in 1957, "To solve the problem for low-income people, the fundamental measure would be to create a health insurance system for everyone. There is no other way."[22]

There was controversy over whether municipalities or prefectures should have administrative responsibility in the proposed mandatory NHI. The Advisory Council on Social Security proposed the prefecture option. They believed having a big pool would diversify risk. Some MHW bureaucrats favored the municipality option based on political calculations. Inbe said in retrospect, "In my opinion, if we compare the organizational power of health insurance associations [in big companies] and medical associations, the latter were much politically powerful than the former. . . . Therefore, it was necessary to connect the municipality heads with the health insurance associations and balance out the power of the JMA. It was based on taking into consideration the overall system."[23] As an MHW official, Inbe did not mention what the impact would be on the power of bureaucrats, but obviously his comment implies that the municipality option was better for the bureaucrats in maintaining power over the JMA and the health insurance system. The municipality option, the status quo, was chosen in the end.

In March 1958, a bill was introduced in the Diet to amend the National Health Insurance Act. The Diet was dissolved in April, and the bill was thus abandoned. It was reintroduced in an extraordinary Diet session in September. In December 1958, finally, the Diet passed the National Health Insurance Act Amendment, known as the new National Health Insurance Act (Shin Kokumin Kenkō Hoken Hō), to make all municipalities cover their residents. In January 1959, the Diet stipulated that all municipalities would have to implement the legislation by March 1961. The act also made the government provide 20 percent of the insurers' administrative expenditures, with the NHI covering 50 percent of out-of-pocket health care costs of the insured and their dependents.[24]

Japan achieved universal coverage by making the NHI mandatory for those not covered by existing insurance programs. The NHI filled in the coverage gap. But the NHI was qualitatively different from the two employment-based programs in the HI, in both program benefits and political dynamics. The NHI was the weakest program. Right before the amendment passed, Tokuo Kojima, managing director of the All-Japan Federation of National Health Insurance Organizations, expressed his concern that the NHI not only had weak finances but also had weak grassroots support. He wrote at that time, "We should not forget that public management has a defect. . . . NHI mainly targets agricultural workers and owners of microenterprises, which were not organized as much as the labor unions that engaged in the administration of the Health Insurance Act. Therefore, as we move to strengthen the power of municipalities in the NHI, it is necessary to organize the insured of the NHI."[25]

The government, worried about the financial impact of increasing the number of insured, was hesitant to raise doctors' fees. Takemi pressed the government to undertake other measures to improve JMA members' incomes. What Takemi received was the establishment of the Medical Finance Corporation (Iryō Kin'yū Kōko), which provided doctors with low-interest loans to set up clinics and hospitals. The 1951 special loan program was not satisfactory to the JMA, because the loans were made to any kind of professional, not specifically doctors. The JMA tried to obtain a clearer assurance by getting a program targeting only doctors. In July 1958, the JMA, along with the Japan Dental Association, Japan Red Cross, Saiseikai Imperial Gift Foundation, and National Welfare Federation of Agricultural Cooperatives (Zenkoku Kōsei Nōgyō Kyōdō Kumiai), asked Diet members to create the Medical Finance Corporation.[26]

The Ministry of Finance opposed this proposal. The ministry argued that the government should not create a public loan organization for a specific industry. Newspapers predicted that the proposal would not get through the budget negotiations for fiscal year 1960. Banboku Ōno, an influential LDP politician, asked Takemi to withdraw the proposal. Takemi replied, "Okay then, it would be fine if you say it is impossible. But it looks like an election is coming soon. Without the Medical Finance Corporation, I cannot ask the JMA members to vote for the LDP."[27] He went home after the meeting and received a phone call from Minister of Health and Welfare Michio Watanabe saying the proposal had been approved, and in February 1960, the cabinet decided to establish the Medical Finance Corporation.[28]

Now Japan had universal health care, and Takemi had won the battle to get the Medical Finance Corporation. In addition, he gained compromises on the double-designation system in the expanded NHI.[29] But the mandatory NHI patched one reform onto the existing institutional setting without changing its basic structure and principles. The SMHI covers those who work in big companies; the GMHI is for those in smaller companies with more than five employees; and the NHI is for all those not covered by the employment-based programs. With these various health insurance programs, the government kept its strong power embedded in the health insurance system. Political actors now tried to expand their interests within this institutional setting, and the controversy over the new fee system heated up.

Battle at Daybreak over Universal Health Care

According to Takemi, when Prime Minister Ikeda proposed his "Income-Doubling Plan" (Shotoku Baizō Keikaku), Takemi asked Ikeda whether doctors' incomes would be doubled and got a positive answer.[30] At the same time, the government was trying to get health care costs under control and succeeded in making a new fee system with two fee schedules. Minister of Health and Welfare Ryūgo Hashimoto told Takemi that the two fee schedules would soon be integrated. The political battles heated up in fiscal year 1960. Takemi said in a radio interview that when Ikeda became prime minister in July 1960, "I demanded that the Ikeda administration take strong action to correct the present situation in which the MHW bureaucrats, especially insurance officials, resort to petty tricks, engaging in political intrigues and forgetting the welfare of the people."[31] It was a critical time for the MHW and the JMA because the government had set the deadline for completing universal national health insurance coverage at the end of fiscal year 1960.

In July 1960, Prime Minister Ikeda appointed Masa Nakayama as minister of health and welfare. She was the first woman to become a cabinet member. With universal health care soon to be realized, Nakayama was an important player not only for the MHW bureaucrats but also for the JMA. William Steslicke mentions that MHW bureaucrats were rather disappointed about her appointment because she did not seem to be strong enough to counter political pressures from the JMA and others.[32] Takemi also made a negative comment to Prime Minister Ikeda in person: "Why did you appoint such a fool to be minister of health and welfare?"[33] But the appointment of Nakayama turned out to be favorable for the JMA.

On August 18, 1960, JMA representatives visited Administrative Vice Minister of Health and Welfare Masami Tanaka and submitted a formal statement of "Four Demands" to Minister Nakayama. The petition began, "If Japan starts universal health insurance under current conditions, it will permanently lose the respect of academia, sacrifice the welfare of the people, and strengthen the self-righteous fascism of health insurance bureaucrats."[34] The demands included a fee increase and the integration of the two fee schedules. This was rather a symbolic action, but in Steslicke's words, it "marked the beginning of a JMA campaign to secure favorable governmental action on the Four Demands."[35]

The demands included abolishing wartime restrictions on medical treatments (*seigen shinryō*) that could be obtained with health insurance. With the intensive war mobilization, the government had significant power to regulate the content of medical benefits and to keep down the costs.[36] The restrictions remained after the war. Takemi in retrospect stated, "The MHW tried to create a system that would never allow for increases in health costs. With the restrictions on medical treatment, doctors could not use expensive medicines. What kind of medicines could be used and in what order they should be used was all decided and written on the [government's] list. Doctors were not allowed to use new effective medicines."[37] Takemi also said, "If we have universal health care, it is absolutely necessary to abolish the restrictions on medical treatment. The restrictions violate human rights, because people's lives are endangered if academic developments are not supported. Following my academic beliefs, I will never compromise on this issue."[38]

Jirō Arioka explains why the JMA made the proposal at the time: "Solo practitioners felt worried because they were not sure how universal health care would impact them. . . . Takemi grasped their anxiety and discontent and asked for a substantial raise in the fee, the abolishment of medical treatment restrictions, and other things."[39] In September, Nakayama directed MHW officials to accept the JMA's requests.[40] But Nakayama soon resigned when Ikeda formed a new cabinet in December.

The new health and welfare minister, Yoshimi Furui, faced a difficult situation. As a result of the previous minister's sympathetic attitude toward the JMA, the association built up confidence to put forward its demands. Furui, however, knew how to fight the JMA. He was a former Home Ministry bureaucrat and became its vice minister in August 1945 at the young age of forty-two. Although he was purged by General Headquarters, he was elected to the lower house in 1952.[41] He consistently showed a confrontational attitude toward the JMA.

Dealing with Takemi, however, was not the only task Furui faced. He had to solve the problem of strikes in big hospitals. Around 1960, not only doctors but also nurses and other hospital staff were frustrated by the low fees. Strikes in hospitals began to spread. In November 1960, thirty-one Red Cross hospitals were shut down by strikes.[42] Akira Sugaya explains the cause of the strikes: "To achieve universal health insurance, the new National Health Insurance program drastically increased the coverage. But it was by expanding the NHI program, which was the worst [among various programs]. . . . The nationwide strikes by hospitals were the clear result."[43] The strikes were to improve the economic status of hospital officers and doctors.[44]

The JMA set up a subcommittee of hospital administrators and asked for an across-the-board fee increase of 30 percent. In January 1961, when the budget plan for the next fiscal year was discussed, the LDP's Special Committee on Medical Care (Iryō Taisaku Tokubetsu Iinkai) made a counterproposal of a 15 percent fee increase. Worse, in the view of the JMA, the MHW made a counterproposal of a 10 percent fee increase with more fee increases for hospitals. The JMA intensely opposed the MHW proposal. JMA executive board member Shigesada Marumo stated, "The MHW's proposal, in a word, is a policy to stamp out private solo practitioners."[45] This conflict led to the JMA's big campaign to intimidate the government by threatening to quit health insurance practice in 1961.

The JMA's Resistance in 1961

The National Health Insurance Act Amendment was supposed to be fully implemented to achieve universal health care by the end of March 1961. Except for a part of Kagoshima, all municipalities set up their NHI associations by the deadline.[46] With what he had experienced in the past few years, Takemi concluded that the JMA had to be prepared for a more aggressive fight against government control. Arioka describes the context of the battle:

> About a decade after the war, national health insurance was expanded, and many smoldering problems began to emerge in 1957. The MHW

tried to use the introduction of universal health care as a means to strengthen its control over not only health insurance programs but also the overall health care system. It tried to restrain private practitioners' medical practices and keep down health care costs. At the same time, the JMA under Takemi sniffed out the MHW's intention to seize bureaucratic control in order to nationalize medicine and conducted a strong opposition movement.[47]

Takemi began his serious efforts to counter the government when universal health insurance was to be introduced. In 1958, he stopped sending JMA representatives to the Central Social Insurance Medical Council (hereafter Chūikyō) after the disturbance of San'eki Kanzaki (described in chapter 5). Because he believed that the JMA should be the single authority in medicine, Takemi could not allow Kanzaki to claim to represent the interests of the Japan Hospital Association. The JHA movement matched the government's agenda of diminishing the JMA's power.

The MHW fought back. In July 1961 it created, under the supervision of the minister of health and welfare, the Health Security Advisory Committee, the so-called five-member committee, which had no JMA representative but did have a JHA representative. The members included Kōki Naganuma (former administrative vice minister of the Ministry of Finance), Yoshisuke Kasai (former administrative vice minister of the MHW), and Hirotoshi Hashimoto (president of the JHA). In March 1959, the committee released its final report, broadly affirming what the MHW was trying to do. The JMA attacked the report, saying that instead of listening to the policy recommendations of the Advisory Council on Social Security, the MHW created a new committee to gather favorable opinions.[48] Hideo Yoshida, social security scholar at Hosei University, supported this view. He had served as a representative of labor when the Advisory Council on Social Security was established in 1949. He wrote, "The MHW in the past created such and such committees in a reckless manner. . . . The other government agencies also had the same attitude, but I cannot help feeling the administrative agencies' irritability, sneakiness, and craftiness, particularly the MHW."[49] Bunji Kondō, a prominent social security scholar at Osaka City University, pointed out that "the report did not have concreteness in its proposal" and called it "a rigged sumo match."[50]

Despite the JMA's opposition, the budget for fiscal year 1961 was approved in line with the government's wishes. In January 1961, the JMA organized a meeting of prefectural medical association presidents, who decided to form the Headquarters for Fighting the Medical Crisis (Iryōkiki Toppa Tōsō Sōhonbu) specifically to counter the government's proposal. The executive directors also decided to have a one-day nonconsultation strike on February 19 and to hold local meetings on that day to discuss medical affairs with the people.[51]

Takemi negotiated with the LDP leaders to reach a compromise, but nothing came of these negotiations. The JMA held a nonconsultation day campaign. It was on a Sunday, and about 40 percent of private practitioners joined the discussion meetings with the public. The board of directors praised the event, saying, "We achieved the goal of telling the people about current medical problems."[52] But the major media did not report on the meetings. Instead, they asked Takemi about the possibility of sick patients' not getting health services during the strike. Media reported that he replied, "It was their fault if they were sick on the nonconsultation day." Takemi later said, "What I meant was it will be unfortunate for people who become sick on that day."[53] The media reported on the event not as an issue concerning the health care system but as an instance of Takemi's arrogant attitude.[54]

Takemi continued to fight. He threatened to have another nonconsultation day on March 5 and to make JMA members resign from health insurance practice by the end of March. On March 3, after negotiations with the government, Takemi won a one-yen increase in the price per point. This was big win for Takemi because the MHW had tried to set the price at ten yen, which would give the government more discretion to manipulate fee increases, such as setting higher fees specifically for hospitals. On March 7, the extraordinary session of the Diet approved what Takemi had negotiated with the LDP.[55]

LDP politicians promised that the fee increase would happen in September. In the extraordinary House of Delegates meeting, Takemi said, "All members were united for the event of the century. The result we had was the first time in the history of social insurance. . . . Between now and September is an important transition. We are changing from the fighting phase to the monitoring phase, and we will carefully watch [what the government does]."[56] This comment demonstrates that Takemi still felt uncertain about whether the agreement with the LDP would hold.

As Takemi had predicted, the Federation of Health Insurance Societies and its allies tried to revise what the government had agreed on with the JMA. The federation and its allies had Health and Welfare Minister Furui as their strong supporter. He met with Chūikyō when representatives of the JMA and JDA were absent and only one medical provider representative from the JHA was present. Furui received advice from the council on the MHW proposal that differed from what the LDP and the JMA had agreed on. As Furui hoped, the council proposed that the MHW keep ten yen for the price per point, not change drug prices or materials costs, and increase the fee by 12.5 percent with changing points for medical services. The fee increases mostly favored hospitals.[57]

When Prime Minister Ikeda reorganized his cabinet on July 18, 1961, Health and Welfare Minister Furui stepped down. According to Takemi, Furui once said, "In fact, I have thought about dissolving the JMA and solving the problem at once."[58] Hirokata Iwai, a close supporter of Takemi's, wrote, "Have international trade and industry ministers considered dissolving the Japan Business Federation (Keidanren) and the Japan Chamber of Commerce and Industry? Have justice ministers considered dissolving the Japan Federation of Bar Associations? Does Minister Furui know that the JMA includes the Japanese Association of Medical Sciences (Nihon Igakukai)?"[59]

The next Health and Welfare minister was Hirokichi Nadao. Like Furui, he was a former Home Ministry bureaucrat. Ironically, as director of the Hygiene Bureau, Nadao had witnessed Taichi Kitajima's anguished speech just before the JMA was turned into a state organization in 1943. Nadao was elected as a Diet member after GHQ's purge was lifted. Ikeda and Nadao both were from Hiroshima Prefecture and knew each other very well. When Ikeda asked Nadao to be the new minister, Nadao said to Ikeda with a bitter smile, "You are putting me in a tough place." Ikeda replied, "There is no one but you [who can deal with the current situation]. You must accept it."[60]

Nadao could not keep Takemi from concluding that the new cabinet was not serious about keeping the negotiated promise.[61] Takemi directed JMA members to resign from insurance practice starting August 1, 1961. The top priority of the JMA was to have a fee increase by changing the unit price per point. Because the change of fee schedule in 1958 was done without JMA input, Takemi was worried that the unit price per official point would be set at ten yen.[62]

In the end, Takemi once again directly negotiated with an influential LDP politician, Kakuei Tanaka, chairman of the party's Policy Research Council. They were both from Niigata Prefecture and had a long-standing relationship.[63] Tanaka sent a nearly blank note to Takemi on which was written, "With these conditions, the JMA will stop doing its [nonparticipation in insurance] plan." The note meant that Takemi could write in whatever conditions he wanted. He wrote four conditions: (1) fundamental reform of the health insurance system; (2) a strong connection between the improvement of medical research and education and the improvement of the people's welfare; (3) respect for the free private relationship between doctor and patient; (4) establishment of a fee schedule based on the idea of a free economy.[64] On July 31, three top leaders of the LDP, Health and Welfare Minister Nadao, JDA president Hiroshi Kawamura, and JMA president Takemi met at LDP headquarters. They accepted what Tanaka had requested. This looked like a big victory for Takemi, but it lacked any specific substance. Steslicke writes of this result, "While the JMA failed to receive all it had demanded, the compromise was an important symbolic victory which not only established its consultancy status in medical politics but also forced recognition of its influence and power as a veto group."[65]

The Battle over the Fee-Setting Process

Takemi continued the battle. He called for a reorganization of Chūikyō. Established right after the war when the JMA was weak, the council was a tool MHW bureaucrats used to keep down health care costs. The case of Kanzaki ignited the JMA's long-term frustration. As previously described (chapter 5), the JMA and the MHW fought over how to deal with the problem of Kanzaki, who was recommended by the JMA as a council member but ended up opposing the JMA's policy. Because Chūikyō had considerable power to decide the fee schedule, the JMA and the MHW devoted themselves to increasing their allies there.

In June 1959, on the day of the upper house election, Health and Welfare Minister Michita Sakata suggested that the JHA should be allowed to send a representative to Chūikyō. Takemi resisted by boycotting the council. Kazuo Miwa later wrote, "Takemi's boycott of Chūikyō blighted both the MHW and the JMA. While the MHW lost a discussion space for important agendas, the JMA lost opportunities to fight back."[66]

At the time, however, Takemi believed that a boycott would help the JMA show off its political power. He also needed to take the action in order to be seen by JMA members as politically strong, an image that helped him get reelected in April 1960. The JMA presidential election in April 1960 was a symbolic election asking whether the JMA under Takemi or the traditional pre-Takemi JMA was preferred. The opposition, led by former JMA president Korekiyo Obata, nominated Akira Takahashi. He was a prominent scholar and the former and first president of the reorganized JMA after the war. But Takemi won in an overwhelming victory.[67]

Takemi went on to insist that Chūikyō should be reorganized. He had three goals. The first was to increase the JMA's share of council members by diminishing, first, the power of the insurers and, second, the power of the public interest members as much as possible. The old council had four components, representing four interest groupings: insurers, employers and the insured, medical service providers, and public interests. Each component had six members. The JMA objected to business having such a large influence by participating both as employer and as insurer of the SMHI. Moreover, the JMA did not like that the government chose the public interest members at its convenience. These were usually economists who tried to keep down medical costs from only an economic perspective, which often turned out to be the government policy preference. The JMA often became the minority in the council.

It was not easy to resolve the conflict. In April 1961, during the JMA campaign for doctors to resign from health insurance practice, Health and Welfare Minister Furui proposed a reorganization plan. His proposal was that medical service providers, payers, and public interest representatives each have eight members on the council. Takemi was not happy that the proposal came from the MHW. He demanded that the reorganization plan should be introduced by members of the Diet and that the public interest nominees should be approved by the other members.[68]

The Diet changed the number of Chūikyō's components from four to three. The group of medical service providers secured eight members. The group of insurers also had eight members. Takemi would have preferred the council to have only one public interest member, who would play a role as "judge." But the number of public interest members ended up being four. Even with the compromise about the public interest members, the result was a victory for Takemi.[69] With the new arrangement, the JMA gained a bigger voice in the council (table 6.1).

The JMA's second goal in reorganizing the Central Social Insurance Medical Council was to ensure that the JMA would be the only medical service provider organization with the right to approve members. Taku Nomura read Takemi's intention: "It seemed that Takemi had the idea of preventing any medical administration from bypassing the JMA and to make the JMA more powerful versus the governmental and administrative agencies."[70] Because who would represent the medical providers' interests was not articulated in the reorganization plan itself, a political decision was needed. After the new council was established, it took one year and seven months to solve this problem and hold the first meeting. The JMA refused to participate until it secured a guarantee from Health and Welfare Minister Eiichi Nishimura that the JHA would not nominate its own representative for the council.[71]

In the process of creating the new council, the JMA cooperated with the Japan Pharmaceutical Association. It was, in the JPA's words, "a historical moment" for both organizations.[72] Doctors and pharmacists had fought over the separation of medical treatment and the sale of medicines since the Meiji era. Now the

TABLE 6.1 Members of the Central Social Insurance Medical Council

Pre–reorganization	Insurers	Employers and the insured	Medical service providers	Public interest
	6	6	6	6
Post–reorganization		Payers	Medical service providers	Public interest
		8	8	4

JMA, which usually cooperated with the Japan Dental Association, added a new ally. The three organizations, commonly called the Fellows of Three Professions (Sanshikai), began to cooperate more closely in the battle over national health insurance fees. They were opposed by the following six organizations: the Federation of Health Insurance Societies, the Organization of National Health Insurance Associations, the Japan Federation of Employers' Associations, the Japanese Confederation of Labor Unions, the National Federation of Industrial Organizations, and the JHA.[73]

In order to respond to the criticism that the JMA had squeezed the JHA out of the council so that the hospital organization did not have a voice in the fee-setting process, the JMA created the All-Japan Hospital Association (Zennihon Byōin Kyōkai) for midsize and small hospitals in July 1962. Takemi installed Yoshio Ozawa, professor emeritus of medicine at Osaka University and director of the Osaka Industrial Accident Compensation Hospital, as the association's president. Takemi had previously sought to make Ozawa president of the JHA in order to take over the organization, but this attempt failed. Takemi therefore created a new hospital organization. The organizational principle was "walking the path with the JMA." The new organization had members who were hospital directors who were not happy about the JHA confronting the JMA. Of course, there was a counteraction. The National Municipal Hospital Association (Zenkoku Jichitai Byōin Kyōgikai) was created for hospitals run by municipalities.[74]

As Takemi's struggle with hospitals continued, he successfully prevented the further growth of public hospitals. In September 1962, the Diet passed a law prohibiting public hospitals from increasing their number of beds without the prefectural governor's approval. The MHW and the Federation of Health Insurance Societies had opposed the law, but Takemi convinced influential politicians to support it. This regulation of the number of public hospital beds (byōshō kisei) shaped the balance between public hospitals and private hospitals: the latter continued to outnumber the former.[75]

The JMA's last goal was to make the council more independent from the MHW. In July 1962, the Social Insurance Agency (Shakaihoken Chō) was created as part of the reorganization plan. Since the early 1950s, the JMA had been saying it was wrong for the MHW to be the insurer of the GMHI because the MHW also played a role in making final decisions about the fee schedule.[76] The head of the Bureau of Social Insurance had participated in the old council as a member of the insurers. As a solution to this problem, the work-site operation section of health insurance and pensions was separated from the MHW and was included in the Social Insurance Agency.[77] The establishment of the new agency resulted from the collaboration of Nadao and Takemi.[78]

It can be concluded that Takemi won the battle to increase the JMA's voice in the fee-setting process. As usual, Takemi used his personal connections with influential LDP politicians to get what he wanted. But the MHW continued to have a large influence. Political scientist Hiroyasu Yūki points out that the organizational reforms did not change the environment in which the MHW drafted proposals and others, including JMA representatives, discussed issues within the framework of the MHW's proposals.[79] Both the JMA and government understood that they were not at the end of their political contest. The real battle was over how the various public health insurance programs should be improved and integrated.

The Battle over Fundamental Reform

While stakeholders engaged in the battle over the fee rate or fee system, they also fought about the overall restructuring of the health care system. Japan achieved universal health insurance in 1961. But as many have pointed out, Japan was not fully prepared for the development at that time. Sugaya writes, for example, that "overall, the benefits were not high. The program administration did not have unitary management. The programs were not coordinated. These were serious problems left for the future."[80] In the new era of universal health care, the most controversial issue was how the various health insurance programs should be integrated to improve the universal health care system.

These were old pending issues. Soon after the end of World War II, as described in chapter 4, GHQ and reformist government officials and scholars pushed for the integration of the various health insurance programs as part of improving social security. Taketo Tomonō, head of the Health Insurance Division, said, "I think many people hoped that the integration of social insurance would be advanced by the Advisory Council on Social Security."[81]

A unified administration would be not only more financially efficient but also more egalitarian. There was an inequality between the wealthy SMHI associations, which required patients to pay very limited out-of-pocket expenses, and the poor NHI associations, which required a 30 percent (50% for dependents) co-payment. After universal health care was achieved, political actors engaged in a discussion about how to close this gap, and debate about a radical reform became part of this discussion.

As a result of the 1961 strike threat campaign, Takemi had assurances from Tanaka that fundamental reform of the health insurance system would take place. Takemi had an agreement with Tanaka and other LDP leaders that an Informal Conference on Medical Affairs (Iryō Kondankai) would be established to discuss fundamental health care issues. Steslicke writes that the JMA's strike threat was a success in "exposing the inadequacies of the present health insurance system and the necessity for fundamental reform."[82] It appeared that the JMA would have a leadership role in the new Informal Conference. As Takemi demanded, it had ten members from the JMA and other medical provider groups and ten members from the payment side and others. The meetings were held in August 1961 and reached an overall conclusion that the inequality among the health insurance programs should be resolved.[83]

Meanwhile, in August 1962, the Advisory Council on Social Security came up with its Report on the Comprehensive Adjustment and Recommendations for Advancement of the Social Security System (Shakaihoshō no Sōgōchōsei ni kansuru Tōshin oyobi Shakaihoshō no Suishin ni kansuru Kankoku). The proposal included the goal that Japan should achieve the same level of social security expenditures as Western European countries. The Advisory Council also proposed integrating the multiple social security programs.[84] The momentum for program integration intensified.

In 1967, the Diet passed the Special Measures for Health Insurance Act (Kenkō Hoken Tokurei Hō), which included a condition that fundamental reform be achieved within two years. Responding to a request from the LDP's Investigation Committee on Fundamental Medical Problems (Iryō Kihon Mondai Chōsakai), the MHW submitted a proposal. It included expansion of health insurance benefits, compensation of the public programs' deficits, and financial coordination (zaisei chōsei) among health insurance programs. Fearing that the rich SMHI associations would have to contribute to balance the poorer programs, the Federation of Health Insurance Societies opposed the proposal. The federation insisted that it was wrong to discuss financial coordination without proposing any specific reforms in regard to the fee schedule, the insurance doctor system, and the medical service provider system.[85] Former MHW officials Kenji Yoshihara and Masaru Wada point out that the Federation of Health Insurance Societies sounded too much like it was protecting the SMHI and not the people, showing their "egoism."[86]

The JMA made a counterproposal in October 1968. Before that time, Takemi confirmed with Zenkō Suzuki, chair of the LDP's Research Committee, that the MHW's proposal would not be the basis for the discussion and that the JMA and the Research Committee would have equal weight in the discussion. The main thrust of the JMA's proposal was that the health insurance system should be reformed into a system with three components: one for industrial accidents, another for the elderly, and the last for residence-based health insurance programs administered by prefectures. He believed that the SMHI's health insurance societies allowed big companies to manage personnel and that, being financially better off, the societies could provide extra benefits for their members without taking financially weaker programs into consideration. Other JMA proposals included introducing a public health insurance program for the elderly (over the age of sixty-five); abolishing co-payments for NHI enrollees (dependents' co-payments would be reduced from 50% to 30%), making the NHI the same as the SMHI; and integrating the divided two fee schedules into the No. 2 fee schedule.[87]

The Federation of Health Insurance Societies and the JMA led the two opposing camps on how to achieve radical reform. The LDP's Research Committee could not reach a conclusion by the 1969 deadline. In May, the LDP released its proposed policy outline, which satisfied neither side. The JMA was not happy that its plan for a three-pillar system was rejected. The Federation of Health Insurance Societies opposed any measure that would lead to an increase in the federation's financial burden. The resulting legislation, called the Concerning the Exceptional Measures on the Health Insurance Act, was passed in the Diet with a stipulation that the MHW implement fundamental reform by August 1971. The end of 1970, however, saw no progress in the discussion about fundamental reforms.[88]

The introduction of universal health insurance did not mean a sufficient medical safety net for the entire population. Another step was needed to improve the health insurance system as a whole. However, the government did not give up its power in the existing institutional arrangements. On the other hand, although Takemi had exceptionally strong power as the JMA president to raise health insurance fees and change the proportion of the JMA members in the fee-setting organization, he mainly used his power to maximize benefits within the given institutional setting. To make things worse, around this time, Japan began to face a slowdown in its economic development. With a shrinking budgetary pie, it became even more difficult for political actors to reach an agreement on fundamental reform of the health care system. To break the deadlock, Takemi took a bold step in 1971.

MAKING UNIVERSAL HEALTH INSURANCE SURVIVE

Japan's rapid economic development from 1965 to 1970, known as the "Izanagi economic boom," resulted in Japan becoming the second-greatest economic power in the world. The "3Cs" (cars, color televisions, and coolers or air conditioners) became widely available in Japan. But the 1973 oil crisis was a serious challenge to the Japanese economy, which had been able to develop with a stable crude oil price. The country now entered a new phase of economic and political circumstances in which the economy showed it was not as strong as the Japanese people had thought. Government officials began to realize that the era of Japan's rapid economic growth was over. In a reaction to the post-Olympic recession in 1965, the government began to issue government bonds to cover its deficit. By the 1980s, the national debt had risen beyond 20 percent of GDP.[1]

In this period, Japan experienced peak health insurance expansion and then the beginning of the retrenchment of benefits. In 1972, the government passed a law giving free care to the elderly. But because of economic stagnation and rapidly rising health care costs, the government soon abolished this benefit and also required higher co-payments and harshly reduced the overall health care budget. Meanwhile, the government needed to respond to the pressures caused by an aging society. In an expanding economy, health care benefits are likely to be increased, as politicians seek to please their constituencies. In a stagnating economy, reducing health care benefits can really harm politicians. Political scientist Paul Pierson summarizes these differences in general: "Welfare state expansion involved the enactment of *popular* policies in a relatively underdeveloped interest-group environment. By contrast, welfare state retrenchment generally requires elected officials to pursue unpopular policies that must withstand the scrutiny of both voters and well-entrenched networks of interest groups."[2] In the politics of retrenchment, Pierson also stresses, avoiding blame for unpopular policies is important. He describes three measures a government may take to protect its image: (1) "play off one group of beneficiaries against another," (2) "develop reforms that compensate politically crucial groups for lost benefits," and (3) "lower the visibility of reforms."[3]

How much the government can succeed avoiding blame depends not only on the political and economic environment but also on the institutional arrangements of health insurance policy. Despite the JMA's demand for a fundamental reform of the health insurance system starting in the mid-1960s, the government successfully resisted and held on to its power in the system. The path dependence effect from previous decades persisted. Beginning to face fiscal austerity, the government succeeded in satisfying Pierson's conditions. To play off one group against another and avoid blame, in particular, the government looked for scapegoats, and the JMA became one of its targets. By then, the public had strengthened its negative view of the JMA's aggressive campaigns against the government. Tarō Takemi, who had been a strong fighter against the government, decided to step down as head of the JMA in 1982. He might have predicted what would happen long before that time. The JMA's revolt in 1971 was his last big political fight against the government.

The JMA's Revolt in 1971

The JMA repeatedly threatened the government by saying the organization would resign from health insurance practice unless compromises were made. With intensifying debate about fundamental reform in 1971, Takemi decided the JMA should actually quit accepting health insurance payments. The JMA began its strike on July 1. The strike lasted for a month before Takemi was able to reach an agreement with Prime Minister Eisaku Satō and Health and Welfare Minister Noboru Saitō. Although the action demonstrated that Japan's universal insurance system needed to be improved, the relationship between the JMA and the government did not improve, and the strike left negative feelings toward the JMA among the population.

Takemi's decision to undertake the action was triggered by a February 1971 discussion memo entitled "Regarding the Optimization of the Fee Schedule" that MHW bureaucrats prepared for the Central Social Insurance Medical Council (hereafter Chūikyō). Takemi took it not just as a discussion memo but as representing the government's effort to nationalize medicine. The JMA had increased its political power in the reorganized Chūikyō in 1963, which ensured that all of the medical provider representatives were basically approved by the JMA. The reorganization, nevertheless, did not much diminish the power of the MHW. Social welfare scholar Yasuhiro Yūki writes, "In general, while the JMA was first considered to be at the center of the discussion of the new fee schedule, the bureaucrats [of the Medical Affairs Section of the MHW] took the initiative in the discussion."[4]

The memo suggested that the cost of medicines should be separated from medical services more clearly, that medical services requiring more complex technology should be evaluated at a higher fee, that fees should not be based on charges for drugs and services but should be based on the nature of the disease, and that fees should vary depending on the number of patients a doctor had.[5] Takemi was particularly upset because he believed that the bureaucrats were using the public-interest council members to try to reinstate restrictions on medical treatments that had been abolished. Doing so would violate the agreement between Takemi and Kakuei Tanaka that had ended the JMA's resignation threat ten years earlier.[6]

Takemi's determination to actually quit accepting national health insurance astonished the officials in the MHW and also the public. Many people had not believed that the JMA would do such a thing, because a doctors' strike would cause a huge controversy. Many underestimated the level of the JMA's seriousness, however, and Takemi moved forward. About 90 percent of the JMA membership, or approximately seventy thousand doctors, stopped accepting national health insurance as payment.[7]

Takemi justified his decision by saying that the MHW submitted its memo "in a sneaky manner" that set a tone for expanding the government's control and depressing the fee schedule.[8] Takemi wrote later, "When we pursued the resignation from health insurance practice, journalists mistook it as a 'strike.' . . . They were totally ignorant because we did it to return health care to the people, as the unjust health insurance system had been serving bureaucrats, business, and large labor unions."[9] As Takemi put it, the doctors were not striking: they simply did not offer medical services covered by health insurance. Clinics and hospitals were still open. Patients could pay out of pocket and get reimbursed later. Takemi also directed the membership to make an exception for patients with National Health Insurance, which offered poorer benefits than other public programs.[10] He wanted to make sure people understood that his enemy was the government, the Federation of Health Insurance Societies, and their allies.

Internal JMA politics also affected Takemi. From 1957 to 1966, he won all the presidential elections by increasingly large margins (figure 7.1). But in 1970, for the first time, his margin declined from the previous election. He needed something to demonstrate that he was still a strong leader.

William Steslicke wrote of the politics within the JMA:

> Within the Association the level of interest and participation on the part of rank-and-file members tends to be fairly low. This means that a small, active minority of members, most of whom hold an elective or appointive office, are able to exercise considerable control over the management of the Association's affairs and activities. It also means that this active minority is able to mobilize the relatively inactive majority at special times and for special purposes.[11]

Takemi had concluded that it was time to reenergize his political base in the JMA by coming up with a special and dramatic occasion to tell the JMA members what dangers they were facing from the government and who must lead the fight against the government. Rank-and-file members, without knowing too much about the policy details, were convinced that they faced a serious threat and followed their leader's decision. The JMA, which had been based on solo practitioners, now had a problem with the increasing number of hospitals and hospital doctors (figure 7.2). As the government gradually made the national health insurance fee more favorable for hospitals, more doctors turned their clinics into hospitals. They joined both the JMA and the hospital associations.[12] Takemi was not happy with the situation, but he was especially frustrated when, in February 1964, the public-hospital-based Japan Hospital Association, led by San'eki Kanzaki, joined the Japan Hospital Federation (Zenkoku Kōshi Byōin Renmei).[13] Takemi could not force JMA members not to open hospitals, but what he could do was take dramatic action against the government. He needed to remind JMA members that he was working hard on their behalf.

To come to an agreement with the government, Takemi had three televised debates with Health and Welfare Minister Saitō, moderated by Ichirō Nakayama, who was a prominent economist and professor emeritus from Hitotsubashi University. Finally, Takemi had a televised debate with Prime Minister Satō, arranged by Chief Cabinet Secretary Noboru Takeshita. Takemi and Satō agreed on twelve items, which basically confirmed the points that Takemi and Tanaka had agreed on ten years earlier.[14] This repetition underscored that the LDP politicians had not fulfilled their promises made a decade ago.

Takemi's strategy worked well within the JMA, as he demonstrated that he still had a strong power to negotiate with the government. But to many others, Takemi's strategy appeared unreasonable. The government and major newspapers criticized the doctors' walkout as irresponsible. The general public believed that doctors were wealthy and did not understand what the JMA was trying to do.[15] Public and media antipathy toward Takemi increased. Writer Yasumasa Ikura wrote in 1979:

> By nature, doctors are intellectual elitists. They are calm technicians who deal with people's lives though medicine. The JMA represents these doctors, but it made an enemy of the public through Takemi's blistering remarks and audacious behavior that disrupted politicians and bureaucrats. President Takemi's speeches and behaviors looked strange to people who expected the doctors with whom they entrusted their lives to behave graciously.[16]

Government officials who hoped to diminish the JMA's voice in health politics made use of this opportunity to criticize the JMA.

Eiichi Yūki, who served as the JMA's executive board member from 1976 to 1983, doubted the media's reporting on the drama. He later wrote, "Newspapers and television did not focus on what the conflict was about; they just liked to report on Dr. Takemi's 'harsh language' when he attacked MHW bureaucrats."[17] Taku Nomura supports Yūki's view. He points out that, given rising prices and wage levels, the JMA's request for a fee increase was not totally out of bounds. He writes, "I wonder why the media reports it as an 'unreasonable and unfair demand' and as the JMA's grumbling. The Japan Federation of Employers' Associations [Nikkeiren] always plays the villain role in the annual wage struggle, but it can be a champion of justice by supporting the Federation of Health Insurance Societies in attacking the JMA."[18]

The media-led public criticism of the JMA was not the only negative legacy of the association's 1971 withdrawal campaign. The JMA had repeatedly threatened to withdraw from health insurance practice. But in 1971, it finally did so as a last resort. Threatening to use a hidden sword is different from using it. As Yūki points out, once the tactic was actually used, its political effectiveness was weakened. After the 1971 withdrawal action, the JMA continued to use the noncooperation strategy in response to the government's mandatory program of checkups at schools and vaccinations, but the association did not exert such strong pressure.[19]

Free Health Care for the Elderly

During the period of economic growth, a policy innovation took place at the local level. Even when universal health care was achieved in 1961, many elderly people in the NHI program suffered because of the required 50 percent (later 30 percent) co-payment. In 1960, Sawauchi Village in Iwate Prefecture began to cover the co-payment for these outpatients out of its general revenues. Heads of other municipalities and prefectures copied this policy, seeing it as a way to respond to the needs of the elderly to gain their support. Tokyo Prefecture governor Ryōkichi Minobe introduced such a measure in 1969. Minobe had won the election in 1967 as the candidate of both the Socialist and the Communist Parties.[20] Meanwhile, Osaka and Kyoto Prefectures and many municipalities also elected non-LDP leaders. These were known as progressive prefectures and municipalities (*kakushin jichitai*). Minobe promised aggressive measures to fight pollution and to have more generous social welfare programs. Free medical care for those over seventy was included in his program. By 1972, all prefectures except two had adopted such measures.[21]

The movement to create free health care for the elderly was a response starting at the local level to address a problem that the LDP had not responded to adequately at the national level. In the mid-1960s, the central government began to pay attention to the problem of medical care for the elderly. Over the decade 1955 to 1965, the number of those over seventy increased by 30 percent, from about 28 million to 36 million. The MHW tried in fiscal year 1969 to get the government to cover part of the co-payments (above 2,000 yen for hospitalization and 1,000 yen for outpatient care), but the budget proposal was not accepted because of the Finance Ministry's opposition. Some also believed that such a proposal should be part of the reform of the national health insurance system.[22] Thus, innovation at the local level filled in the gap for the elderly.

When the LDP had poor results in the election, the party began to become serious about a national plan to cover co-payments for the elderly. The heads of prefectures and municipalities also pushed for national legislation in order to reduce their financial burdens. The JMA and labor unions backed the plan so that retirees could have access to medical care without expense. Furthermore, the Japan Federation of Senior Citizens Clubs (Zenkoku Rōjin Kurabu Rengōkai), which had not previously been politically active, mobilized its members to petition the government to pass such legislation.[23] In June 1972, the Diet passed an amendment to the Social Welfare for the Elderly Act (Rōjin Fukushi Hō) that would cover NHI and HI co-payments by dividing the contribution so that two-thirds came from the central government, one-sixth came from the prefectures, and one-sixth came from municipalities. Although the amendment set an income cap for beneficiaries, about 90 percent of people over seventy now could have free medical care. Margarita Esteves-Abe writes, "The LDP 'stole' the program to rid itself of the negative Economy First image and campaigned that the government would provide greater welfare benefits."[24]

Although the LDP took the lead in creating the new national policy, the MHW and the Advisory Council on Social Security, along with the MOF, which typically opposed the expansion of social programs, did not actively support the way the policy was set up. The original Social Welfare for the Elderly Act was passed in 1962 to confirm Article 25 of the Constitution, which stipulated that the central government and local public bodies would be responsible for the welfare of the elderly. But health insurance was not part of the original act.[25] Without changing the health insurance system itself, the government sought to deal with the problem of senior care by using the amended program to subsidize free medical care for the elderly. The MHW was concerned that this method did not fit in with the existing health insurance system. The ministry was also worried that the new policy would lead to the elderly using more medical services than anticipated, which would undermine existing health insurance programs, especially the NHI program. The new policy covered co-payments, but it did not cover expanded health insurance payments. Pointing out that the new policy was created rather hastily, the Advisory Council on Social Security suggested that the policy should be a temporary measure to be incorporated into national health insurance with an increase in the national subsidy in the near future.[26] As Toshimitsu Shinkawa points out, the amendment was designed under the leadership of the LDP, more specifically by the prime minister, who tried to create an eye-catching policy that would help him in the coming elections. The capstone was the hallmark of the campaign by Prime Minister Tanaka and the LDP to promote 1973 as "the first year of the real welfare state" (*fukushi gannen*).[27]

With free elderly care, the number of patients grew more than estimated. The government had budgeted 3.4 billion yen to subsidize the program of free care for seniors, but the actual spending was more than what was budgeted.[28] The program was soon criticized for creating a moral hazard—old people getting more doctors' consultations, medicine, and hospital stays than necessary—which pushed up health care costs.[29] In what was called "social hospitalization" (*shakai-teki nyūin*), some old people asked for hospital accommodations not because of their health conditions but because of such nonmedical situations as being left home alone. Many critical commentators noted that hospitals had become like salons for the elderly.[30]

Unfortunately for supporters of free medical care for the elderly, the economic downturn hit Japan soon after free health care was nationally implemented in January 1973. The first oil shock occurred in October. This gave the Ministry of Finance a reason to advocate ending the new measure. In 1975, because of shrinking revenues, the MOF demanded a co-payment. LDP Prime Minister Takeo Miki opposed this demand because he did not want the public to think he was cutting social welfare. The party backed Miki because of the coming lower house election in December 1976. The LDP, however, lost the election largely because of the Lockheed scandal, which resulted in former prime minister Tanaka being arrested. Taking responsibility for the election loss, Miki resigned. The next LDP prime minister, Takeo Fukuda, took a nuanced position toward free health care for the elderly. He promised to keep the policy as it was while saying it was not an ideal policy.[31]

The failure of free care for the elderly could have damaged the LDP. Interestingly, though, the government did not lose much as a result. The program helped the LDP mobilize its base with older voters in rural areas. During the late 1970s, the LDP's electoral power base was weakening, and the Japan Socialist Party and other progressive parties gained seats in the Diet. This shift prompted Prime Minister Tanaka to take the lead in creating the free elderly care program. When free senior care began to be criticized as a moral hazard, the LDP blamed the Socialist Party and its allies for having initiated the program. There was one other group that the LDP successfully made the target of blame: the JMA.

The End of Doctors' Preferential Tax Treatment

Under the free elderly care policy, doctors were criticized for agreeing to provide unnecessary care and medicines. Under the fee-for-service system, the more that doctors provided, the more income they received. The government and media claimed that doctors encouraged seniors' moral hazard. The JMA was put into a defensive position. Then, an old issue came back to bite the JMA: preferential tax treatment for doctors.

As described in chapter 5, preferential tax treatment for doctors was first negotiated during Shigeru Yoshida's administration and was made law in 1954. The measure allowed doctors to deduct 72 percent of their income as a necessary business expense. Takemi, who had just resigned as vice president under JMA president Tamiya, was JMA's liaison with Yoshida and Finance Minister Hayato Ikeda. Ikeda refused Takemi's request for fee increases but offered him preferential tax treatment for doctors as an alternative. This was to be a temporary measure until the government completed fundamental health insurance reform.[32]

The MOF was not happy about Ikeda's compromise and continually fought the JMA. When a new national health insurance fee system was discussed in 1957, for example, the JMA asked for a big fee raise. The MOF pressured the MHW by threatening that if the fee was raised, the MOF would abolish the preferential tax treatment.[33] Takemi insisted that the preferential tax treatment should continue because the government had not, at least in Takemi's view, undertaken fundamental reform. He wanted a structural reform that would abolish the employment-based programs and integrate the various health insurance programs into a residence-based health insurance program. His aim was to re-duce the power of the Federation of Health Insurance Societies and the govern-ment, which were the insurers of the Society-Managed Health Insurance and the Government-Managed Health Insurance, respectively. Takemi's proposal was blocked, and the preferential tax treatment continued, with doctors beginning to see the temporary measure as a vested right.

In 1971, things changed. The JMA could not convey its rationale clearly to the public when it decided on withdrawal from health insurance practice. The pub-lic's negative image of the JMA and Takemi, influenced by the media, strength-ened. The MOF used the situation to counterattack. The MHW also saw this as an opportunity to increase its negotiation power against the JMA. In the mid-1970s, government officials previously cowed by Takemi, who had often bypassed them and negotiated directly with the LDP, began to try to convince the public that the preferential tax treatment was unfair and gave doctors special advantages.

Takemi resisted the government's attack. In 1978, he wrote of the strong power of the Federation of Health Insurance Societies: "The preferential tax treatment for doctors is now a target of criticism, but there are about twenty such special tax considerations. It is strange that only the one for doctors is regarded with enmity while the others are not. This demonstrates one of the characteristics of the LDP, that it has a cozy relationship with big business."[34] He later stated, "The government succeeded in forcing low-paying health care on doctors in exchange for the preferential tax treatment. While the treatment was grudgingly contin-ued, doctors were nevertheless forced to survive by getting commissions from selling medicine. Not the JMA but the government should be held responsible for keeping the special tax treatment for such a long time."[35]

The oil shocks in the 1970s and the beginning of the slowing down of the Japanese economy put the JMA on the defensive. The government tried to re-vise all the tax codes to maintain revenues. Furthermore, the public began to have an image that medicine was a cushy profession.[36] The public supported the government's efforts to abolish the preferential tax treatment for doctors. In Oc-tober 1974, the Government Tax Commission (Zeisei Chōsakai) submitted a report to Prime Minister Tanaka proposing this revision.[37]

In December 1974, Takeo Miki succeeded Tanaka, who resigned as prime minster after the influential monthly magazine *Bungeishunjū* exposed his accep-tance of bribes in the Lockheed scandal. Miki had promised to correct social unfairness, and stopping the preferential tax treatment for doctors became one of his priorities with strong public support. The Takeo Fukuda administration (December 1976–December 1978) continued Miki's policy objective. Fukuda, a former MOF official, was determined to end the special tax treatment. In December 1978, the LDP's Tax Commission approved revision of the preferential tax to be completed by March 1979.[38]

The determination of prime ministers along with public support for abolishing the preferential tax treatment eventually led the JMA to accept the change as inevitable. The exemption rate varies presently depending on doctors' incomes. It is 72 percent for doctors with income under 25 million yen; 70 percent for those making 25–30 million yen; 62 percent for 30–40 million yen; 57 percent for 40–50 million yen; and 52 percent for those making more than 50 million yen. Takemi expected that JMA members would be satisfied with the compromise, because most solo practitioners made less than 25 million yen.[39]

The end of the preferential tax, however, led to Takemi's losing control of the JMA. Hirokata Iwai, a close ally of Takemi's, defended his position: "Some of the JMA members criticized Takemi for having weak political power as he had said that he would never allow an end to the preferential tax treatment. But thanks to his strong energy, its abolishment was delayed for some years."[40] Doctor and writer Kazuo Miwa points out, "It was very important for Takemi to protect the preferential tax treatment for doctors. It was almost synonymous with protecting his presidency."[41] Miwa also indicates why Takemi may have lost this battle: "Small companies are usually allowed to exempt necessary expenses up to 50 percent of their revenues. . . . I wonder why solo practitioners were always compared with salaried workers, who have no exemptions. Probably, Takemi's overreaction [to the government] worked against him."[42] Takemi's struggle in the preferential tax treatment battle can be seen, in retrospect, as symbolic of the decline of his stature.

Takemi's Resignation

The withdrawal from health insurance practice in 1971 seemed to temporarily solidify Takemi's political base in the JMA. But his support was gradually eroding. The first sign came in the election of 1972. Makoto Watanabe, president of the Kyoto Medical Association and a good friend of Takemi's from their university days, ran against him.[43] Watanabe represented the frustrated JMA membership. The result was Takemi's second-worst showing after his first election in 1957. Eiichi Yūki explains the reasons for the vote: "Some did not participate in the withdrawal campaign, and some of those who experienced a decrease in income for a month and had the feeling, 'Takemi is too aggressive and dangerous.'"[44] It must have been a shock to Takemi, who had just led the withdrawal campaign and achieved an agreement with Prime Minister Saitō.

The results of the three other elections in the 1970s were not bad for him (see figure 7.1). These results were both fortunate and unfortunate for Takemi. On the one hand, Takemi continued to provide the JMA with access to influential politicians. On the other hand, he became more arrogant and isolated from those running the organization. He began to be more self-interested in selecting the JMA's important leadership positions, and members gradually lost trust in him.[45] They were further disappointed when he lost the battle over the preferential tax treatment.

The JMA also suffered from decreasing members. Despite Takemi's visible political performance, after the late 1960s, the percentage of the JMA members among doctors continued to decline (see figure 7.2). The reason was largely that the number of solo practitioners decreased. Clinic owners accounted for 48.1 percent of all doctors in 1965, but the percentage declined to 39.5 percent in 1980.[46] The decrease in membership meant that the JMA lost its power in medicine.

The accumulated distrust and anxiety toward Takemi showed itself in the election of 1980. Kanji Hanaoka challenged Takemi. Hanaoka garnered 82 votes, while Takemi received 133. It was the closest result since Takemi was first elected. Hanaoka said after the election, "The fact that I received more votes than the previous challengers showed that many disliked Takemi's self-righteous attitude.

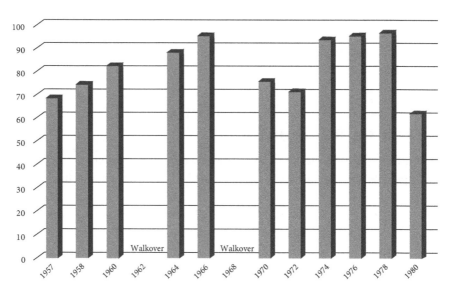

FIGURE 7.1. Votes obtained by Tarō Takemi (% of votes, 1957–1980)

Source: Nihon Ishikai Sōritsu Gojusshūnen Kinen Jigyō Suishin Iinkai, Nihon Ishikai Sōritsu Kinenshi: Sengo Gojūnen no Ayumi (Anniversary of the founding of the Japan Medical Association: Fifty-years of progress after World War II) (Tokyo: Nihon Ishikai, 1997).

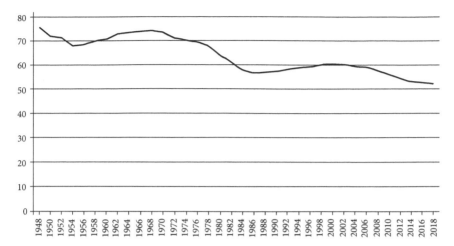

FIGURE 7.2. Proportion of JMA membership among physicians (percentage, 1948–2018)

Source: Japan Medical Association, "Nihon Ishikai Kaiinsū no Suii" (JMA membership numbers).

The election was the beginning of the JMA's modernization."[47] Hanaoka prepared to run in the next election.

The 1980 election result brought Takemi his thirteenth victory, but he had to face political difficulties not only within the JMA but also with the government. In addition to the growing public negative image of Takemi, rising health care costs put the JMA on the defensive. With an aging society and a shrinking economic pie, it was obvious to the government and the public that some new policy scheme would be needed to keep health care costs under control. In this environment, it was difficult for the JMA to ask for fee increases.

Takemi also had to deal with his own physical deterioration. In 1980, he was seventy-five years old. Right after the presidential election, on May 22, he was diagnosed with stomach cancer. He underwent surgery, and although the operation was successful, he did not recover sufficiently to carry on the JMA leadership position. He expressed his desire to retire in April 1981. After his retirement, he experienced recurring hospitalizations. He died on December 20, 1983.

Takemi repeatedly emphasized that it was important for the public and doctors to consider the country as a whole. He wrote, "Individual egos, regional egos, and all sorts of egos prevented Japan from moving forward. Egos can be a positive factor in a nation's progress only when they go through a social filter that gives them a desire for social progress. . . . If Japanese people stay stuck with their individual egos, their future prospects are decidedly pessimistic."[48] Many commentators are sympathetic to Takemi that many doctors were not seriously thinking about medical science, the health care system, and Japan more broadly. But Takemi, ironically, needed to keep this constituency satisfied in order to continue his presidency. To do so he had to take a very aggressive attitude toward the bureaucrats and stay close to influential LDP politicians so as to earn material benefits for doctors, usually fee increases. But the basic structure of the health insurance system remained almost the same. Influential LDP politicians did promise Takemi to undertake a radical reform, but they did not have the strong collective will to achieve it. It was easier for them to give fee increases to doctors. With the need for fiscal austerity starting in the 1970s, the LDP politicians no longer had the luxury to continue fee increases. As Takemi served as JMA president, furthermore, he became isolated from the membership, health care bureaucrats, and the public. The way he ended his presidency must not have been what he dreamed of. But he had to end his journey.

The Nakasone Administration and Retrenchment Policy

At the beginning of the 1980s, the Japanese government needed to figure out a new policy paradigm that would deal with slower economic development and an expanded social welfare budget, with a rapidly aging population. Political leaders who advocated a neoliberal and "small government" policy had gained popularity in many advanced countries. Fiscal consolidation, privatization, and market deregulation were the keynotes of neoliberal policy. President Ronald Reagan (1981–88) of the United States advocated cutting the size of the federal government, claiming, "Government is not the solution to our problem, government is the problem."[49] Prime Minister Margaret Thatcher (1979–90) of Britain argued, "A man's right to work as he will, to spend what he earns, to own property, to have the State as servant and not as master, these are the British inheritance."[50] Japan was also part of the neoliberal and small-government movement.

"Administrative reform" (*gyōsei kaikaku*) became the key phrase in the small-government movement in Japan. Pressured by big business, which opposed tax increases, Prime Minister Zenkō Suzuki (July 1980–November 1982) promised to reconstruct finances without tax increases (*zōzei naki zaisei saiken*). Soon after he won the election, he got the Diet to pass legislation creating the Extraordinary Administration Investigating Committee (Rinji Gyōsei Chōsakai) to carry out this goal. He got Toshio Dokō, a former president of the Japan Business Federation, to lead the committee and make concrete policy proposals. The committee's proposals included abolishing the sale of government bonds to finance deficit spending and privatizing Japanese National Railways, Nippon

Telegraph and Telephone Public Corporation, and Japan Tobacco and Salt Public Corporation.[51]

Political scientist Toshimitsu Shinkawa points out how pressure from big business distorted the discussion about administrative reform:

> Administrative reform should have started with goals for what the future administration should be like and then address how administrative organizations and regulations should be rationalized and improved to achieve them. But constrained by the political situation [pressure from big business], the Extraordinary Administrative Investigation Committee began by focusing exclusively on fiscal reconstruction.[52]

There was similar political pressure from big business in the United States and Britain to retrench health care budgets, but the debate over health care reform in Japan was conducted more by financial concerns without a wide discussion.

Although the Suzuki administration was short lived, the next prime minister, Yasuhiro Nakasone (November 1982–November 1987), became a symbolic figure for administrative reform. As director general of the Administrative Management Agency (Gyōsei Kanri Chō), Nakasone had previously been actively engaged in the discussion about administrative reform during the Suzuki administration. In July 1983, he established the Extraordinary Administrative Reform Promotion Council (Rinji Gyōsei Kaikaku Suishin Shingikai) as a replacement for the Extraordinary Administration Investigating Committee. The new council was again led by Dokō. It pushed for the government's goal of structural reform (kōzō kaikaku) and cutting the budget.[53] Serving for five years, Nakasone successfully achieved privatization of the public corporations. The Nakasone administration also took an aggressive step to reduce the budgets of social security programs, which were a large share of the overall budget. Health care was not an exception.

In preparing the fiscal year 1982 budget, Nakasone prohibited all ministries from increasing their budgets from the previous year. In the following year, the ministries were to follow what was called a "minus ceiling," that is, cutting 5 percent from the previous year.[54] With an aging society pushing up health care costs, the MHW had to figure out ways to cut its budget. The MHW's first target was free care for the elderly.

Ending free care for the elderly was an important turning point in the development of health insurance policy. In August 1982, the Elderly Health Care Act (Rōjin Hoken Hō) was passed for those over seventy-five (figure 7.3). Medical care for the elderly was changed from a welfare scheme to a social insurance scheme. The act introduced fixed co-payments to 400 yen for one-month outpatient service and 300 yen for one-day hospitalization. The financial-coordination mechanism was introduced: all insurers were required to make financial contributions

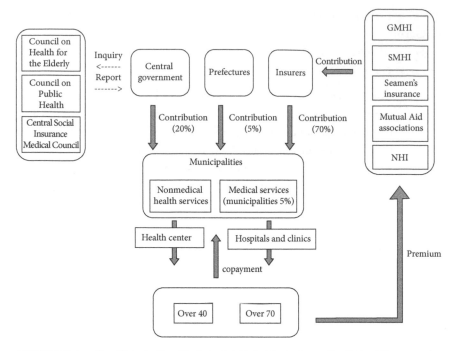

FIGURE 7.3. The Elderly Health Act of 1982. Made from Kenji Yoshihara and Masaru Wada, *Nihon Iryōhoken Seidoshi* [History of Japanese health insurance] (Tokyo: Tōyō Keizai Shuppansha, 1999), 308.

to the new program. As former MHW bureaucrats Masaru Wada and Kenji Yoshihara write, "The Elderly Health Care Act did away with the policy of free care for the elderly, which was the hallmark of 'the first year of the real welfare state.' It changed the course of Japan's social security and health insurance policy, which up until then had been consistently covering more people, providing better benefits, and reducing patients' financial burdens."[55]

One of the reasons the Elderly Health Care Act was able to pass was that the LDP won 284 seats out of 511 in the 1980 lower house election. The LDP also found someone to blame. Former Tokyo governor Minobe and other progressive leaders of prefectures and municipalities were accused of having loose fiscal administrations, with free care for the elderly epitomizing their programs.[56] Lastly, the JMA's opposition to the act was not effective largely because the organization had been struggling with the public's negative image of the JMA, and because Takemi was ending his presidency and losing his power vis-à-vis the government.

One MHW bureaucrat played an especially important role in preventing the government from becoming a target of blame. In January 1983, Jin Yoshimura, head of the Insurance Bureau in the MHW, claimed in a national conference for health insurance and pension administrators that "rising health care costs will kill Japan."[57] In March, Yoshimura published an article in *Shakaihoken Shunpō*, an influential magazine of social welfare policy, to repeat his argument and introduced the idea of a "prophecy of the country's ruin by health care" (*iryō bōkoku ron*).[58] After seeing health care costs continuing to increase, he concluded that something had to be done to change people's views on health care. The words "prophecy of the country's ruin by health care" brought the idea of a national crisis in health care costs to the public. The phrase became a powerful weapon the government used in pushing its agenda, and it diminished the power of the post-Takemi JMA.

Some said that Yoshimura was taking revenge on the JMA, which under Takemi had attacked MHW bureaucrats for many years. Indeed, Yoshimura did have a personally difficult relationship with Takemi. But Yoshimura believed in the government's more powerful role in health care. He claimed that not the JMA but the MHW should take the initiative to rationalize the medical care system and break through the financially difficult situation. He commented about the JMA, "With the fee-for-service payment [for doctors] and in-kind payment [for patients], doctors do not well understand that health care funds are limited and that the system itself is under criticism from the public."[59] Yoshimura was well known for his strong, innovative, and challenging personality, and he played a great role in revitalizing the MHW.[60] In August 1984, he became the administrative vice minister of the MHW and continued to put pressure on the JMA and to push for health insurance reform.

The Health Insurance Act Amendment of 1984 was another important piece of legislation for the government's retrenchment policy. The amendment mainly concerned the problem of those who lost HI coverage after retirement and enrolled in the NHI before age seventy-five. The problem was twofold. First, the more people retired, the worse the NHI's finances became, because the retired seniors used more medical services. The central government and municipalities were under pressure to increase the subsidy. Second, retirees had less generous benefits under the NHI than under the HI. Workers did not have a co-payment under the HI; however, once they retired, they had to pay a 30 percent co-payment. Large labor unions, such as the General Council of Trade Unions of Japan and the Japanese Confederation of Labor (Dōmei), claimed that the same level of benefits should be provided to former HI enrollees.[61] With the Health Insurance Act Amendment, the Medical Care Service Program for Retired Employees (Taishokusha Iryō Seido) was established. To finance the program, the amendment required the HI's primary insured to make a co-payment of 20 percent (10% until the Diet approved the increase) for the first time. With the co-payment, the government could reduce its subsidy to the NHI, which now moved retirees into the new program.

Along with the Elderly Health Care Act, the Health Insurance Act Amendment was something the government had to create to avoid being blamed for financial cutbacks in health care. The JMA and other groups expressed their opposition to the legislation, but, unusually, it was enacted without being postponed until another Diet. Masaru Wada explains the reason for such unusually rapid legislation: "Necessity knows no law. Financial pressure caused it."[62] The amendment was to introduce a system of beneficiaries' sharing expenses. Meanwhile, the amendment also lowered the premiums of active HI enrollees. This was, in Pierson's words, an example of developing "reforms that compensate politically crucial groups for lost benefits."[63]

The MHW, moreover, sought to portray HI enrollees as a privileged group compared with NHI enrollees. The Insurance Bureau, for its part, produced a pamphlet titled "Why Should We Reform Health Insurance Now?" that included a cartoon showing NHI insurers with their 30 percent co-payment angry at white-collar HI male insureds relaxing and smoking without any co-payments.[64] The strategy was, again in Pierson's words, to "play off one group of beneficiaries against another."[65] The government successfully obtained reforms by avoiding public blame.

The Post-Takemi JMA

While the government took bold steps to reduce its health insurance financial burden, the JMA appeared to be uncertain about the best way to respond. Steslicke pointed out the general characteristics of interest groups in Japan:

> A look at the structure of postwar Japanese pressure groups reveals that they are not composed of individuals who have joined forces because of a common desire to attain specific goals. On the contrary, these groups are composed of individuals who feel close to one another mostly because they live in the same area, because they work in the same office or factory, etc. . . . Moreover, not having specialized goals, they tend strongly to concentrate more upon pursuing positions of power and authority than upon seeking enactment and implementation of specific policies. This explains why many groups try to get their own members elected to the Diet, and why relationships between pressure groups and Diet members tend to be strongly personalized.[66]

What the post-Takemi JMA presidents had to do was either continue Take-mi's way of doing politics or adopt a new way of pressuring the government. Takemi used his personal connections with influential LDP politicians to gain compromises. Kenji Hanaoka won the election in April 1982 against Mamoru Kikegawa, whom Takemi had backed, and Hanaoka chose not to follow Take-mi's methods.

Hanaoka was unsure, however, about how to increase the JMA's political le-verage against the LDP, which had momentum for its retrenchment policy. Med-ical journalist Hajime Mizuno points out that Hanaoka neither tried to find new leaders nor trained up a new generation. Right after assuming office, Hana-oka had to face the debate over the Elderly Health Care Act. He protested to the MHW minister, Motoharu Morishita, that "separating people over seventy and creating a new medical system for them neglects the human rights of the elderly. It is not acceptable."[67] Despite the JMA's opposition, the Elderly Health Care Act passed. Mizuno explains that Takemi's one-year absence from politics because of illness might have given the MHW time to advance the bill, and Hanaoka's protest was too late to have an impact.[68] But the main reason for the act's pas-sage was that the government created a mood of crisis and took the leadership role to reform the health insurance system. It was a bad start for Hanaoka—a clear contrast to the compromises Takemi had wrested from the government after he was elected in 1957 during the rapid expansion of the economy.

Hanaoka also fought the Health Insurance Act Amendment of 1984. The JMA was joined by the Japan Dental Association and the Japan Pharmaceutical As-sociation in opposition to the proposal. The opposition was unsuccessful. JMA members saw that Hanaoka could not win even small compromises from the LDP.

Because of the disappointment of many JMA members with Hanaoka, Har-uto Haneda defeated Hanaoka in the presidential election in April 1984. Takemi had served for twenty-six years, and Hanaoka ended up with only one two-year term. He tried to change the JMA leadership, but he did not have time to de-velop his team, while the way the government ran things did not change. Mean-while, the Tokyo Medical Association, an influential actor with Takemi in the JMA for twenty-six years, led the anti-Hanaoka movement. The association sought to regain power in the early period of the Hanaoka presidency. Accord-ing to Mizuno, it was an intra-JMA political conflict that gave Haneda the pres-idential win.[69]

Haneda had organizational management skills and had an interest in medi-cal ethics issues. In his eight years as JMA president, Haneda took the lead to establish and promote the Life Ethics Council to discuss organ transplants from patients with brain death, medical treatment for the terminally ill (including euthanasia), and informed consent. Haneda's quest for informed consent was in clear contrast to Takemi's passive attitude regarding this issue. Mizuno states that Takemi had a more paternalistic attitude toward patients.[70]

Although he was good at managing internal JMA affairs, Haneda seemed to have difficulty managing external affairs with MHW bureaucrats and LDP politicians. The reason was partly the way his presidency began, as a result of intra-JMA political conflict. More importantly, LDP politicians did not have an incentive to go along with the JMA, given the budgetary restraints pressed by the prime minister. In this difficult political environment, the JMA could have appealed to the politicians, bureaucrats, and the public with detailed data to refute or correct government policies. But the JMA lacked a system for conducting research and promoting its own policy proposals.[71] That was a negative legacy of the long-term Takemi presidency, which relied on Takemi's personal connections and negotiation skills.

The Hanaoka and Haneda presidencies could not substantially affect the Health Insurance Act Amendment, which passed in the Diet in August 1984. Jirō Arioka writes, "The report from the Special Advisory Council on Enforcement of Administrative Reform provided a favorable wind for the government and the majority party [LDP], which had a strong will to pursue 'fiscal reconstruction without a tax increase' and to achieve health insurance reform. That was how they overcame the opposition of the minority parties and the JMA."[72] Haneda served for eight years, until 1992, but he did not regain much of the political leverage against the government that Takemi had.

Hanaoka, Haneda, and the following JMA presidents were haunted by Takemi's legacy. Because of Takemi's personal political power, the JMA became a powerful interest group to counter the government. Because of Takemi, however, the public's confidence in the JMA eroded. The JMA's revolt in 1971 retrospectively was a big turning point for the organization. Fiscal austerity further turned the tide to the government's advantage. Then Takemi left the stage. The government was prepared for this moment, but the JMA was not. Globalization added another difficulty to the JMA by justifying the government's position of maintaining an austere budget and reducing health care costs.

JAPANESE HEALTH CARE IN THE GLOBALIZATION ERA

Japan experienced an economic bubble beginning in the mid-1980s. In December 1989, the stock market hit the unprecedented high of 38,957 yen. After the bubble burst in 1991, Japan struggled to recover for a long time. In 2003, the stock market fell to 7,607 yen, the lowest since the collapse of the bubble economy. To revitalize the economy, the Liberal Democratic Party continued to push a neoliberal policy and reduce the government budget. In April 2001, Jun'ichiro Koizumi was elected as prime minister with a promise to conduct further structural reforms, including the privatization of another large state-owned firm, the Japan Post (Nihon Yūsei Kōsha). But economic conditions did not improve much, and the LDP experienced heated internal conflicts. As a result, the LDP lost popular trust.

In 2009 the Democratic Party of Japan (DPJ) came to power with Prime Minister Yukio Hatoyama (September 2009–June 2010). The DPJ stayed in the power with Naoto Kan (June 2010–September 2011) and Yoshihiko Noda (September 2011–December 2012). The DPJ administrations, however, could not develop a clear alternative path to the LDP's neoliberal policy. Then, in December 2012, the LDP regained the majority in the House of Representatives, and Shinzō Abe became prime minister.

These prime ministers have had to deal with deepening globalization. With increasing globalization, the government has found it harder to increase tax revenues, especially from corporate taxes, as many companies have chosen to move their factories and even their headquarters to countries with cheaper labor costs and lower taxes. Along with the worsening business climate caused by long-term economic stagnation after the economic bubble burst, the advance of globalization has played a large role in reducing government revenues and adding to the national debt.

Reform in the health insurance system since the 1990s has continued to be driven by policy path dependency. While maintaining the basic institutional arrangements, Koizumi began in earnest to carry out what Nakasone had begun by keeping down the health care budget as much as possible by controlling the fee-setting process. However, Koizumi sought to do the same as was done with the Japan Post reform: introduce private businesses into the system. This change could have brought a fundamental transformation to the health insurance system; but at this time, interestingly, the Japan Medical Association fought to protect the existing institutional arrangements. The JMA has tried to change its organizational goals, policies, and strategies. In particular, the association has tried to reach out to the public. However, the JMA is still struggling to earn the public's trust and to gain power to deal with the government, which still largely controls the health insurance system.

Two events may have had a substantial impact on the health insurance system. The first was the adoption of the Long-Term Care Insurance Act of 1997. Although the act was seen by the government largely as another fiscal adjustment measure to patch the problem of care for the elderly, the legislation caused an unprecedented public debate because the act touched not only on the elderly care issue but also the gender issue. The health insurance issue was, for the first time, discussed widely by others beyond the regular stakeholder players. In terms of historical institutionalism, this act may have had a layering effect by adding a new institution that could bring a gradual change to the existing health insurance system.[1] Another event was the spread of COVID-19 beginning early in 2020. The rapid spread of the pandemic, as a result of deepening globalization, became a big external pressure on the Japanese health care system. This chapter ends with some early observations about how the pandemic will affect the discourse of health insurance policy.

The Long-Term Care Insurance Act

The Elderly Health Care Act of 1982 and the Medical Care Service Program for Retired Employees of 1984 made the health insurance system more financially sustainable, at least from the perspective of the government. The legislation reduced the number of social hospitalizations (*shakaiteki nyūin*). But these laws did not solve the problems of older people with chronic diseases and disabilities. Care for such people was considered a private matter: in many cases, women were expected to do the caregiving.[2] But as the traditional multigenerational family unit gradually became less common, with more women working outside the home, elderly people began to need more intermediate facilities and services.

The government started planning for this issue in the late 1980s. This planning took place at the same time as there was a debate about introducing a 3 percent consumption tax. The government had depended for revenue on direct taxes, such as income tax and corporate tax, and began to consider introducing a consumption tax to increase and stabilize revenue. But the consumption tax was not popular among the people, and the LDP lost a number of seats in the election of July 1989. As part of the LDP's hope to gain women's votes, the Ministry of Health and Welfare, Ministry of Finance, and Ministry of Home Affairs (Jichi Shō) jointly created the Ten-Year Strategy for Health and Welfare for the Elderly (Kōreisha Hoken Fukushi Suishin Jukkanen Senryaku), known as the Gold Plan, which allocated 6 trillion yen for the next ten years to increase and improve nursing homes and short-stay care facilities and to compensate caregivers.[3]

The movement to create the Long-Term Care Insurance Act gained momentum when a non-LDP government was formed in August 1993. Morihiro Hosokawa, the founder of the Japan New Party (Nihon Shintō), formed the government with six other parties.[4] This was the first government without the LDP since 1955, when the LDP was formed. In his first administrative policy speech, Hosokawa emphasized planning something new for the elderly: "To make a society in which the elderly are healthy and secure, I will fundamentally reexamine the Ten-Year Strategy for Health and Welfare for the Elderly, what we call the Gold Plan. I plan to improve the quality of medical care services, so they meet the various needs of patients."[5]

The Hosokawa administration formed the Council on Welfare Vision for an Aged Society (Kōrei Shakaifukushi Bijon Kondankai), which was led by Isamu Miyazaki, an economist and a former Economic Planning Agency bureaucrat. The council concluded that the social security system should change so that long-term health care would be better connected with both medical and welfare services, helping to ensure that all seniors could receive necessary care. The discussion continued in the Task Force on Long-Term Care for the Elderly (Kōreisha Kaigo Taisaku Honbu), established in April 1994.[6] When Tomiichi Murayama, head of the Socialist Party of Japan, became prime minister in June 1994 in a coalition with the LDP and the New Party Sakigake, he directed his cabinet's project team on welfare policy to study health insurance policy, to conduct public opinion surveys, and to make the ongoing discussion open to the public. The Murayama administration revised the existing Gold Plan and presented a New Gold Plan, with more ambitious goals for facilities and services for the elderly and plans for new long-term care legislation.[7]

In July 1995, the Advisory Council on Social Security also sent a policy recommendation affirming the importance of long-term care insurance. The council made a comprehensive proposal, "Recommendations for Reconstruction of the Social Security System: A Twentieth-First Century Society Where Needs Are Met" (Shakaihoshō no Saikōchiku (Kankoku): Anshin Shite Kuraseru 21 Seiki no Shakai wo Mezashite), describing what Japanese social security should be like in the coming twenty-first century. While the council's proposal claimed that "the social security system of our country, except for some areas, is not inferior to other advanced countries," the proposal also admitted that social security was in danger. The proposal added: "Around 1980, we began to see a conflict between the social security system, on the one hand, and the economy and society, on the other hand. We must look carefully at the reality and see that social security has become stagnant or even regressed." The council proposed reconstructing the social security system according to five principles: universalism, fairness, coordination, human rights, and effectiveness. The proposal situated long-term care insurance among these principles and proclaimed that "the right to live has been only minimally guaranteed for those who have physical and mental handicaps or those who are old and need care at home or outside the home. From now on, this right must be part of a social security system that is based on human dignity, and it must be improved."[8] The proposal was important for further pushing for reforms, including long-term care.[9]

In June 1996, the MHW consulted with the Advisory Council on Social Security and the Council on Health and Welfare for the Elderly (Rōjin Hoken Fukushi Shingikai) to create an outline for a Long-Term Care Insurance Act (Kaigo Hoken Hō Yōkō). During summer 1996, the LDP, which come to power by allying with the Socialist Party of Japan, set up a team that held hearings all over Japan to hear from stakeholders. Kenji Yoshihara and Masaru Wada point out, "It was the first time that the majority party [the LDP] took strong leadership in introducing such a bill."[10]

Another important aspect of the policymaking process leading up to the Long-Term Care Insurance Act was that civil society was mobilized to participate. The leading group was the 10,000 Citizens Committee (Ichimannin Shimin Iinkai). The committee was established in August 1996. It had two prominent representatives, Keiko Higuchi, professor at Tokyo Kasei University and a well-known writer and activist, and Tsutomu Hotta, a prosecutor in the Lockheed bribery scandal. Both had been actively engaged in discussions about the problem of care for the elderly.[11]

A unique aspect of the 10,000 Citizens Committee was that it included many professionals, such as scholars, bureaucrats at the national and local levels, and journalists. The committee set a goal of collecting 100 million yen by asking ten

thousand people to contribute ten thousand yen each. The money was successfully used to gather information, prepare pamphlets and newsletters, and hold
a symposium and workshops. The Citizens Committee did not engage in street
demonstrations but made counterproposals to the government. The committee
successfully modified some parts of the Long-Term Care bill. For example, the
committee got a provision to have representatives of residents on the governing
board. The Citizens Committee opposed the paternalism of the Japanese welfare state and promoted citizens' participation.[12] The emergence of the new deliberation space could change the policymaking process in the long run.

Even after the lower house election in November 1996 led to a one-party LDP
government, the LDP continued to push for the long-term care insurance policy. The LDP's experience in the coalition government with the Socialist Party
of Japan and the New Party Sakigake gave the policy a positive push like "a tail-
wind that propelled it forward to establishment."[13]

The health and welfare minister at the time, Jun'ichiro Koizumi, explained
to the lower house the purpose of the act:

> In our country, those who need long-term care are sharply increasing
> because of our rapidly aging society. As the period in which necessary
> care is longer and the family unit is smaller than before, long-term care
> is the most serious concern for people contemplating life in their older
> years. . . . This act was introduced to respond to this situation. We want
> to restructure the existing system based on the idea of cooperation and
> solidarity and build a new system in which the entire society supports
> long-term care for those who need it.[14]

In December 1997, the Long-Term Care Insurance Act passed, and in April 2000,
the act became operative.

The Long-Term Care Insurance Act targeted two groups. First, No. 1 Insured
was for people over sixty-five. Their premium was deducted from their pensions.
Out-of-pocket expense was 10 percent for the service cost. Major costs were covered by a 50 percent premium plus public subsidy (50%: 25% from the central
government, 15% from prefectures, 15% from municipalities). Those covered
with No. 1 Insured could get long-term care if they were admitted by municipalities to access the care. Second, No. 2 Insured was for those between forty
and sixty-four. Their premium was paid by the national health insurance premium. Those with designated diseases, such as late-stage cancer, rheumatoid ar-
thritis, and amyotrophic lateral sclerosis, for example, had access to long-term
care.[15]

The establishment of the Long-Term Care Insurance Act was important in
the development of Japan's social security system. Long-term care was the fifth

social security policy category after medicine, pensions, industrial accidents, and unemployment. Japan had been lagging behind many other industrialized countries in developing institutions to provide the elderly with long-term care. The legislation was also important in the development of health insurance policy. The act reaffirmed the social insurance scheme with a heavy government subsidy as the core of the social security system.[16]

In the late 1990s, along with the Long-Term Care Insurance Act of 1997, fundamental reform of the various national health insurance programs was again under discussion. Largely because of the financial contribution for care of the elderly, not only the National Health Insurance and the Government-Managed Health Insurance but also the Society-Managed Health Insurance programs were in crisis. In fiscal year 1996, 1,293 SMHI societies out of 1,815 were in deficit, a sharp increase from 346 in fiscal year 1991. The government pushed companies' health insurance societies with deficits to improve their financial situations, but now it began to allow them to dissolve themselves. The dissolution pushed their beneficiaries into the GMHI, which cost the government more.[17] Although fundamental reform needed to be discussed, establishing long-term care insurance ironically played a role in further delaying discussion of fundamental reform.

Meanwhile, overall administrative reorganization took place in line with the top-down small government policy. In June 1998, the Hashimoto administration succeeded in gaining passage of the Act for Enforcement of Acts Related to the Central Government Reform (Chūōshōchō tō Kaikaku Kihon Hō). One of Hashimoto's campaign promises was to downsize government agencies and make them more efficient. The Prime Minister's Office was upgraded to the Cabinet Office, strengthening the power of the prime minister over the agencies. The act reorganized the government agencies and reduced their number from twenty-two to twelve. The merger of the MHW and the Ministry of Labor into the Ministry of Health, Labor, and Welfare (MHLW) was part of the reform.

The new ministry had a mandate to "deal with the declining birth rate and aging population, the demand for gender equality, and the changing economic system." Its guiding principle was as follows: "For the security and improvement of the peoples' lives, economic development, social welfare, social security, and public health should be promoted integrally and comprehensively with the improvement of the workplace environment, job security, and human resource development."[18] Although the purpose of integrating the ministries was explained as being to improve people's welfare, this reorganization was driven by the financial goal of downsizing agencies rather than making policy administration function better. The Koizumi administration, which followed Hashimoto's, made the policy direction even clearer.

Koizumi Administration Reforms

Koizumi became prime minister in April 2001.[19] Many initially thought that Ryūtarō Hashimoto, who was the head of the largest faction in the LDP and ran again after having served two and half years, would be elected. But Koizumi ran a strong campaign with help from Makiko Tanaka, who was popular particularly among women, as one who would bring fresh energy to stalemated politics. Koizumi used a simple slogan to appeal to the LDP's non-Diet party members—"Destroy the LDP" (*Jimintō wo bukkowasu*), which sounded like drastically reforming the LDP from the inside—and won the primary election.[20] He gradually gained momentum and eventually won a landslide victory against Hashimoto.

Koizumi opposed the factional politics of the LDP and formed his cabinet in an unusual way: he chose his cabinet members without having recommendations from the faction leaders. He appointed Heizō Takenaka, an economics professor at Keio University who was not a Diet member, as minister of state for economic and fiscal policy.[21] Takenaka advocated bold deregulation and the introduction of the market mechanism. He was critical of the existing social security programs. As a core cabinet member, he previously played a major role in the Council on Economic and Fiscal Policy (Keizai Zaisei Shimon Kaigi), which was established in 2001 as part of the Hashimoto administration's agency reorganization. The prime minister serves as the chair of the council. Koizumi actively used the council to make economic and social security policies, and Takenaka had a great influence on the Koizumi administration reforms.[22]

Koizumi used the slogan, "Without structural reform, there can be no economic recovery." He claimed that there were no exceptions in his structural reform: his idea was called "structural reform with no sacred cows" (*seiiki naki kōzō kaikaku*). His structural reform mostly meant creating small government through privatizing state organizations. He sought to reduce the role of the central government by empowering the prime minister. Particularly, he sought to diminish the power of the bureaucrats.

Privatization of the postal services was one of the major promises of Koizumi's campaign. He faced opposition even within his own party, and the privatization bill once died in the upper house. Then he dissolved the lower house and asked for the people's approval of his postal reform plan. He won the election of September 2005 by a landslide. His postal services privatization bill passed in the Diet in October.[23] In January 2006, the Japan Post (Nippon Yūsei Kōsha), a government-owned special corporation, was replaced by the Japan Post Group, which comprised four divisions.

Another of Koizumi's targets was health care. He used the same logic to reform health care: the more the government budget could be reduced, and the market mechanism included, the more economically efficient the administration could be. Koizumi's first task was cutting the government's health care expenditure. In December 2001, he quickly moved to substantially raise the health insurance premium. The fee schedule was cut by 2.7 percent; the fee for medical services was cut by 1.3 percent. Moreover, in 2003, the premium of the HI was increased by starting to collect from a twice-a-year bonus, and the co-payment of the HI insured increased from 20 percent to 30 percent, the same level as the NHI.[24] Koizumi explained these reforms with the phrase "*sanpō ichiryō zon*," or sharing the pain equally among three parties: medical providers (by lowering the fees), patients (by increasing the co-payment), and the insures (by increasing their contribution to the premium).[25]

Koizumi's next task was to introduce the private sector into health care. He believed that introduction of the market mechanism into health care would lower the government's financial burden and overall medical costs. In June 2001, Koizumi's cabinet approved his Basic Policies for Economic and Fiscal Management and Reform (Keizai Zaisei Un'ei to Kōzō Kaikaku ni Kansuru Kihon Hōshin). The cabinet decision, for the first time, included a plan for mixed treatment (*kongō shinryō*), which would allow patients to receive combined treatments in which some treatments were and others were not covered by national health insurance. If one procedure out of many was not included in the government fee schedule, with few exceptions, the cost of the entire treatment had to be paid as out-of-pocket expense. The Koizumi administration sought to loosen the regulation by letting patients choose how they were treated and allowing private industry to sell new technology and medicine.

In September 2004, in the Council on Economic and Fiscal Policy, Koizumi urged quick introduction of this plan, saying, "Mixed treatment has been discussed for a long time. I want to have approval of it by the end of this year." Because of a successful opposition campaign led by the JMA (discussed later in this chapter), however, the Koizumi administration achieved almost none of its initial aims.[26]

Another important piece of legislation was the Advanced Elderly Medical Service System (Kōki Kōreisha Iryōseido) of 2006. The Elderly Health Care Act of 1982 introduced co-payments and financial coordination among insurers into health care for the elderly. But while the cost of care increased over time, the co-payment remained unchanged. The insurers had to meet the financial burden because the act required insurers to contribute 50 percent of the entire cost. In 1999, the insurers conducted a campaign to protest their increasing contribution. In 2000, the co-payment was changed from a fixed amount to a fixed percentage, 10 percent. Meanwhile, the government promised to come up with a basic policy for the problem of care of the elderly by 2002, the year that the elderly were required to increase their co-payments. The Advanced Elderly Medical Service System Act was introduced in February 2006 and passed in June of that year.[27]

The most important thing about the Advanced Elderly Medical Service System was that it separated care of those over seventy-four more clearly from care for the rest of the population. Under the previous Elderly Health Care Act, the elderly had enrollee status in both the elderly care program and their health insurance program, and many of them were NHI program enrollees. Under the Advanced Elderly Medical Service System, everyone seventy-five or older was moved into one program. This change played a large role in creating a public image of the Advanced Elderly Medical Service System as a system for granny dumping. In Japanese folklore, there is the idea that old people are abandoned in the mountains, "*ubasuteyama*," by younger family members to save on food costs.[28]

Koizumi's health care reform ended up mostly consisting in reducing the government's financial burden. Doctor and medical economist Ryū Niki called the Koizumi reform a further advancement of Japan's "strictest reduction of health care costs in the world," which started in the 1980s.[29] The government tried to avoid becoming the target of public blame for the cutbacks as much as possible. Koizumi's simple yet powerful "one-phrase politics" using simple slogans successfully spread among the population the feeling of there being a national financial crisis and convinced them of a need for *sanpō ichiryō zon*. Meanwhile, the government continued to dominate the decision-making process.

As economic deflation persisted, however, more people began to question Koizumi's policy, which connected his structural reforms with economic recovery. His term as the head of the LDP was over in September 2006. As time passed, it started to be recognized that neoliberalism policy worked for some industrial sectors but not so well for the health care sector, at least not for the government's purposes. It came to be understood that introducing private businesses into the health care sector actually led to an increase in overall health care costs.[30] Furthermore, by decreasing fees, many hospitals had to close financially weak departments, such as pediatrics and obstetrics and gynecology. The number of doctors in Japan has almost always been smallest among Group of Seven (G7) countries (figure 8.1). The media sensationally reported that pregnant women were rejected by many hospitals and died in ambulances.[31] The media began to use the phrase "collapse of medical care" (*iryō hōkai*), which gained the public's attention.[32] Now the direction of health care reform needed to be reconsidered.

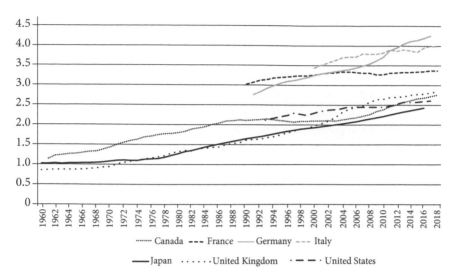

FIGURE 8.1. Number of doctors per 1,000 inhabitants, 1960–2018

Source: Organisation for Economic Co-operation and Development, "Doctors," https://data.oecd.org/healthres /doctors.htm, accessed March 15, 2020.

Post-Koizumi Administrations

After Koizumi resigned, Shinzō Abe took over as prime minister. His first administration was beset with many troubles and scandals. One of the most serious scandals involved the Social Security Agency's mishandling of pension records. People often have multiple pension records because of changing their jobs and work status. When the agency changed from printed records to electronic data, as many as 50 million pension records were not integrated. The scandal was called "the problem of disappeared pensions" (*kieta nenkin mondai*). In the public's disappointment, Abe resigned in September 2007 after serving for only one year.

Two more LDP prime ministers, Yasuo Fukuda (September 2007–September 2008) and Tarō Asō (September 2008–September 2009), followed. But they could not change the public's negative image of the LDP. The Democratic Party of Japan took advantage of the LDP's failures and had a landslide victory in August 2009, winning 308 out of 480 seats in the Diet. Three DPJ politicians became prime minister: Yukio Hatoyama (September 2009–June 2010), Naoto Kan (June 2010–September 2011), and Yoshihiko Noda (September 2011–December 2012).

The DPJ had been formed in 1996 as part of the reorganization efforts of minority parties. Ichirō Ozawa, who left the LDP in 1993, sought to establish a large political counterforce to the LDP. Ozawa played a major role in creating the New Frontier Party in 1994 by merging the Japan Renewal Party, the New Komeito, the Japan New Party, and others. Yukio Hatoyama took another route to counter the LDP. With high popularity as a grandson of Ichirō Hatoyama, the first president of the LDP, Hatoyama won election to the lower house in 1983 as an LDP candidate. In 1993, he left the LDP to form the New Party Sakigake with Masayoshi Takemura. In 1996, Hatoyama gathered Diet members mainly from the New Party Sakigake and the Socialist Party of Japan to form the DPJ.[33] In the late 1990s, the Socialist Party of Japan was in rapid decline, and party realignments took place. It was significant that former LDP politicians like Ozawa and Hatoyama took the lead in party realignments by absorbing many center-right and center-left political forces.

In 2009, when the LDP lost the public's trust and Hatoyama's DPJ won the majority in the Diet, the DPJ needed to provide the public with an alternative to the LDP's economic and social welfare policy. But the DPJ was not able to provide a clear policy stance other than a strong opposition to bureaucracy, somewhat similar to Koizumi's plan.

As a symbolic move in the area of social security policy, the DPJ opposed the Advanced Elderly Medical Service System. Abolishing the law that had recently passed under the Koizumi administration was an important part of the DPJ's manifesto in the 2009 election to distinguish the party from the LDP.[34] The DPJ proposed that enrollees in the Advanced Elderly Medical Service System should be returned to their NHI or HI programs. Furthermore, the DPJ proposed that the national health insurance programs should be eventually integrated in a residence-based program.[35] However, the DPJ could not convince the public that the party's proposal would bring a better solution for the aging society.

For one thing, prefectural governors opposed the DPJ's proposal. The governors had spent about two years preparing for the new system under the guidance of the reformed MHLW. The governors claimed that their investment of time and human resources would be wasted if the Advanced Elderly Medical Service System was abolished. Prefectural governors were also worried that they would have a greater financial burden under the DPJ plan. The negative public image of the program had also weakened. Once the program started, 69 percent of former NHI enrollees found they had lower health insurance premiums.[36] Furthermore, because it was the first time that the DPJ had the majority in the Diet, the party did not have the capacity and mature political skills to develop the proposal in detail. Finally, the DPJ had to face the reality that government debt was rising. By 2000, the Japanese government's debt became much higher than that of the other Organization for Economic Cooperation and Development (OECD) countries (figure 8.2). Koizumi's structural reform did not succeed in pushing it down. The DPJ did not have the luxury of creating a generous program for the aging population. In

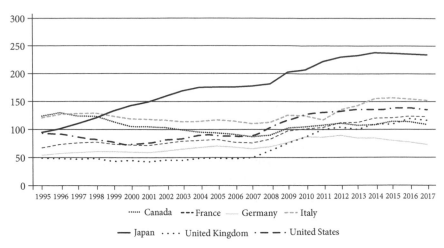

FIGURE 8.2.   Government debt (% of GDP, 1995–2017)

Source: Organisation for Economic Co-operation and Development, "General Government Debt," https://data .oecd.org/gga/general-government-debt.htm, accessed March 15, 2020.

June 2012, Yoshihiko Noda, the last of the three DPJ prime ministers, almost gave up the plan altogether in order to get an agreement with the LDP and Komeito to raise the consumption tax. The DPJ lost the upper house election in 2010, and there was no way for the party to push for its plan without the cooperation of the LDP and Komeito.[37] Public disappointment ended the period of DPJ administrations, and there was no alternative other than going back to the LDP.

Shinzō Abe again became prime minister in December 2012. On August 24, 2020, he became the longest consecutively serving prime minister, with his administration having lasted for 2,799 days. What the Abe administration has been trying to do overall is in line with the Koizumi plan for keeping down health care costs. But Abe has apparently admitted that the Koizumi neoliberal reforms went too far and created public anxiety and that his administration needed to respond to the public concern. Abe commented on the difference between Koizumi's health care reform and his: "While Prime Minister Koizumi was a very powerful [Western-style] drug, I am Kanpō medicine."[38] Ryū Niki points out that the Council on Economic and Fiscal Policy and other actors that pushed for US-type neoliberal reforms became less prominent under Abe's administration.[39] To discuss his reform plans, Abe created the Social Security System Reform Conference in 2013. Led by Atsushi Seike, president of Keio University, the conference gathered policy experts, mostly university professors, to study a wide range of social security issues, including health insurance matters.

While health insurance reform was discussed, the MHLW suffered from scandals and had difficulty gaining public trust. This experience was a sort of déjà vu for Abe. In 2015, personal information in the Japan Pension Service was leaked out. Names, date of birth, and basic pension numbers of more than a million people were exposed. The ministry was criticized for its slow and inappropriate response. In 2018, it came out that the ministry intentionally and institutionally tried to distort the data about the average wage. Although the ministry was required to research all employers with more than five hundred workers, it excluded more than 10 percent of employers in Tokyo and other big prefectures, which lowered the average wage statistic. As a result, the amount of the unemployment insurance payment, which is determined by the statistical data, was lowered. This scandal created a public negative image of the MHLW and, more broadly, the government.[40]

This scandal led to a discussion about reorganizing the MHLW by dividing it into two parts, one for labor and one for health and welfare—in other words, a reversal of what was done in 2001. One of the major problems was that the MHLW had become too big for senior officers to be able to check on operations in detail. As of 2020, it was not clear whether the plan would go through or not. But what is clear is that to regain public trust and have a sound discussion about health insurance, the government has to do more than just reorganize the ministry. But the government has a limitation.

What is needed is a mature civil society that bridges the people and the government and creates venues where a wide range of individuals and groups can have input into the policymaking process. One of the key actors should be the JMA, not as an interest group but as a mediator. The question is, How can the JMA as a medical-professional organization more actively reach out to the public to make the discussion more deliberate and productive through cooperating with other health care professional groups, educating the population, and connecting them with the government? But the JMA still seems to have a hard time figuring out how it should play a role in civil society.

The JMA's Challenges

In April 1996, Eitaka Tsuboi was elected JMA president. He had served as an executive board member and vice president under the previous presidents. But the victory of Tsuboi, who is based in Fukushima Prefecture, was seen as challenging the status quo, in which the Tokyo Medical Association had a large influence. Tsuboi promised to reform the JMA, particularly its internal money politics. He was originally recruited as "an interesting man" by Takemi when Tsuboi was active in the local medical association.[41] He began to attend Takemi's private study meetings. In a sense, Tsuboi succeeded in Takemi's goal, at least in his early terms, of breaking through the JMA's organizational cultures. But Tsuboi sought to do so in a different way.[42]

Tsuboi knew that, unlike Takemi, he did not have strong personal connections to influential LDP politicians. He also saw the limitations of the way Takemi engaged in politics. Tsuboi said, "Takemi had a theory but no policies."[43] Tsuboi tried to find a new means of influencing the policymaking process by creating the JMA's own think tank to strengthen its policymaking capacity. From being a member of the government's council, he concluded that the JMA needed its own research organization to check and refute the data and future predictions of the Statistics and Information Department of the MHW, which had grown to become a large organization as a result of conditions in World War II and afterward.[44]

In April 1997, President Tsuboi took the lead in establishing the Japan Medical Association Research Institute (Nihon Ishikai Sōgō Seisaku Kenkyū Kikō). He recruited Jūnen Nakamura from Tokyo Marine, a large insurance company, to head the institute.[45] Its principle is "to strive to achieve health care that is humane." The institute's mission includes (1) drafting health care policy options for the public to decide among, (2) creating a consensus-building process centered on the people, and (3) providing reliable data and information.[46] The JMA Research Institute, right after its establishment, showed off its strong presence by correcting government statistical data concerning future health care costs.[47]

At the same time, Tsuboi actively engaged in the debate about what Japanese health care should be like in the future. In 1997, the JMA presented its own idea for structural reform of health care. This not only included reform proposals for health insurance, including fee schedules, but also emphasized changing the way doctors, other medical providers, and patients used medical information technology and sought to make people think more seriously about health care costs.[48] This idea led the JMA to further work on reform plans and to propose in March 2000 its "Grand Design of Medicine for 2015," which gained the public's attention. Tsuboi also published his own book, Waga Iryō Kakumei Ron (The theory behind my medical revolution), to share his vision with the public.[49] It was the first time an incumbent JMA president published a book with detailed proposals.[50] Whereas Takemi tried to connect the JMA with the LDP, Tsuboi tried to connect the JMA directly with the public.

Tsuboi explained why he actively participated in policy discussions, "Health care policymaking has always been finance-centered: money has been the deciding factor in shaping health care policies. As a result, the official committees have not discussed whether people have sufficient health care to maintain their health and lives." One of the proposals that gained public attention was the idea of self-support investment. This is similar to the idea behind health savings accounts in the United States, which allow people some tax benefits when they save specifically for medical needs. Tsuboi claimed that "to improve social security and allow the people to plan their lives without worry, it is necessary for them to be motivated to support social security. For people to plan healthy lives, they should rely not only on subsidies from the central government and premiums but also on investment in self-support."[51]

This claim sounded to some like a neoliberal policy. Tsuboi admitted that the Japanese health insurance system would face serious financial problems in the near future and that the Japanese people should contribute more to solve them in innovative ways. He did not deny the importance of social security, however. He argued that public works, such as infrastructure construction projects, tend to provide one-shot economic stimulation, while social security has a long-lasting economic impact. He stressed that the government should invest more in health care. But the reality of politics went against Tsuboi's wishes.[52]

Tsuboi gradually lost his power base in the JMA as Koizumi's health care reform moved forward. When the new administration suggested a 2.7 percent reduction of the fee schedule in 2001, the JMA first resisted, but eventually Tsuboi decided to accept it. He concluded that it would not be good for the JMA to resist the Koizumi administration's overall reform direction. But those who were not happy with Tsuboi's decision challenged him in the 2002 JMA presidential election, which had been expected by many to present him with no challengers.[53]

Tsuboi's efforts to transform the JMA continued after his bitter victory. His new executive board included two female doctors for the first time in the JMA's history.[54] But it meant that the JMA had lagged behind with having females in its leadership. Still, as of 2020, the JMA has had no female presidents. In contrast, the American Medical Association had its first female president, Nancy Dickey, in 1997. This backwardness reflects the small number of female doctors in Japan. In 1966, female doctors made up 9 percent of the overall total. By 2015, the proportion had increased to 20.3 percent. But the number is still at the bottom of all OECD countries: the average of these countries was 46.1 percent (United Kingdom 45.8%, Germany 45.2%, France 44.3%, Canada 41.2%, Italy 40.3%, United States 34.1%).[55] Japan has had a stronger tradition that doctors should be men and nurses should be women. This tradition helped the JMA to have a paternalistic culture and superiority over nurses' organizations.

When Tsuboi retired at the end of his term in the spring of 2004, it was revealed that the Japan Dental Association was guilty of committing bribery in the Central Social Insurance Medical Council (hereafter Chūikyō), giving the government an excuse to reduce the JMA's political power. The Japan Dental Association bribed two council members, Takeshi Shimomura from the Federation of Health Insurance Societies and Katsutoshi Katō from the Japan Trade

Union Confederation, to favor the JDA in the council. The JDA also bought off some Diet members.[56] In response to the scandal, in 2006, Chūikyō was reorganized to add two more public-interest members. In 2008, after the minister of Health, Labor, and Welfare, Yōichi Masuzoe, claimed that the council needed to be more transparent, the JDA weakened the power to recommend members to Chūikyō.[57] The scandals increased the public's overall distrust in the fee-setting process and in the medical interest groups.

While the Koizumi administration continued to pressure the JMA, the association pushed back by going to the public. When Koizumi pushed hard for mixed treatment, many in the media and other commentators went along. The JMA counterattacked by cooperating with thirty-five other medical organizations in a campaign opposing mixed treatment. In October 2004, JMA president Haruo Uematsu set up an umbrella organization, the People's Medicine Promotion Council (Kokumin Iryō Suishin Kyōgikai). Within one month, the organization collected about 6 million signatures on a petition opposing mixed treatment. The petition, which included 320 signatures of Diet members, was submitted to the chairpersons of the upper and lower houses. It was unanimously adopted in the plenary session in December 2004.

When the Trans-Pacific Strategic Economic Partnership Agreement (hereafter TPP) caused heated debate in 2011, the JMA, along with the JDA and the Japan Pharmaceutical Association, again took a strong position against the agreement. The TPP was negotiated among twelve Pacific Rim countries, including Japan and the United States, to enhance trade among them. The agreement would not only significantly lower tariffs but also set common rules about labor, public services, intellectual property rights, investment, and so on. The Japanese debated whether the United States would pressure Japan to privatize medical care, introduce mixed treatment, and destroy the existing national health insurance system. In a press conference at the Ministry of Health, Labor, and Welfare in November 2011, the opposition health organizations officially requested the government to guarantee that national health insurance would not be negotiable. Although their worry ended when Donald Trump decided to withdraw the United States from the TPP in January 2017, it had given the JMA another opportunity to publicly defend the national health insurance system.[58] Once again, the JMA defended the status quo while the government challenged it.

While the TPP was on the negotiation table, Yoshitake Yokokura won the JMA presidential election in April 2012. He became the first president based in Fukuoka, Kyushu, in the southern part of Japan. In an interview for a business magazine, he said, "What I wanted to do the most after I became president was to get rid of the public image that the JMA was a pressure group [for self-interest]."[59]

Yokokura took a path similar to Tsuboi's by actively engaging in policy debates. In March 2019, the JMA released its "Grand Design of Medicine for 2030." In the proposal, Yokokura explains that the intention is to discuss what medicine can do in response to Japan's decreasing population and labor power, increasing income gap, and super aging society. He states that the purpose of the "Grand Design" is to answer questions that doctors face:

> The rapid advances in science and technology have brought human beings to a place we have never before experienced. How should medical practitioners evaluate and effectively use this new knowledge? Medical institutions, culture, and professional groups are challenged by this development. People living in Japan should keep in mind the question of what medicine should be. How should it be planned for, improved on, and administered?[60]

While the JMA tried to engage with the public, the association still needed venues for more directly affecting policymaking. But the JMA appeared to be uncertain about how to be an influential actor in the decision-making process. In the upper house election of 2019, Toshi Hanyūda, former JMA vice president, was recommended by the JMA to the LDP's list for the proportional election.[61] Although he won the fourteenth place on the list in the election, the Japan Pharmaceutical Association and the Japan Nursing Association mobilized more votes for their own representative candidates, Akiko Honda in the twelfth place and Masahiro Ishida in the tenth place. One of the leading members of the JMA said, "The victory itself does not mean much. We have to be at the top of the proportional election. Otherwise, the LDP thinks that the JMA is not enthusiastic about [supporting the LDP] in the election."[62]

The JMA has been suffering as an organization because more and more doctors work in hospitals. The JMA in the twenty-first century cannot follow Takemi's way of holding JMA members together by threatening the public and the government that members would quit health insurance practice. The JMA cannot continue to make its members happy by getting increased fees, which are unavailable with a tightening government budget. What the JMA can do is to transform itself from being the representative organization of private solo practitioners into an organization that engages more in cultivating the discussion space for health care problems and improving civil society. The result of the upper house election of 2019 is a great opportunity for the JMA to seriously consider becoming a professional organization for improving the entire health care system. Yokokura was elected three times, but he was limited in what he could do to change the health insurance system. His response to COVID-19 at the end of his presidency symbolized this limitation.

COVID-19

At the beginning of 2020, COVID-19 began to spread and threaten many countries. The cases and death toll increased rapidly. The quick spread of the infectious disease resulted from globalization. Japan was no exception. As of February 8, 2021, the number of infections and deaths was 404,128 and 6,373 respectively. The number of deaths per 100,000 people in Japan was 5.04, which was much lower than the other G7 countries: United Kingdom (168.91), Italy (150.59), France (117.84), United States (141.26), Canada (55.86), and Germany (74.22). But neighboring countries and regions had a lower mortality rate: South Korea (2.85), China (0.35), and Taiwan (0.04).[63] The Japanese government has made difficult policy choices to balance the resumption of economic activities with infection control.

On January 19, 2020, the first case of infection was reported in Japan. As the number of cases gradually increased, in January 30, the government established the Novel Coronavirus Response Headquarters (Shingata Korona Uirusu Kansenshō Taisaku Honbu) in the cabinet. On February 14, the government formed the Novel Coronavirus Expert Panel (Shingata Korona Uirusu Kansenshō Taisaku Senmonka Kaigi) as the advisory body to the headquarters.[64] On February 28, Prime Minister Abe called for all schools to close. On March 11, the World Health Organization declared that COVID-19 was officially a pandemic.

Prime Minister Abe and many others became concerned about whether Japan would still able to hold the Tokyo Olympics and Paralympics of 2020 in the coming summer. The Olympic torch arrived in Japan on March 20, and Prime Minister Abe tried to be positive about holding the games. But the situation quickly became worse. On March 23, seeing the inevitability of rescheduling the Tokyo Olympics, Tokyo Governor Yuriko Koike mentioned the possibility of a lockdown in Tokyo. On March 24, the International Olympics Committee and the Tokyo 2020 Organizing Committee made a joint announcement to postpone the Tokyo Olympics for about a year.[65] A more shocking event to many people was that a very famous comedian, Ken Shimura, died from the coronavirus infection at the age of seventy, on March 30. On April 7, Prime Minister Abe declared a state of emergency over COVID-19 for seven prefectures including Tokyo; the state of emergency was soon extended to include all other prefectures. The reported cases of infection began to go down in mid-April, and on May 25, the state of emergency was ended.

As the first wave ended in late May, the cases and the death toll were lower than in other G7 countries. What was more surprising to foreigners was that Japan achieved this outcome with a "soft" lockdown. While many European countries enforced hard lockdowns with force and penalties, the Japanese government asked for self-restraint and achieved significant control of people's behavior. Some claim that Japan was simply lucky because it has a culture of bowing for greetings, not shaking hands and hugging, and that Japanese people already have the custom of wearing masks and washing their hands often. Some point out that the mandatory Bacillus Calmette–Guérin (BCG) vaccine for tuberculosis may lower the possibility of infection.

The Japanese health care system worked well for some aspects of the pandemic and not so well for others. Universal health insurance allowed all residents to have treatment without a heavy financial burden. Moreover, health centers, developed during World War II to prevent tuberculosis and improve the health of babies and mothers, worked to provide polymerase chain reaction (PCR tests) and to prevent one cluster of COVID-19 cases from creating another.[66] But some argue that the health centers could have more effectively prevented the spread of COVID-19 if the government had not cut the budget for the centers.[67] In 1992, there were 852 health centers in Japan, but the number had decreased to 472 in 2019. Critics also point out that the government has invested too little in the National Institute of Infectious Disease (Kokuritsu Kansenshō Kenkyūjo). Compared with its US counterpart, the Centers for Disease Control and Prevention (CDC), Japan's institute has 1/42 of the number of personnel and a budget that is 1/1077 of the CDC's.[68] Finally, it became obvious that there were not enough hospitals in Japan with the capacity to care for infected patients. The reason is largely that the government has not sufficiently invested in large public hospitals because of the JMA's opposition.

The JMA, on the other hand, showed its presence when cases increased in March and April. On April 1, JMA president Yokokura made an announcement of the state of medical emergency and urged the government to declare that medical facilities have been driven into a corner to handle the infected people.[69] Frustrated by the government's slow response, on April 6, the Tokyo Medical Association made the same announcement. Haruo Ozaki, the president of the association, said, "If an 'overshoot' [a term not widely used outside Japan, meaning explosive rise] occurs, we will not only face a shortage of hospital beds in Tokyo but also risk exposing medical staffs to the virus. Moreover, because infection prevention equipment will be in short supply, we cannot provide sufficient medical services for serious cases and our medical care system will break down."[70] The statement was widely reported on television and in newspapers and paved the way for the government to declare the state of emergency on April 7.

But it appeared to the public that making these announcements was the only role the JMA played in dealing with the COVID-19 pandemic. The JMA was criticized when it held its presidential election while the situation was getting worse. Yokokura unofficially said that he would not run for a fifth term, but he decided to declare his candidacy. Toshio Nakagawa, the longtime vice president, ran against Yokokura. While Yokokura had a strong personal connection to the LDP leaders, including Deputy Prime Minister Tarō Asō, Nakagawa tried to show a more unbiased attitude. Yokokura was a better candidate for the LDP, but Nakagawa won the election. The heated electoral campaign was widely reported, and the JMA was criticized for its members' quarrels among themselves.[71]

Furthermore, the JMA was under attack when it opposed the use of online diagnostics, which stood to benefit both patients and medical staff by preventing the spread of COVID-19. The JMA argued that doctors and patients must have trust in face-to-face consultations and that fake doctors might appear and endanger patients. But the JMA's opposition was seen as a means to protect clinics and small hospitals. The JMA eventually accepted online diagnostics as an emergency measure in April. But the JMA was seen as being hypocritical in being inflexible on a measure to protect patients while declaring that the health care system was in crisis.[72]

The JMA has represented the interest of private practitioners. But during the COVID-19 pandemic, the main medical actors were health centers with public doctors and nurses and hospitals with highly skilled medical staff and the technology to deal with the infectious disease. COVID-19 in a sense gave the JMA an opportunity to reconsider what social role it should play. In June 2020, newly elected Nakagawa said, "The JMA will be reborn as a stronger and genuinely open 'new Japan Medical Association.'"[73] But there is no strong sign yet from his presidency. The JMA's struggle should be a beneficial opportunity for the Japanese people to think about the future of their health care system.

CONCLUSION

For the Future of Health Insurance Politics

Health care policy affects how people are born, live, and die. People's health is about not only the quantity of years they live but also the quality of their lives. Health care policy affects people's happiness and the form of their civil society—in other words, how they interact with others and engage in community. Health care policy is also a tool for governing the nation. The government needs people's good health to develop the economy, win wars, and stabilize society. Interest groups are expected to mediate between individuals and the government to develop civil society. Among interest groups, doctors, who have medical knowledge and experience, play an important role in the health care policy deliberation. The government and doctors, therefore, are the two major players shaping health care policy.

The relationship between governments and doctors is not static. The historical development of political institutions and policy affects the politics between the two players. Drastic policy changes restrained their policy preferences and political strategy in subsequent periods. Once a new policy develops, it continues to exist whether or not it is the most effective measure to deal with problems. In this book we learn how Japan has come to adopt the health insurance system it has now by examining which historical events caused policy changes and what institutional and political contexts drove subsequent policy development.

As Naoki Ikegami and John Campbell point out, the Japanese health insurance system is relatively low-cost and has an egalitarian design.[1] The historical process that expanded health insurance coverage and controlled costs is important. The top-down creation of a medical education and administration after the Meiji Restoration empowered the government to intervene in health care. Such intervention may have been a natural consequence for a late-developing country like Japan. Soon the democratic movement took place, and elite doctors tried to form medical associations for professional and financial reasons. But the democratic movement was oppressed by the government, fearing socialism. Medical associations stagnated as a result of a difficult relationship with the government. Elite doctors found it very difficult to be independent from government power, because the best partner for doctors to gain power would be the government.

These institutional and political developments gave the government strong political leverage when World War II required high-level war mobilization. As good health was deeply connected with the national defense policy, the radical expansion of public health insurance was achieved during the war. With wartime budget constraints, however, the government created new programs as cheaply as possible and, to keep down health care costs, introduced a fee-setting mechanism; the government combined these developments with patriotic propaganda about the necessity of making sacrifices for victory. The government used all human resources in pursuit of winning the war. The JMA was dissolved and turned into a state organization.

This radical policy change brought in its wake a deep policy path dependence after the war. The postwar political environment also contributed to this path dependence. General Headquarters' reforms ended up working with the conservative political parties and bureaucrats to consolidate Japan's wartime policies. Postwar financial difficulties prodded the government to keep health care costs under control. With the Liberal Democratic Party continuing to lead the government after 1955, health care policy was geared to appeal to party constituencies but was always subordinate to economic development policy. Universal coverage was achieved in 1961, but this achievement was reached by expanding the weakest program, the National Health Insurance program, to cover the uninsured. The basic structure of health insurance remained the same, and the economic boom allowed the government to improve program benefits. But the elderly still suffered from the heavy co-payment in the NHI program. Municipalities and prefectures first and then the central government responded to the problem by introducing free elderly care as part of the government's welfare program.

When economic development slowed, welfare retrenchment began. The government shifted its policy toward "small government" through privatizing state-owned firms, relaxing regulations, and cutting back on social welfare programs. However, the government achieved the retrenchment policy without losing much of the people's trust. For the first time, the government successfully introduced financial coordination among financially strong and weak health insurance programs. By promoting the idea that high health care costs would lead to the nation's ruin, the government managed to keep down health care costs without too much of the people's blame.

With institutional developments in which the government continued to be the most powerful actor, what could the JMA do to survive as a professional organization, contribute to medical science, improve the people's health, and develop civil society? Although Takemi's legacy has been overstated by some, he did not break up the foundation of existing health care institutions. What he achieved was to maximize the JMA's (and his own) interests within the given institutional arrangements. The institutional orders were so robust that Takemi had no other option but to go to the influential LDP politicians to gain material benefits, such as an increase of the national health insurance fee, that would appease JMA members and assure his reelection. Because of Takemi's special connections with people at the center of politics, he succeeded very well in this effort. Perhaps he succeeded too well, as he did not need to consider other ways of building up the JMA, such as reaching out to the public and becoming an alternative to the government for making policy. Takemi, in a sense, was a "monster" created by the historical development of health care policy.

When the monster disappeared, the JMA had difficulty finding new ways to survive. The JMA needs to build on the approach the association took when opposing mixed treatment as proposed by the Koizumi administration and in dealing with the Trans-Pacific Strategic Economic Partnership Agreement: to cooperate more with other health care professional organizations. The JMA also needs to work together with civic organizations like the coalition that emerged to improve the Long-Term Care Insurance Act. It may be more difficult than what doctors might imagine because the JMA has long been proud of standing on its own as the leading professional organization.

While the basic structure of health insurance has not changed much since the end of World War II, the culture of health care administration faces a difficult time adjusting to the new era of the twenty-first century. In 2003, for example, former Prime Minister Yoshirō Mori commented, "It is not appropriate that women who do not have children rely on the public old-age pension."[2] In 2007, the minister of health, labor, and welfare, Hakuo Yanagisawa, stated in a public meeting, "The number of baby-making machines between fifteen and fifty cannot be changed. [To solve the problem of the declining of birth rate] each woman must make an effort [to increase her productivity]."[3] The media heavily criticized this comment by summarizing it as follows: "Women are birth machines."[4] The LDP politicians do not seem to learn from their mistakes. More recently in 2019, Tarō Asō and Yoshitaka Sakurada asserted that women have an obligation to procreate. Although Asō and Sakurada retracted their comments, calling them slips of the tongue, their words are the result of Japan's not only traditional gender bias but also the culture of health care administration, which tends to see human resources as belonging to the nation.

People's lives and health in Japan have traditionally been considered as tools for nation building, national defense, and national economic development. Debate on health care policy has been limited to a small group, with the government setting the terms of the argument. Financial concerns have always been at the forefront of the discussion. Although financial considerations are very important in making the health insurance system more sustainable, health insurance policy cannot be sustainable without engaging more actors and developing a better deliberation process.

Japan has recently become more diverse with more foreign residents. In 2017, Japan ranked fourth among countries in accepting international migration, after Germany, the United States, and the United Kingdom.[5] Japan not only has many people from abroad but also many new ideas from all over the world. Young people particularly look into new ways of life and use new venues, such as social networking, to voice their opinions. With a more diverse population with different ways of life, the government cannot continue with its traditional politics, policy, and culture.

Doctors also have to change their ways of engaging in politics and culture. This is not a simple task. As people live longer with chronic diseases, doctors are having to cooperate with long-term care managers, nurses, and others. The JMA is losing its status as the dominant organization in medicine. Furthermore, advances in information technology and artificial intelligence have changed the way people experience the practice of medicine and the social role of medical professionals. Medical information is more available to the public, and artificial intelligence and robots can already perform important tasks that doctors used to do, such as make diagnoses and assist in surgery.

Lastly, the COVID-19 pandemic reminds us how deep globalization is in a world in which this infectious disease spread so quickly, as well as how strong the borders of cities and countries are during lockdown. The pandemic reveals the positive and negative aspects of health care systems, not only in Japan, but also in other countries. I do hope that this crisis will soon be over, and more people will begin to discuss what health care system they want to live with. It is time to discuss how to create a truly sustainable health care system, so that people can live for their own happiness and that of others. There is no such thing as a perfect health care system. Countries have to make the best policy choices within their own given institutional, political, and historical contexts. To do so, it is necessary to understand how each country has adopted its current health care system. Countries also have to learn what has succeeded and failed in other countries in order to further consider policy options. I hope this book will be a guide for such endeavors.

Appendix

TABLE A.1 Prime ministers and ministers of health and welfare (1938–2021)

PRIME MINISTER	MINISTER OF HEALTH AND WELFARE	PERIOD
Fumimaro Konoe	Kōichi Kido	1/11/1938–5/26/1938
		5/25/1938–1/05/1939
Kiichirō Hiranuma	Hisatada Hirose	1/05/1939–8/30/1939
Nobuyuki Abe	Naoshi Ōhara	8/30/1939–11/29/1939
	Kiyoshi Akita	11/29/1939–1/16/1940
Mitsumasa Yonai	Shigeru Yoshida	1/16/1940–7/22/1940
Fumimaro Konoe	Eiji Yasui	7/22/1940–9/28/1940
	Tsuneo Kanemitsu	9/28/1940–7/18/1941
Hideki Toujō	Chikahiko Koizumi	7/18/1941–10/18/1941
		10/18/1941–7/22/1944
Kuniaki Koiso	Hisatada Hirose	7/22/1944–2/10/1945
	Katsuroku Aikawa	2/10/1945–4/7/1945
Kantarō Suzuki	Tadahiko Okada	4/7/1945–8/17/1945
Naruhikoou Higashikuninomiya	Kenzō Matsumura	8/17/1945–10/9/1945
Kijūro Shidehara	Hitoshi Ashida	10/9/1945–5/22/1946
Shigeru Yoshida	Yoshinari Kawai	5/22/1946–5/22/1947
	Shigeru Yoshida	5/22/1947–5/24/1947
Tetsu Katayama	Tetsu Katayama	5/24/1947–6/1/1947
	Sadayoshi Hitotsumatsu	6/1/1947–3/10/1948
Hitoshi Ashida	Giichi Takeda	3/10/1948–10/15/1948
Shigeru Yoshida	Shigeru Yoshida	10/15/1948–10/19/1948
	Jōji Hayashi	10/19/1948–6/28/1950
	Takeo Kurokawa	6/28/1950–7/4/1951
	Ryōgo Hashimoto	7/4/1951–1/18/1952
	Eichi Yoshitake	1/18/1952–10/30/1952
	Katsumi Yamagata	10/30/1952–1/9/1954
	Ryūen Kusaba	1/9/1954–12/10/1954
Ichirō Hatoyama	Yūsuke Tsurumi	12/10/1954–3/19/1955
	Hideji Kawasaki	3/19/1955–11/22/1955
	Eizo Kobayashi	11/22/1955–12/23/1956

(continued)

TABLE A.1 *(continued)*

PRIME MINISTER	MINISTER OF HEALTH AND WELFARE	PERIOD
Tanzan Ishibashi	Tanzan Ishibashi	12/23/ 1956–12/23/1956
Nobusuke Kishi	Hiroshi Kanda	12/23/1956–2/25/1957
		2/25/1957–7/10/1957
	Kenzō Horiki	7/10/1957–6/12/1958
	Ryōgo Hashimoto	6/12/1958–1/12/1959
	Michita Sakata	1/12/1959/–6/18/1959
	Yoshio Watanabe	6/18/1959–7/19/1960
Hayato Ikeda	Masa Nakayama	7/19/1960–12/8/1960
	Yoshimi Furui	12/8/1960–7/18/1961
	Hirokichi Nadao	7/18/1961–7/18/1962
	Eiichi Nishimura	7/18/1962–7/18/1963
	Takeji Kobayashi	7/18/1963–7/18/1964
Satō Eisaku	Hiroshi Kanda	7/18/1964–11/9/1964
		11/9/1964–6/3/1965
	Zenkō Suzuki	6/3/1965–12/3/1966
	Hideo Bō	12/3/1966–11/25/1967
	Sunao Sonoda	11/25/1967–11/30/1968
	Noboru Saitō	11/30/1968–1/14/1970
	Tsuneo Uchida	1/14/1970–7/5/1971
	Saito Noboru	7/5/1971–7/7/1972
Kakuei Tanaka	Shunji Shiomi	7/7/1972–12/22/1972
	Kunikichi Saitō	12/22/1972–11/11/1974
	Kenji Fukunaga	11/11/1974–12/9/1974
Takeo Miki	Masami Tanaka	12/9/1974–9/15/1976
	Takashi Hayakawa	9/15/1976–12/24/1976
Takeo Fukuda	Michio Watanabe	12/24/1976–11/28/1977
	Tatsuo Ozawa	11/28/1977–12/7/1978
Masayoshi Ōhira	Ryūtarō Hashimoto	12/7/1978–11/9/1979
	Kyōichi Noro	11/9/1979–7/17/1980
Zenkō Suzuki	Kunikichi Saitō	7/17/1980–9/19/1980
	Sunao Sonoda	9/19/1980–5/18/1981
	Tatsuo Murayama	5/18/1981–11/30/1981
	Motoharu Morishita	11/30/1981–11/27/1982
Yasuhiro Nakasone	Yoshirō Hayashi	11/27/1982–12/27/1983
	Kōzō Watanabe	12/27/1983–11/1/1984
	Hiroyuki Masuoka	11/1/1984–12/28/1985
	Isamu Imai	12/28/1985–7/22/1986
	Jūro Saitō	7/22/1986–11/6/1987

PRIME MINISTER	MINISTER OF HEALTH AND WELFARE	PERIOD
Noboru Takeshita	Takao Fujimoto	11/6/1987–12/27/1988
Sōsuke Uno	Jun'ichirō Koizumi	12/27/1988–6/3/1989
		6/3/1989–8/10/1989
Toshiki Kaifu	Saburō Toida	8/10/1989–2/28/1990
	Yūji Tsushima	2/28/1990–12/29/1990
	Shinichirō Shimojyo	12/29/1990–11/5/1991
Kiichi Miyazawa	Tokuo Yamashita	11/5/1991–12/12/1992
	Yūya Niwa	12/12/1992–8/9/1993
Morihiro Hosokawa	Keigo Ōchi	8/9/1993–4/28/1994
Tsutomu Hata		4/28/1994–6/30/1994
Tomiichi Murayama	Shōichi Ide	6/30/1994–8/8/1995
	Chūryō Morii	8/8/1995–1/11/1996
Ryutarō Hashimoto	Naoto Kan	1/11/1996–11/7/1996
	Jun'ichirō Koizumi	11/7/1996–7/30/1998
Keizō Obuchi	Sōhei Miyashita	7/30/1998–10/5/1999
Yoshirō Mori	Yuya Niwa	10/5/1999–4/5/2000
		4/5/2000–7/4/2000
	Yūji Tsushima	7/4/2000–12/5/2000
Jun'ichirō Koizumi	Chikara Sakaguchi	12/5/2000–4/26/2001
		4/26/2001–9/27/2004
	Hidehisa Ōtsuji	9/27/2004–10/31/2005
	Jirō Kawasaki	10/31/2005–9/26/2006
Shinzō Abe	Hakuo Yanagisawa	9/26/2006–8/27/2007
Yasuo Fukuda	Masuzoe Yōichi	8/27/2007–9/26/2007
		9/26/2007–9/24/2008
Tarō Asō		9/24/2008–9/16/2009
Yukio Hatoyama	Akira Nagatsuma	9/16/2009–6/8/2010
Naoto Kan		6/8/2010–9/17/2010
	Ritsuo Hosokawa	9/17/2010–9/2/2011
Yoshihiko Noda	Yōko Komiyama	9/2/2011–10/1/2012
	Wakio Mitsui	10/1/2012–12/26/2012
Shinzō Abe	Norihisa Tamura	12/26/2012–12/24/2014
	Shiozaki Yasuhisa	12/24/2014–8/3/2017
	Katsunobu Katō	8/3/2017–10/2/2018
	Takumi Nemoto	10/2/2018–9/11/2019
	Katsunobu Katō	9/11/2019–9/16/2020
Yoshihide Suga	Norihisa Tamura	9/16/2020–present (3/2/2021)

Note: On January 6, 2001, the Ministry of Health and Welfare was reorganized as the Ministry of Health, Labor, and Welfare.

TABLE A.2 Administrative heads of the Ministry of Health and Welfare (1938–2021)

NAME	PERIOD
Hisatada Hirose	1/11/1938–1/5/1939
Fumihide Okada	1/7/1939–4/5/1940
Masasuke Kodama	4/5/1940–3/26/1941
Kyūichi Kodama	3/26/1941–11/4/1941
Gunji Takei	11/4/1941–4/18/1944
Katsuroku Aikawa	4/18/1944–2/10/1945
Keinoshin Nakamura	2/13/1945–8/22/1945
Kōichi Kameyama	8/22/1945–1/25/1946
Seiichiro Yasui	1/25/1946–7/23/1946
Kinji Itō	7/23/1946–3/16/1948
Yoshisuke Kasai	3/16/1948–5/8/1951
Taichi Miyazaki	5/8/1951–9/1/1953
Chūjirō Kimura	9/1/1953–1957/5/20
Shigeo Tanabe	5/20/1957–7/10/1959
Iwao Yasuda	7/10/1959–6/17/1960
Masami Takada	6/17/1960–11/17/1961
Hirokuni Dazai	11/17/1961–12/10/1963
Kōun Takada	12/10/1963–2/9/1965
Tadasu Ōyama	2/9/1965–6/2/1965
Yoshito Ushimaru	6/2/1965–6/6/1967
Masayoshi Yamamoto	6/6/1967–8/12/1969
Masao Kumazaki	8/12/1969–1/8/1971
Yoshimasa Umemoto	1/8/1971–7/1/1971
Teiichiro Sakamoto	7/1/1971–7/27/1973
Masakata Tozawa	7/27/1973–6/11/1974
Takeji Katō	6/11/1974–7/8/1975
Gen Takagi	7/8/1975–10/15/1976
Rikio Kitagawa	10/15/1976–8/23/1977
Kyūjirō Okina	8/23/1977–12/12/1978
Ikuo Soneda	12/12/1978–3/4/1980
Tetsuo Yagi	3/4/1980–8/26/1981
Seiji Ishino	8/26/1981–8/27/1982
Maomi Yamashita	8/27/1982–8/28/1984
Hitoshi Yoshimura	8/28/1984–6/13/1986
Masataka Kōda	6/13/1986–6/7/1988
Kenji Yoshihara	6/7/1988–6/29/1990
Tatsuhiko Sakamoto	6/29/1990–7/1/1992
Takehiro Kuroki	7/1/1992–6/29/1993
Teijirō Furukawa	6/29/1993–9/2/1994
Hiroshi Tada	9/2/1994–7/2/1996

NAME	PERIOD
Nobuharu Okamitsu	7/2/1996–11/19/1996
Fumio Sasaki	11/19/1996–11/22/1996
Takehiko Yamaguchi	11/22/1996–8/31/1999
Shingo Haketa	8/31/1999–1/5/2001
Jungorō Kondō	1/6/2001–8/30/2002
Yōtarō Sawada	8/30/2002–8/29/2003
Tetsuo Tsuji	9/1/2006–8/31/2007
Takeshi Erikawa	8/31/2007–7/24/2009
Kunio Mizuta	7/24/2009–7/30/2010
Shinji Asonuma	7/30/2010–9/10/2012
Junichi Kaneko	9/10/2012–7/2/2013
Atsuko Muraki	7/2/2013–10/1/2015
Kazuo Futagawa	10/1/2015–7/11/2017
Motomichi Kamohara	7/11/2017–7/31/2018
Toshihiko Suzuki	7/31/2018–9/14/2020
Hideki Tarumi	9/14/2020–present (3/2/21)

Note: English translations of the position's name have changed over the years: health and welfare vice minister from January 11, 1938, to June 1, 1949; health and welfare administrative vice minister from June 1, 1949, to January 5, 2001; and health, labor, and welfare administrative minister from January 5, 2001, to present.

TABLE A.3 Presidents of the Japan Medical Association (1916–2021)

NAME	HOME MEDICAL ASSOCIATION	PREVIOUS POSITIONS	TERM
Shibasaburō Kitazato	n/a	Dean of Keio University Medical School, head of Kitazato Institute	11/1923–6/1931
Taichi Kitajima	n/a	Dean of Keio University Medical School	7/1931–1/1943
Ryukichi Inada	n/a	Professor of Kyushu Imperial University and Tokyo Imperial University	2/1943–3/1946
Toshihiko Nakayama	Tokyo Medical Association	President of Tokyo Medical Association, member of House of Peers	4/1946–3/1948
Akira Takahashi	Tokyo Medical Association	Professor of Tokyo Imperial University Medical School	3/1948–3/1950
Takeo Tamiya	Tokyo Medical Association	Dean of Tokyo Imperial University Medical School	4/1950–8/1950
Yasaburo Taniguchi	Kumamoto Medical Association	President of Kumamoto Medical Association, professor of Kumamoto Medical Technical School, member of House of Councillors	8/1950–1/1952
Takeo Tamiya	Tokyo Medical Association	Dean of Tokyo Imperial University Medical School	2/1952–3/1954
Junzo Kurosawa	Tokyo Medical Association	President of Tokyo Medical Association, professor of Nippon Medical School, director of Ogawa Ophthalmic Hospital	4/1954–9/1955
Korekiyo Obata	Tokyo Medical Association	President of Tokyo Medical Association, director of Hamada Hospital	10/1955–3/1957
Taro Takemi	Tokyo Medical Association	Vice president of the JMA, owner of Takemi Clinic	4/1957–3/1982
Kenji Hanaoka	Nagano Medical Association	President of Nagano Medical Association, owner of Jikeikai Yoshida Hospital	4/1982–3/1984
Haruto Haneda	Tokyo Medical Association	President of Tokyo Medical Association, owner of Haneda Clinic	4/1984–3/1992
Toshio Murase	Tokyo Medical Association	Vice president of the JMA, owner of Murase Clinic	4/1992–3/1996
Eitaka Tsuboi	Fukushima Medical Association	Vice president of the JMA, owner of Tsuboi Hospital	4/1996–3/2004
Haruo Uematsu	Osaka Medical Association	President of Osaka Medical Association, owner of Uematsu Clinic	4/2004–3/2006
Yoshihito Karasawa	Tokyo Medical Association	President of Tokyo Medical Association, owner of Karasawa Clinic	4/2006–3/2010
Katsuyuki Haranaka	Ibaraki Medical Association	President of Ibaraki Medical Association, associate professor of Tokyo University, chief director of Ohata Hospital	4/2010–3/2012
Yoshitake Yokokura	Fukuoka Medical Association	Vice president of the JMA, president of Fukuoka Medical Association, owner of Yokokura Hospital	4/2012–6/2020
Toshio Nakagawa	Hokkaido Medical Association	Vice president of the JMA, executive director of Hokkaido Medical Association	6/2020–present (3/2/2021)

TABLE A.4 Causes of death per 10,000 inhabitants, 1920–2018

YEAR	DEATH	CANCER	HEART DISEASE	VASCULAR BRAIN DISEASE	TUBERCULOSIS	PNEUMONIA, BRONCHITIS	GASTROENTERITIS	INFANT MORTALITY
1920	142.2	4.0	3.5	8.8	12.5	22.8	14.2	33.5
1925	121.0	4.2	3.9	9.6	11.5	16.4	14.2	29
1930	117.0	4.5	4.1	10.4	11.9	12.8	14.2	25
1935	116.1	5.0	4.9	11.4	13.2	12.9	11.9	23.3
1940	118.6	5.1	4.5	12.7	15.3	13.3	11.4	19
1947	113.8	5.3	4.8	10.1	14.6	13.6	10.6	16.5
1950	90.4	6.4	5.3	10.5	12.1	7.7	6.8	14
1955	69.3	7.7	5.4	12.1	4.6	4.3	2.8	6.0
1960	70.6	9.3	6.8	15.0	3.1	4.6	1.9	4.9
1970	70.0	10.6	7.5	17.2	2.2	3.6	1.2	3.0
1965	71.2	11.9	8.9	18.1	1.5	3.5	0.8	2.5
1975	70.2	13.6	9.9	17.4	1.0	3.7	0.6	1.9
1980	72.2	16.1	12.3	16.2	0.6	3.9	0.4	1.1
1985	75.2	18.7	14.1	13.4	0.4	5.1	0.2	0.7
1990	82.0	21.7	16.5	12.1	0.3	7.1	0.1	0.5
1995	92.2	26.2	13.9	14.6	0.3	7.9	0.1	0.5
1996	89.6	27.1	13.8	14.0	0.3	7.1	*	0.5
1997	91.3	27.5	14.0	13.9	0.3	7.9	*	0.4
1998	93.6	28.4	14.3	13.8	0.3	8	*	0.4
1999	98.2	29.1	15.1	13.9	0.3	9.4	*	0.4
2000	96.2	29.5	14.9	13.3	0.3	8.7	*	0.4
2001	97.0	30.1	14.8	13.2	0.2	8.5	*	0.4
2002	98.2	30.5	15.3	13.0	0.2	8.7	*	0.4

(continued)

TABLE A.4 *(continued)*

YEAR	DEATH	CANCER	HEART DISEASE	VASCULAR BRAIN DISEASE	TUBERCULOSIS	PNEUMONIA, BRONCHITIS	GASTROENTERITIS	INFANT MORTALITY
2003	101.5	31.0	16.0	13.2	0.2	9.5	*	0.3
2004	102.9	32.0	16.0	12.9	0.2	9.6	*	0.3
2005	108.4	32.6	17.3	13.3	0.2	10.7	*	0.3
2006	108.4	32.9	17.3	12.8	0.2	10.7	*	0.3
2007	110.8	33.6	17.6	12.7	0.2	11	*	0.3
2008	114.2	34.3	18.2	12.7	0.2	11.5	*	0.3
2009	114.2	34.4	18.1	12.2	0.2	11.2	*	0.3
2010	119.7	35.3	18.9	12.3	0.2	11.9	*	0.2
2011	125.3	35.7	19.5	12.4	0.2	12.5	*	0.2
2012	125.6	36.1	19.9	12.2	0.2	12.4	*	0.2
2013	126.8	36.4	19.7	12.3	0.2	12.3	*	0.2
2014	127.3	36.8	19.7	11.4	0.2	12	*	0.2
2015	129.0	37.0	19.6	11.2	0.2	12.1	*	0.2
2016	130.8	37.3	19.8	10.9	0.2	11.9	*	0.2
2017	134.0	37.3	20.5	11.0	0.2	9.7	*	0.2
2018	136.2	37.3	20.8	10.8	0.2	9.5	*	0.2

Source: Ministry of Health and Welfare, "Jinkō Dōtai Tokei" [Demographic statistics]; Ministry of Health, Labor, and Welfare, "Jinkō Dōtai Chōsa" [Demographic research].

Note: As a result of a revised classification of diseases (compliant with the World Health Organization's International Classification of Diseases and Related Health Problems 10), the classifications of "pneumonia/bronchitis" and "gastroenteritis" were abolished in 1995.

Notes

INTRODUCTION

1. John C. Campbell and Naoki Ikegami, *The Art of Balance in Health Policy: Maintaining Japan's Low-Cost, Egalitarian System* (New York: Cambridge University Press, 1998). It has been noted that Japan, because it used different definitions of long-term and preventive care before 2010, ranked lower in the amount of expenditures than the country should have. Japan's health care expenditure per capita remains low, however, even though the country is the fastest-aging society in the world. See Japan Medical Association, "International Comparison of Health Care Data: OECD Health Statistics 2016," http://dl.med.or.jp/dl-med/teireikaiken/20160907_1.pdf, accessed December 18, 2017.

2. English translations of Japanese acts, committees, and other bodies are based on the database of the Ministry of Justice. The Ministry of Justice, "Japanese Law Translation," http://www.japaneselawtranslation.go.jp/?re=01, accessed December 31, 2019. If a particular name does not have a translation, I refer to similar ones.

3. Campbell and Ikegami, *The Art of Balance in Health Policy.*

4. Yoneyuki Sugita, *Japan's Shifting Status in the World and the Development of Japan's Medical Insurance Systems* (Singapore: Springer, 2019).

5. Kawakami Takeshi, *Gendai Nihon Iryōshi* (History of modern Japanese health care) (Tokyo: Keisō Shobō, 1965).

6. Sugaya Akira, *Nihon Iryō Seidoshi* (History of Japanese medical institutions) (Tokyo: Hara Shobō, 1976); Akira Sugaya, *Nihon Iryō Seisakushi* (History of Japanese medical policy) (Tokyo: Nihon Hyōronsha, 1977).

7. Yoshihara Kenji and Wada Masaru, *Nihon Iryōhoken Seidoshi* (History of Japanese health insurance) (Tokyo: Tōyō Keizai Shuppansha, 1999). Other works on the health insurance system include Shimazaki Kenji, *Nihon no Iryō: Seido to Seisaku* (Medical care in Japan: Institutions and policy) (Tokyo: Tokyo Daigaku Shuppankai, 2011).

8. Sōmae Kiyosada, *Nihon Iryō no Kindaishi: Seido Keisei no Rekishi Bunseki* (A modern history of Japanese health care: Historical analysis of institutional development) (Kyoto: Minerva Shobō, 2020).

9. Paul Pierson, "Not Just What but When: Timing and Sequence in Political Process," *Studies in American Political Development* 14, no. 1 (Spring 2000): 72.

10. Ruth B. Collier and David Collier, *Shaping the Political Arena: Critical Junctures, the Labor Movement, and Regime Dynamics in Latin America* (Princeton, NJ: Princeton University Press, 1991).

11. Pierson, "Not Just What but When," 75.

12. William E. Steslicke, *Doctors in Politics: The Political Life of the Japan Medical Association* (New York: Praeger, 1973).

13. Nomura Taku, *Nihon Ishikai* (The Japan Medical Association) (Tokyo: Keisō Shobō, 1976).

14. For a detailed history of Japanese medicine, see Sakai Shizu, *Nihon no Iryōshi* (Medical history of Japan) (Tokyo: Tokyo Shoseki, 1982).

15. Kosoto Hiroshi, *Kanpō no Rekishi* (The History of Kanpō) (Tokyo: Taishūkan Shoten, 2014), 120–24. Wake was another prominent medical family that served in the court.

16. Ogawa Teizō, *Igaku no Rekishi* (History of Medicine) (Tokyo: Chūōkōron Shinsha, 1964), 54.

17. Kosoto, *Kanpō no Rekishi*, 152–57.

18. Ōtomo converted to Christianity in 1578.

19. Ogawa, *Igaku no Rekishi*, 96–98; Margaret Powell and Masahira Anesaki, *Health Care in Japan* (London: Routledge, 1990), 19–20.

20. Sugaya, *Nihon Iryō Seidoshi*, 3.

21. Ogawa, *Igaku no Rekishi*, 98; Sugaya, *Nihon Iryō Seidoshi*, 4.

22. Sōmae, *Nihon Iryō no Kindaishi*, 55.

23. Kosoto, *Kanpō no Rekishi*, 177–81. Kosoto mentions that the number of published medical books in that period in Japan may be more than there are in contemporary China.

24. Ryōtaku Maeda, the Nakatsu Domain's official doctor, helped with the translation.

25. This is the predecessor institution of the Medical School of Nagasaki University.

26. Ogawa, *Igaku no Rekishi*, 166.

27. Ogawa, *Igaku no Rekishi*, 156.

28. The institute was initially established as a place for research and smallpox prevention.

29. Ogawa, *Igaku no Rekishi*, 149, 161–62.

1. WESTERNIZING MEDICINE

1. The Second Sino-Japanese War began in July 1937.

2. Ogawa Teizō, *Igaku no Rekishi* (History of Medicine) (Tokyo: Chūōkōron Shinsha, 1964), 164.

3. Of the 266 domains, 96 had systems of medical education and medical regulations. Kawakami Takeshi, *Gendai Nihon Iryōshi* (History of modern Japanese health care) (Tokyo: Keisō Shobō, 1965), 163.

4. Kawakami, *Gendai Nihon Iryōshi*, 122.

5. Sugaya Akira, *Nihon Iryō Seidoshi* (History of Japanese medical institutions) (Tokyo: Hara Shobō, 1976), 6.

6. Kawakami, *Gendai Nihon Iryōshi*, 91.

7. Kosoto Hiroshi, *Kanpō no Rekishi* (The history of Kanpō) (Tokyo: Taishūkan Shoten, 2014), 216.

8. Sugaya, *Nihon Iryō Seidoshi*, 7–8.

9. Kanokogi Toshinori, "Meiji Shonen no Doitsu Igaku no Dōnyū ni tsuite" (The introduction of German medicine at the beginning of the Meiji era), *Journal of Tokyo University Archives* 7 (March 1989): 3.

10. Sugaya, *Nihon Iryō Seidoshi*, 8–9.

11. Sugaya, *Nihon Iryō Seidoshi*, 11–12.

12. Sugaya, *Nihon Iryō Seidoshi*, 12.

13. Murakami Kimiko, "Rodōgyōsei no Sōshutsukatei: Shokusankōgyō Seisaku to Jinryoku Seisaku no Tōgō" (The development of Japanese industrial policy and human resources management in the Early Meiji Era), *Journal of the Department of Social Welfare, Kansai University of Social Welfare* 14, no. 2 (March 2011): 58; Kawakami, *Gendai Nihon Iryōshi*, 105.

14. Sugaya, *Nihon Iryō Seidoshi*, 24.

15. Sugaya, *Nihon Iryō Seidoshi*, 23.

16. For an account of the establishment of Tokyo Imperial University's medical faculty, see Ogawa, *Igaku no Rekishi*, 170.

17. With Takamori Saigo's assistance, Willis moved to the Satsuma Domain with an exceptionally high salary. Kanokogi, "Meiji Shonen no Doitsu Igaku no Dōnyū ni tsuite," 5–14.

18. Sugaya, *Nihon Iryō Seidoshi*, 51–52, 56.

19. Sugaya, *Nihon Iryō Seidoshi*, 59.

20. Margaret Powell and Masahira Anesaki, *Health Care in Japan* (London: Routledge, 1990), 30.

21. Sugaya, *Nihon Iryō Seidoshi*, 63.

22. Sugaya, *Nihon Iryō Seidoshi*, 39.

23. Sugaya, *Nihon Iryō Seidoshi*, 42.

24. Sugaya, *Nihon Iryō Seidoshi*, 42.

25. Existing solo practitioners and their sons were allowed to practice without passing the exam. Sugaya Akira, *Nihon Iryō Seisakushi* (History of Japanese medical policy) (Tokyo: Nihon Hyōronsha, 1977), 39.

26. Sugaya, *Nihon Iryō Seisakushi*, 101.

27. Kōseishō Gojūnenshi Henshū Iinkai, *Kōseishō Gojūnenshi* (Fifty-year history of the Ministry of Welfare, documentary volume) (Tokyo: Chūō Hōki Shuppan, 1988), 57. There were 28,262 medical doctors: 23,015 doctors of Kanpō medicine and 5,247 doctors of Western medicine.

28. Fuse Shōichi, *Ishi no Rekishi: Sono Nihonteki Tokuchō* (History of doctors: Its Japaneseness) (Tokyo: Chūō Kōronsha, 1979), 146.

29. Yoshihara Kenji and Wada Masaru, *Nihon Iryō Hoken Seidoshi* (History of Japanese health insurance) (Tokyo: Tōyō Keizai Shinpōsha, 1999), 24.

30. Ogawa, *Igaku no Rekishi*, 210.

31. Ando Yūichiro, *Edo no Yōseijo* (Yōseijo Hospital of Edo) (Tokyo: PHP Kenkyūjo, 2005).

32. Kōsei Rōdō Tōkei Kyōkai, "Nihon no Iryōseido no Tokuchō wa sono Rekishi kara Umareta" (The uniqueness of how the Japanese medical system originated and its history), *Kōsei no Shihyō* 63, no. 11 (September 2016): 50, http://www.hws-kyokai.or.jp /images/book/chiikiiryo-3.pdf, accessed July 5, 2019.

33. Sugaya, *Nihon Iryō Seidoshi*, 96–109. In addition, the war led the Tokugawa shogunate to create its Naval Training Center in 1867, and in the following year the shogunate transformed its School of Medical Science into the Navy and Army hospitals.

34. Sugaya, *Nihon Iryō Seidoshi*, 42.

35. For more on the history of Juntendo Hospital, see Sakai Shizu, "Juntendo Iin no Konjaku" (The Past and Present of Juntendo Hospital), https://www.juntendo.ac.jp/corp /history/time, accessed November 10, 2019.

36. For the history of Jikei Hospital, see "Enkaku" (History and development), https:// www.hosp.jikei.ac.jp/about/history.html, accessed November 10, 2019.

37. Sugaya, *Nihon Iryō Seisakushi*, 102, 146.

38. Regarding the administrative agency, there was a difference between the western region and eastern region. In the early Meiji era, many former domain hospitals were turned into public hospitals in the west. But since not so many domains in the east had hospitals, people established voluntary hospitals. Sugaya, *Nihon Iryō Seidoshi*, 122.

39. Sugaya, *Nihon Iryō Seisakushi*, 42; Sugaya, *Nihon Iryō Seidoshi*, 109–7.

40. Sugaya, *Nihon Iryō Seisakushi*, 38.

41. Sugaya, *Nihon Iryō Seidoshi*, 124.

42. Kawakami, *Gendai Nihon Iryōshi*, 33, 193. The Boshin War (1868–69) was fought between the Tokugawa shogunate and forces that sought to establish a new government under the emperor. The Satsuma Rebellion or Seinan War (1877) was the largest civil war fought by descendants of the samurai class in the Meiji era, the last domestic war in Japan.

43. Sugaya, *Nihon Iryō Seidoshi*, 18. Japan's Hygiene Bureau was established seventy-four years after France's, twenty-eight years after Britain's, and a few years after the United States'. Kawakami, *Gendai Nihon Iryōshi*, 115.

44. For more on Nagayo's life, see Matsumoto Jun, Nagayo Sensai, Ogawa Kenzo, and Sakai Shizu, *Matsumoto Jun Jiden, Nagayo Sensai Jiden* (Biography of Matsumoto Jun and biography of Nagayo Sensai) (Tokyo: Heibonsha, 1980).

45. Sugaya, *Nihon Iryō Seisakushi*, 38.

46. Sugaya, *Nihon Iryō Seidoshi*, 18–22.

47. Sōmae Kiyosada, *Nihon Iryō no Kindaishi: Seido Keisei no Rekishi Bunseki* (A Modern history of Japanese health care: Historical analysis of institutional development) (Kyoto: Minerva Shobō, 2020), 77.

48. Sugaya, *Nihon Iryō Seisakushi*, 39–41.

49. Kōseishō Gojūnenshi Henshū Iinkai, *Kōseishō Gojūnenshi*, 141.

50. Sugaya *Nihon Iryō Seidoshi*, 240; Kawakami, *Gendai Nihon Iryōshi*, 231.

51. Sugaya *Nihon Iryō Seidoshi*, 242.

52. Medical vocational schools developed mainly for those who studied for the national licensing exam. Most of the schools did not have any requirements to enter and complete the program, because many students studied there simply to pass the exam. In 1903, these vocational schools were standardized as medical vocational schools (*igaku senmon gakkō*). Ikegami Naoki, *Nihon no Iryō to Kaigo* (Japan's health and long-term care system) (Tokyo: Nihon Keizai Shimbun Shuppansha, 2017), 15.

53. Sugaya, *Nihon Iryō Seidoshi*, 243. Sōhaku Asai served as an official doctor for the Tokugawa shogunate and later for the Imperial Household in addition to practitioners of Western medicine. Kosoto, *Kanpō no Rekishi*, 193–98.

54. Kawakami, *Gendai Nihon Iryōshi*, 231–32. See also William E. Steslicke, *Doctors in Politics: The Political Life of the Japan Medical Association* (New York: Praeger, 1973), 38. Although the regulations prohibited doctors from being licensed exclusively in Kanpō, licensed doctors were allowed to practice Kanpō as part of their treatments.

55. Sugaya, *Nihon Iryō Seisakushi*, 39

56. Kosoto, *Kanpō no Rekishi*, 217.

57. Sugaya, *Nihon Iryō Seisakushi*, 47.

58. Sugaya, *Nihon Iryō Seidoshi*, 49.

59. Kawakami, *Gendai Nihon Iryōshi*, 155; Ogawa, *Igaku no Rekishi*, 211–12. Asada Sōhaku, another prominent Kanpō doctor, had died in 1895.

60. Sugaya, *Nihon Iryō Seidoshi*, 241.

61. The second imperial university, Kyoto Imperial University, was established in 1897.

62. Steslicke, *Doctors in Politics*, 40. See also Sugaya, *Nihon Iryō Seidoshi*, 47.

63. William E. Steslicke, "The Political Life of the Japan Medical Association," *Journal of Asian Studies* 31 no. 4 (1972): 845.

64. Nihon Ishikai Sōritsu Gojusshūnen Kinen Jigyō Suishin Iinkai, *Nihon Ishikai Sōritsu Kinenshi: Sengo Gojūnen no Ayumi* (Anniversary of the founding of the Japan Medical Association: Fifty years of progress after World War II) (Tokyo: Nihon Ishikai, 1997), 6. The Japan Doctors Alliance (Nihon Rengō Ishikai) was formed in 1914 and became a precursor of the Greater Japan Medical Association.

65. Kitasato did not receive the Nobel Prize. It was awarded to his research colleague, Emil von Behring. For more about Kitasato, see Christopher Aldous and Akihito Suzuki, *Reforming Public Health in Occupied Japan, 1945–52: Alien Prescription?* (London: Routledge, 2012), 28–31.

66. Ogawa, *Igaku no Rekishi*, 199. Morimura Ichizaemon was a wealthy merchant. Fukuzawa Yukichi was the founder of Keio University, a private university. Kitasato later helped Fukuzawa create the medical faculty for Keio University.

67. Kitajima Taichi, *Kitajima Taichi Jiden* (Autobiography of Taichi Kitajima) (Tokyo: Kitajima Sensei Kinen Jigyōkai, 1955), 41.

68. Kitajima, *Kitajima Taichi Jiden*, 92.

69. Miwa Kazuo, *Mōi Takemi Tarō* (The fighting doctor, Tarō Takemi) (Tokyo: Tokuma Shoten, 1995), 161.

70. Nihon Ishikai Sōritsu Gojusshūnen Kinen Jigyō Suishin Iinkai, *Nihon Ishikai Sōritsu Kinenshi*, 7.

71. Kōseishō Gojūnenshi Henshū Iinkai, *Kōseishō Gojūnenshi*, 62. Kanpō doctors rarely performed surgical procedures.

72. Sugaya, *Nihon Iryō Seidoshi*, 441.

73. Kawakami, *Gendai Nihon Iryōshi*, 206–7.

74. Sugaya, *Nihon Iryō Seisakushi*, 38.

75. Kawakami, *Gendai Nihon Iryōshi*, 209–10.

76. Sugaya, *Nihon Iryō Seidoshi*, 445–46.

77. Nihon Ishikai Sōritsu Gojusshūnen Kinen Jigyō Suishin Iinkai, *Nihon Ishikai Sōritsu Kinenshi*, 5.

78. Kawakami, *Gendai Nihon Iryōshi*, 232.

79. Sugaya, *Nihon Iryō Seidoshi*, 445–46.

80. Kawakami, *Gendai Nihon Iryōshi*, 242.

81. Kawakami, *Gendai Nihon Iryōshi*, 212.

2. REACTING TO DETERIORATING HEALTH

1. For the history of political development during the Meiji period, see Carol Gluck, *Japan's Modern Myths: Ideology in the Late Meiji Period* (New York: Columbia University Press, 1985).

2. Elise K. Tipton, *Modern Japan: A Social and Political History* (Oxford: Routledge, 2002), 97.

3. For the nature of the Taishō democracy, see Harukata Yakenaka, *Failed Democratization in Prewar Japan: Breakdown of a Hybrid Regime* (Stanford, CA: Stanford University Press, 2014).

4. For the rise of social movements during this period, see Sheldon Garon, "From Meiji to Heisei: The State and Civil Society in Japan," in *The State of Civil Society in Japan*, ed. Frank J. Schwartz and Susan Pharr (Cambridge: Cambridge University Press 2003), 50–54.

5. Sugaya Akira, *Nihon Iryō Seidoshi* (History of Japanese medical institutions) (Tokyo: Hara Shobō, 1976), 166. The labor movement at this time was influenced by the American Federation of Labor. Akira Sugaya, *Nihon Iryō Seisakushi* (History of Japanese medical policy) (Tokyo: Nihon Hyōronsha, 1977), 66.

6. Sugaya, *Nihon Iryō Seisakushi*, 78–84. For labor history during the Meiji period, see Andrew Gordon, *The Evolution of Labor Relations in Japan: Heavy Industry* (Cambridge, MA: Harvard University Press, 1985), 17–50.

7. Sugaya, *Nihon Iryō Seidoshi*, 172.

8. Murakami Kimiko, "Rodōgyōsei no Sōshutsukatei: Shokusankōgyō Seisaku to Jinryoku Seisaku no Tōgō" (Co-development of Japanese industrial policy and human resources management in the early Meiji era), *Journal of the Department of Social Welfare, Kansai University of Social Welfare* 14, no. 2 (March 2011): 61–62.

9. Gotō Shinpei, "Shitsubyō no Hokenhō" (Sickness insurance), in *Nihon Shakaihoshō Zenshi Shiryō: Shakaihoken*, ed. Shakaihoshō Kenkyūsho (Prehistory of Japanese social security: Social insurance) (Tokyo: Shiseidō, 1981), 6–12.

10. Kawakami Takeshi, *Gendai Nihon Iryōshi* (History of modern Japanese health care) (Tokyo: Keisō Shobō, 1965), 351. The first mutual aid association in a state-owned firm was established as a voluntary program at Yahata Steel Company. Sugaya, *Nihon Iryō Seisakushi*, 67.

11. Sugaya, *Nihon Iryō Seisakushi*, 67–70.

12. Sugaya, *Nihon Iryō Seisakushi*, 286–88.

13. The health of female workers was a problem according to the research results of the Ministry of Agriculture and Commerce. Many female factory workers died from tuberculosis. Moreover, many female workers returned home with tuberculosis and infected others. The health of female workers gained more public attention after Ishihara Osamu's publication in 1914. He analyzed the research results of the Ministry of Agriculture and Commerce. Ishihara Osamu, *Eiseigakujō yori Mitaru Jokō no Genjō* (The state of female factory workers from the perspective of hygiene) (Tokyo: Kokka Igakkai, 1914).

14. Sugaya, *Nihon Iryō Seisakushi*, 78–80. In 1923, the Factory Act Amendment was passed, reducing the number of employees that a firm had to have to be covered by the Factory Act from fifteen to ten. Working hours were also further limited to eleven hours. This was the standard until the Labor Standards Act of 1947.

15. Sugaya, *Nihon Iryō Seisakushi*, 47.

16. For a detailed history of Suzuki and Kato, see Tanaka Shōzō, *Iryō no Shakaika wo Jissen shita Jinbutsu Suzuki Umeshirō* (Suzuki Umeshirō: The person who put socialized medicine into practice) (Tokyo: Ishikenkyūkai, 1995); Takasu Yukio, "Kato Tokijirō nit suite" (About Kato Tokijirō), *Journal of the Japanese Society for the History of Medicine* 60, no. 4 (2014): 417–19.

17. Kawakami, *Gendai Nihon Iryōshi*, 45–46; Sugaya, *Nihon Iryō Seidoshi*, 185–93.

18. Sugaya, *Nihon Iryō Seidoshi*, 193.

19. Iseki Tomotoshi, *Jichitai Byōin no Rekishi: Jūmin Iryō no Ayumi to Korekara* (The history of municipal hospitals: The past and future of grassroots medicine) (Tokyo: Miwa Shoten, 2014), 107–8.

20. Sugaya, *Nihon Iryō Seidoshi*, 197.

21. In 1928, 38 percent of doctors practiced in urban areas. By 1932, however, the percentage had increased to 55 percent, and by 1936 to 58 percent. Sugaya, *Nihon Iryō Seidoshi*, 196–98.

22. Sugaya, *Nihon Iryō Seidoshi*, 201. For more about how the Industrial Cooperative Act played a role in rural areas, see Adam Sheingate, *The Rise of the Agricultural Welfare State: Institutions and Interest Group Power in the United States, France, and Japan* (Princeton, NJ: Princeton University Press, 2001), 67–70.

23. Inazō Nitobe, *Bushido, the Soul of Japan: An Exposition of Japanese Thought* (New York: G. P. Putnam's Sons, 1905); Kagawa Toyohiko, *Shisen wo Koete* (Facing the death lines) (1920; repr., Tokyo: Shakaishisōsha, 1983).

24. Aoki Ikuo, "Tokyo Iryō Riyō Kumiai no Setsuritsuninka wo Meguru Shotairitsu Taikōkankei" (Conflicts and confrontations regarding the Tokyo Medical Cooperative), *Journal of Hannan University the Hannan Ronshu Humanities and Natural Science* 49 no. 2 (March 2014): 95–98.

25. Sugaya, *Nihon Iryō Seidoshi*, 199–201.

26. Sugaya, *Nihon Iryō Seisakushi*, 63–64. The members also received half of their wages after a four-day absence. Mutō Sanji was a Keio University graduate who went to the United States for three years and had a chance to study at the University of the Pacific in San Jose, California. In 1921, he became the president of Kanebo Ltd. He then began to get involved in politics. He formed the Business Fellowship (Jitsugō Dōshikai) Party in 1923 and won a seat in the lower house in 1924. For more about Mutō, see "Sanji Muto: Timeless Messages," https://www.pacific.edu/university-libraries/services/seeds-of-the-sakura.html, accessed December 25, 2019.

27. Mutō Sanji, *Watashi no Minouebanashi* (My life story) (Hyōgo: Mutō Kinta, 1934).

28. Sugaya, *Nihon Iryō Seisakushi*, 66–67. Ajin Mine, which was established in 1888, had the first mutual aid association in Japan.

29. Kawakami, *Gendai Nihon Iryōshi*, 314.

30. Saguchi Takashi, "Kokumin Kenkōhoken to Iryō no Shakaika" (National Health Insurance and the socialization of medicine), *Toshi Mondai* 49, no. 11 (October 1958): 4.

31. Sugaya, *Nihon Iryō Seisakushi*, 24–36.

32. Sugaya, *Nihon Iryō Seisakushi*, 161.

33. Sugaya, *Nihon Iryō Seisakushi*, 115.

34. Sugaya, *Nihon Iryō Seisakushi*, 122.

35. Sugaya, *Nihon Iryō Seisakushi*, 115.

36. Kenneth B. Pyle, *The Making of Modern Japan* (Lexington, MA: Heath, 1978), 170; Kasahara Hidehiko, *Nihon no Iryō Gyōsei: Sono Rekishi to Kadai* (Japanese health-care administration: Its history and problems) (Tokyo: Keio University Press, 1999), 81; Sugaya, *Nihon Iryō Seisakushi*, 119–20. For more on party politics of this period, see Elise K. Tipton, *Modern Japan: A Social and Political History* (New York: Routledge, 2002), 90–94.

37. Kawakami, *Gendai Nihon Iryōshi*, 353; Sugaya, *Nihon Iryō Seisakushi*, 115, 119; Egi Tsubasa and Kataoka Naoyasu, "Shitsubyōhoken Hōan ni tsuiteno Setsumei" (Explanation of the Sickness Insurance Plan), in *Nihon Shakaihoshō Zenshi Shiryō: Shakaihoken*, ed. Shakaihoshō Kenkyūsho (Pre-history of Japanese social security: Social insurance) (Tokyo: Shiseidō, 1981), 42–53, Kōseishō Gojūnenshi Henshū Iinkai, *Kōseishō Gojūnenshi: Kijutsu Hen* (Fifty-year history of the Ministry of Welfare, documentary volume) (Tokyo: Chūō Hōki Shuppan, 1988), 316; Nakashizu Michi, *Iryō Hoken no Gyōsei to Seiji* (Administration and politics of health insurance) (Tokyo: Yoshikawa Kōbunkan, 1998).

38. As quoted in Sugaya, *Nihon Iryō Seisakushi*, 122.

39. Derek Fraser, *The Evolution of the British Welfare State: A History of Social Policy since the Industrial Revolution* (London: Palgrave Macmillan, 1973). With this act, Britain became the first country to have national compulsory unemployment insurance.

40. Michael Stolleis, *Origins of the German Welfare State: Social Policy in Germany to 1945* (Heidelberg: Springer, 2013).

41. Nishimura Mariko, Nihon Saisho no Kenkōhoken Hō (1922nen) no Seiritsu to Shakaiseisaku: Kyūsaijigyō kara Shakaiseisaku heno Tenkan" (Establishment of the first Health Insurance Act [1922] in Japan and social policy: A turning point from charity to social policy), *Keio Journal of Economics* 83, no. 1 (September 1990): 145; Sugaya, *Nihon Iryō Seisakushi*, 116.

42. Kōseishō Imu Kyoku, *Isei Hyakunen* (One-hundred-year history of medicine) (Tokyo: Gyōsei, 1976), 222.

43. Yamamoto Tatsuo, "Daijin no Aisatsu no Yōshi" (Summary of minister's explanation), in *Nihon Shakaihoshō Zenshi Shiryō* (Prehistory of Japanese social security: Social insurance), ed. Shakaihoshō Kenkyūsho (Tokyo: Shiseidō, 1981), 65.

44. The Mining Act was created in 1905 for mining industry workers. When the Factory Act passed in 1916, the Mining Act was amended to provide the same benefits for miners as provided other workers in the Factory Act. See Sugaya, *Nihon Iryō Seisakushi*, 75–76.

45. Dependents were not covered until they began to be covered with a 50 percent co-payment in 1942. For more about the HI program, see Ryūji Kitahara, *Kenkōhoken to Ishikai: Shakaihoken Sōshiki niokeru Ishi to Iryō* (The health insurance system and the JMA: Doctors and medicine at the beginning of social health insurance) (Tokyo: Tōshindō, 1999), 20.

46. Sugaya, *Nihon Iryō Seisakushi*, 132.

47. Kumiai Kanshō Hoken is translated by some as Association-Managed Health Insurance.

48. Sugaya, *Nihon Iryō Seisakushi*, 123–28.

49. Sugaya, *Nihon Iryō Seisakushi*, 132.

50. Yoneyuki Sugita, "The 1922 Japanese Health Insurance Law: Toward a Corporatist Framework," *Harvard Asian Quarterly* 14, no. 4 (2012): 36–43.

51. Sugita, "The 1922 Japanese Health Insurance Law," 41–42.

52. Sakaguchi Masayuki, *Nihon Kenkōhokenhō Seiritsushi Ron* (History of health insurance acts in Japan) (Kyoto: Kōyō Shobō, 1985), 177, 295.

53. For a summary of the JMA's development, see Takakazu Yamagishi, "The Japan Medical Association and Its Political Development," *Academia Social Sciences* 9 (June 2015): 129–39.

54. William E. Steslicke, "The Political Life of the Japan Medical Association," *Journal of Asian Studies* 31, no. 4 (August 1972), 845.

55. Nihon Ishikai Sōritsu Gojusshūnen Kinen Jigyō Suishin Iinkai, *Nihon Ishikai Sōritsu Kinenshi: Sengo Gojūnen no Ayumi* (Anniversary of the founding of the Japan Medical Association: Fifty-years of progress after World War II) (Tokyo: Nihon Ishikai, 1997), 7.

56. Kawakami, *Gendai Nihon Iryōshi*, 242.

57. Sugaya, *Nihon Iryō Seidoshi*, 264.

58. Ikura Yasumasa, *Shindan Takemi Tarō* (Evaluating Tarō Takemi) (Tokyo: Sōshisha, 1979), 50.

59. Kitajima Taichi, *Kitajima Taichi Jiden* (Biography of Taichi Kitajima) (Tokyo: Kitajima Sensei Kinen Jigyōkai, 1955), 18.

60. Saguchi, "Kokumin Kenkōhoken to Iryō no Shakaika," 4.

61. Kawakami, *Gendai Nihon Iryōshi*, 357.

62. Kitahara, *Kenkōhoken to Ishikai*, 71.

63. Kawakami, *Gendai Nihon Iryōshi*, 358.

64. American Medical Association, *Caring for the Country: A History and Celebration of the First 150 Years of the American Medical Association* (Chicago: American Medical Association, 1997).

65. Ikura, *Shindan Takemi Tarō*, 50.

66. Sugaya, *Nihon Iryō Seisakushi*, 355; Nomura Taku, *Nihon Ishikai* (The Japan Medical Association) (Tokyo: Keisō Shobō, 1976), 67.

67. Saguchi, "Kokumin Kenkōhoken to Iryō no Shakaika," 4.

68. Saguchi, "Kokumin Kenkōhoken to Iryō no Shakaika," 4; Kōno Sumiko, "Kenkōhokenhō Seiritsukatei no Shitekikōsatsu" (Historical study of the process of the formation of the Health Insurance Act in Japan), *Shakai Kankyō Kenkyū* 1 (March 1996): 25.

69. As quoted in Nihon Ishikai Sōritsu Gojusshūnen Kinen Jigyō Suishin Iinkai, *Nihon Ishikai Sōritsu Kinenshi*, 5.

70. Sugaya, *Nihon Iryō Seidoshi*, 265.

71. Steslicke, "Political Life of the Japan Medical Association," 847.

72. Kitajima, *Kitajima Taichi Jiden*, 19.

3. IMPROVING PEOPLE'S HEALTH FOR WAR

1. Different countries call this incident by different names. Many Japanese call it the Rokōkyō Bridge Incident; many Chinese and Koreans call it the July 7th Incident. It is called the Marco Polo Bridge Incident in many Western nations, after Marco Polo, who mentioned the bridge in his journal.

2. Naikaku Kanbō, ed., *Naikaku Seido 70 nenshi* (Tokyo: Ōkura Insatsukyoku, 1955); Kōseishō Gojūnenshi Henshū Iinkai, *Kōseishō Gojūnenshi: Shiryō Hen* (Fifty-year history of the Ministry of Welfare, data volume) (Tokyo: Chūō Hōki Shuppan, 1988), 621.

3. Sugaya Akira, *Nihon Iryō Seisakushi* (History of Japanese medical policy) (Tokyo: Nihon Hyōronsha, 1977), 175.

4. Kawakami Takeshi, *Gendai Nihon Iryōshi* (History of modern Japanese health care) (Tokyo: Keisō Shobō, 1965), 379–80; Sugaya Akira, *Nihon Iryō Seidoshi* (History of Japanese medical institutions) (Tokyo: Hara Shobō, 1976), 218–25.

5. Saguchi Takashi, "Kokumin Kenkōhoken to Iryō no Shakaika" (National health insurance and the socialization of medicine), *Toshi Mondai* 49, no. 11 (October 1958): 2.

6. For a more detailed description of how the war's progress affected the development of health insurance policy and health care administration, see Takakazu Yamagishi, *War and Health Insurance Policy in Japan and the United States: World War II to Postwar Reconstruction* (Baltimore: Johns Hopkins University Press, 2011), chap. 3.

7. Furukawa Takahisa, "Kakushinkanryō no Shisō to Kōdō" (The thought and practice of reformist bureaucrats in Japan, 1935–1945), *Shigaku Zasshi* 99, no. 4 (1990): 457–64.

8. Furukawa, "Kakushinkanryō no Shisō to Kōdō," 466–72.

9. Furukawa, "Kakushinkanryō no Shisō to Kōdō," 470.

10. Furukawa, "Kakushinkanryō no Shisō to Kōdō," 474.

11. Furukawa, "Kakushinkanryō no Shisō to Kōdō," 465.

12. Takata Kioaki, *Nadao Hirokichi* (Hiroshima: Chūgoku Shinbunsha, 1991), 57.

13. Kawakami, *Gendai Nihon Iryōshi*, 353.

14. Sugaya, *Nihon Iryō Seisakushi*, 39.

15. "Kokumin no Hoken Kakuritsusaku: 'Eiseishō' Secchi wo Teishō" (Proposal to improve the people's health care: Proposing the establishment of the Ministry of Hygiene), *Tokyo Asahi Shimbun*, June 26, 1936.

16. As quoted in Shō Kashin, *Nihongata Fukushi Kokka no Keisei to Jūgonen Sensō* (The fifteen–year war and the formation of the Japanese welfare state) (Kyoto: Minerva Shobō, 1998), 46.

17. Kojima Kazutaka, "Nihon Shakaifukushi Gyōsei no Keisei to Kōseisho Sōsetsu" (Japanese social welfare administration), *Japan Association of Legal and Political Sciences* 33 (1997): 196.

18. For more about the political role of the military, see Tsutsui Kiyotada, *Shōwa Jūnendai no Rikugun to Seiji: Gunbu Daijin Geneki Bukan Sei no Kyozō to Jitsuzō* (The army and politics from mid-1930s to mid-1940: The virtual image and real image of the system that military ministers are to be active-duty officers) (Tokyo: Iwanami Shoten, 2007).

19. Koizumi was born in 1884 in Fukui Prefecture, the third son of Chikamasa Koizumi, an Army medical doctor. Chikahiko Koizumi earned an MD degree from Tokyo Imperial University in 1908 and a PhD in medicine, also from Tokyo Imperial University, in 1921. From March 1934 to December 1938, he headed the army's Medical Bureau. He became the minister of health and welfare in July 1941 and remained in that position until July 1944. He committed suicide in September 1945. Nihon Kindai Shiryō Kenkyūkai, ed., *Nihon Riku Kai Gun no Seido, Soshiki, Jinji* (Institution, organization, and personal affairs of the Japanese Army and Navy) (Tokyo: Tokyo University Press, 1971), 29.

20. Kojima, "Nihon Shakaifukushi Gyōsei no Keisei to Kōseisho Sōsetsu," 201.

21. As quoted in Kojima, "Nihon Shakaifukushi Gyōsei no Keisei to Kōseisho Sōsetsu," 201.

22. Kōseishō Gojūnenshi Henshū Iinkai, *Kōseishō Gojūnenshi: Kijutsu Hen* (Fifty-year history of the Ministry of Welfare, description volume) (Tokyo: Chūō Hōki Shuppan, 1988), 379.

23. Kawakami, *Gendai Nihon Iryōshi*, 428; Kōseishō Gojūnenshi Henshū Iinkai, *Kōseishō Gojūnenshi*, 342, 380. Under the Meiji Constitution, resignation of the cabinet had to take place if all the cabinet members did not agree.

24. "Kōseishō no Shimei to Igi: Gyōseibunka no Daiisseki" (The significance of the MHW: A step toward division of administrative labors), *Yomiuri Shimbun*, January 8, 1938.

25. Kojima, "Nihon Shakaifukushi Gyōsei no Keisei to Kōseisho Sōsetsu," 197–98.

26. Kojima, "Nihon Shakaifukushi Gyōsei no Keisei to Kōseisho Sōsetsu," 201–3.

27. Kojima, "Nihon Shakaifukushi Gyōsei no Keisei to Kōseisho Sōsetsu," 198.

28. Toshio Tatara, "1,400 Years of Japanese Social Work: From Its Origins through the Allied Occupation, 552–1952" (PhD diss., Bryn Mawr College, 1975), 186; Sugaya, *Nihon Iryō Seidoshi*, 341.

29. Koizumi Chikahiko, *Kokumin Tairyoku no Genjō wo Nobe Kokumin no Funki wo Nozomu* (The current condition of people's strength and my hope for people's action) (Tokyo: Kokumin Seishin Sōdōin Chūō Dōmei, 1938), 4–5.

30. "Kōseishō no Kaisetsu" (Opening of the Ministry of Health and Welfare), *Yomiuri Shimbun*, January 11, 1938.

31. Takei Gunji, *Kōseishō Shōshi: Watashi no Zaikinroku kara* (A short history of the Ministry of Health and Welfare) (Tokyo: Kōseishō Mondai Kenkyūkai, 1952), 3; Kōseishō Nijūnenshi Henshū Iinkai, *Koseishō Nijūnenshi* (Twenty-year history of the Ministry of Welfare) (Tokyo: Kosei Mondai Kenkyūkai, 1960), 118. See also Iwao Yamazaki, "Relief Measures for Soldiers' Families," *Foreign Affairs Association of Japan* 6 (1938): 673; and Miura Toyohiko, *Rōdō to Kenkō no Rekishi* (A history of workers and their health) (Kawasaki, Kanagawa: Rōdō Kagaku Kenkyūjo Shuppanbu, 1988), 383.

32. The Board of Military Protection was separated from the Bureau of Social Affairs as an external ministerial agency in July 1939. The Board of Insurance was reorganized as an internal ministerial agency in November 1942.

33. Tatara, "1,400 Years of Japanese Social Work," 188–90.

34. Kurosawa Fumitaka, *Taisenkanki no Nihon Rikugun* (The Japanese Army between World War I and World War II) (Tokyo: Misuzu Shobō, 2000), 390. The predecessor of the Planning Agency was the Cabinet Research Agency (Naikaku Chōsa Kyoku).

35. Furukawa Takahisa, "Shōwa 12nen–14nen no Kikakuin" (The Board of Planning from 1937 to 1939), *Shigaku Zasshi* 97, no. 10 (1988): 1683.

36. Furukawa, "Shōwa 12nen–14nen no Kikakuin," 1686; Ben-Ami Shillony, *Politics and Culture in Wartime Japan* (Oxford: Clarendon Press, 1981), 7–8.

37. Uemura Kōgorō, "Genka Senjitaisei no Gaiyō" (An overview of the current war mobilization), *Nihon Sangyō Eisei Kyōkai Kaihō* 90 (January 1938): 838; Ikuta Makoto, *Nihon Rikugunshi* (The history of the Japanese Army) (Tokyo: Kyōikusha, 1980), 165.

38. Kitahara Ryūji, *Kenkōhoken to Ishikai: Shakaihoken Sōshiki niokeru Ishi to Iryō* (The health insurance system and the JMA in Japan: Doctors and medicine at the beginning of social health insurance) (Tokyo: Tōshindō, 1999), 166, 221; Kōno Sumiko, "Kenkōhokenhō Seiritsukatei no Shitekikōsatsu" (Historical study about the process of formation of Health Insurance Law in Japan), *Shakai Kankyō Kenkyū* 1 (March 1996), 29. The Great Kanto Earthquake in September 1923 delayed the policy's implementation.

39. Kitahara, *Kenkōhoken to Ishikai*, 228–31. When the HI program was implemented, organized labor staged strikes against it (*kenpo suto*). These strikers claimed that workers now had to pay premiums to get care for occupation-related sicknesses and injuries that the Factory Act and the Miners Act had covered for free. Concerning the strike, see also Kawakami, *Gendai Nihon Iryōshi*, 33; Sugaya, *Nihon Iryō Seisakushi*, 132; Sakaguchi Masayuki, *Nihon Kenkōhokenhō Seiritsushi Ron* (History of health insurance acts in Japan) (Kyoto: Kōyō Shobō, 1985), 9–10, 255; and Kōseishō Gojūnenshi Henshū Iinkai, *Kōseishō Gojūnenshi*, 527.

40. Sugaya, *Nihon Iryō Seisakushi*, 137.

41. Takata, *Nadao Hirokichi*, 59.

42. Sugaya, *Nihon Iryō Seisakushi*, 178–80.

43. Richard M. Titmuss, *Essays on the Welfare State* (New Haven, CT: Yale University Press, 1959).

44. Tuberculosis gained attention during World War I. The Research Council on Health and Hygiene (Hoken Eisei Chōsakai) was established, and it discovered that tuberculosis was an especially serious problem with young people. In 1919, the government enacted the Tuberculosis Prevention Act (Kekkaku Yobō Hō). Sugaya, *Nihon Iryō Seisakushi*, 161.

45. Kōseishō Gojūnenshi Henshū Iinkai, *Kōseishō Gojūnenshi*, 91.

46. Sugaya, *Nihon Iryō Seisakushi*, 189.

47. "Donzoko no Nōmin Kyūsai: Kyūbō ni Mikanete Rikugun mo Tsuini Tatsu" (Relieving farmers: The Army Ministry finally gets involved in the Relief Project), *Yomiuri Shimbun*, June 7, 1932; "Rikugun no Kyūnō Taisaku: Sakujitu Gutaisaku Kōhyō saru" (The army's policy toward poor farmers: Detailed plan was released yesterday), *Chugai Shōgyō*, October 24, 1934.

48. Kawakami, *Gendai Nihon Iryōshi*, 419.

49. Suzuki Hitoshi, "Kokumin Kenkōhoken Seido Yōkōan ni taisuru Ichi Kōsatsu" (A thought about the National Health Insurance Bill), in *Nihon Shakaihoshō Zenshi Shiryō: Shakaihoken* (Early history of Japanese social security: Social insurance), ed. Shakaihoshō Kenkyūsho (Tokyo: Shiseidō, 1981), 114–15.

50. Kōseishō Hoken Kyoku Kokumin Kenkō Hoken Ka (Division of the National Health Insurance, Social Bureau, the Ministry of Health and Welfare) and Kokumin Kenkō Hoken Chūō Kai (National Health Insurance Association), *Kokumin Kenkōhoken Yonjūnenshi* (A forty-year history of National Health Insurance) (Tokyo: Gyōsei, 1979), 4.

51. Kōseishō Gojūnenshi Henshū Iinkai, *Kōseishō Gojūnenshi*, 375.

52. Ōe Shinobu, *Chōheisei* (The conscription system) (Tokyo: Iwanami Shinsho, 1981). Although a conscription system began in 1873, the military had relied mostly on volunteers, except in the case of major international wars, such as the Sino-Japanese War and the Russo-Japanese War.

53. Hirose Hisada, "Shakaihuan wo Nozoku Shakaiseisaku wo" (The establishment of social policy to get rid of social uncertainty), in Kōseishō Nijūnenshi Henshū Iinkai, *Koseishō Nijūnenshi*, 4.

54. "Idai Shigan Dokaheri: Kage Usuragu Igakusei" (A big drop in medical school applicants: A dark cloud over medical school students), *Osaka Asahi Shimbun*, March 24, 1937.

55. As quoted in Kōseishō Gojūnenshi Henshū Iinkai, *Kōseishō Gojūnenshi*, 524.

56. As quoted in Kōseishō Gojūnenshi Henshū Iinkai, *Kōseishō Gojūnenshi*, 524–25.

57. As quoted in Kōseishō Gojūnenshi Henshū Iinkai, *Kōseishō Gojūnenshi*, 525.

58. "Jisei ni Osare Reikō sarenu Kitei," *Tokyo Asahi Shimbun*, March 23, 1931.

59. Sugaya, *Nihon Iryō Seidoshi*, 218.

60. Saguchi Takashi, *Kokumin Kenkōhoken: Keisei to Tenkai* (National Health Insurance: Formation and development) (Tokyo: Kōseikan, 1995), 23; Kawakami, *Gendai Nihon Iryōshi*, 422.

61. Kōseishō Gojūnenshi Henshū Iinkai, *Kōseishō Gojūnenshi*, 526–28. There were two types of NHI associations. One type consisted of associations that were established in a municipality. The other was associations formed by those in the same industry. Already existing medical cooperatives were included as alternative agents for the NHI's administration.

62. Kido Kōichi, "Shukuji" (A congratulatory address), *Nihon Sangyo Eisei Kyōkai Kaihō* 90 (December 1938): 15.

63. Shindō Seiichi, "Nentō no Ji" (New Year's greeting), *Kenkōhoken Jihō* 13 (January 1939): 1.

64. When the Health Insurance Act was discussed in the lower house, the house made a condition to have a study made about a social security program for seamen. Kōseishō Gojūnenshi Henshū Iinkai, *Kōseishō Gojūnenshi*, 534.

65. "Sen'in Kenkō Hoken Hōan" (Bill for Seamen's Insurance), *Shūgiin Giji Sokkiroku* 24 (Tokyo: Tokyo University Press 1939), 564. The formation of Seamen's Insurance had a longer history than the White-Collar Workers' Health Insurance program did. Sugaya, *Nihon Iryō Seisakushi*, 204.

66. Kōseishō Gojūnenshi Henshū Iinkai, *Kōseishō Gojūnenshi*, 532–37.

67. "Shokuin Kenkōhoken Hōan" (Bill for the White-Collar Health Insurance Act), *Shūgiin Giji Sokkiroku* 20 (Tokyo: Tokyo University Press, 1985), 413.

68. Kawakami, *Gendai Nihon Iryōshi*, 440–41; the official history of the MHW also confirms this point. Kōseishō Gojūnenshi Henshū Iinkai, *Kōseishō Gojūnenshi*, 532, 543.

69. Takei, *Kōseishō Shōshi*, 91; Kōseishō Gojūnenshi Henshū Iinkai, *Kōseishō Gojūnenshi*, 422.

70. Kawakami, *Gendai Nihon Iryōshi*, 449–51. In 1929, the number of doctorless villages was 2,909. In 1936 the number increased to 3,243 and in 1939 to 3,600 (one-third of all municipalities).

71. Kawakami, *Gendai Nihon Iryōshi*, 438–39. Hirokichi Nadao, who was a Home Ministry official and became the permanent vice minister in 1945, remembered Koizumi: "Minister Koizumi was a military doctor before. He understood well the importance of preventive medicine and an insurance system. I remember clearly his hard-working spirit, fertile imagination, and passion." Takata, *Nadao Hirokichi*, 74.

72. Nomura Taku, *Nihon Ishikai* (The Japan Medical Association) (Tokyo: Keisō Shobō, 1976), 45–46; Takaoka Hiroyuki, *Sōryokusen Taisei to "Fukushi Kokka": Senjiki Nihon no "Shakai Kaikaku" Kōsō* (Total war political regime and "welfare state": Social reform in wartime Japan) (Tokyo: Iwanami Shoten, 2011), 240–41.

73. Kawakami, *Gendai Nihon Iryōshi*, 446. The National Eugenic Act (Kokumin Yūsei Hō) of 1940 is an example of the totalitarian elements of wartime health care legislation. While the government generally prohibited abortions and encouraged births, it legalized abortions for those it considered genetically inferior.

74. Sugaya, *Nihon Iryō Seisakushi*, 200; Kōseishō Gojūnenshi Henshū Iinkai, *Kōseishō Gojūnenshi*, 458.

75. Kōseishō Gojūnenshi Henshū Iinkai, *Kōseishō Gojūnenshi*, 430–31; Christopher Aldous and Akihito Suzuki, *Reforming Public Health in Occupied Japan, 1945–52: Alien Prescription?* (London: Routledge, 2012), 55.

76. Kōseishō Gojūnenshi Henshū Iinkai, *Kōseishō Gojūnenshi*, 458–60.

77. Kawakami, *Gendai Nihon Iryōshi*, 453.

78. Kōseishō Gojūnenshi Henshū Iinkai, *Kōseishō Gojūnenshi*, 432.

79. Kōseishō Gojūnenshi Henshū Iinkai, *Kōseishō Gojūnenshi*, 423; Takei, *Kōseishō Shōshi*, 91–97; Kawakami, *Gendai Nihon Iryōshi*, 454; Nomura Taku, *Iryō to Kokumin Seikatsu: Shōwa Iryōshi* (Medicine and people's lives) (Tokyo: Aoki Shoten, 1981), 96. By this measure, the government gave the Japan Medical Corporation 1 million yen for five years, and the municipalities could contribute to building hospitals. Kawakami, *Gendai Nihon Iryōshi*, 456.

80. Sōmae Kiyosada, *Nihon Iryō no Kindaishi: Seido Keisei no Rekishi Bunseki* (A modern history of Japanese health care: Historical analysis of institutional development) (Kyoto: Minerva Shobō, 2020), 118.

81. Hirai Akira, "Nentō no Ji" (New Year's greeting), *Kenkōhoken Jihō* 17–18, no.1 (1942): 2–3.

82. Kawakami, *Nihon Iryō Seisakushi*, 440–41.

83. Kōseishō Gojūnenshi Henshū Iinkai, *Kōseishō Gojūnenshi*, 542–43.

84. Kōseishō Gojūnenshi Henshū Iinkai, *Kōseishō Gojūnenshi*, 361. Part of the HI amendment of 1942 was implemented on April 1, 1942, and part on January 1, 1943, and the amendment was implemented in its entirety on April 1, 1943.

85. Kōseishō Gojūnenshi Henshū Iinkai, *Kōseishō Gojūnenshi*, 545–48.

86. Gregory J. Kasza, *One World of Welfare: Japan in Comparative Perspective* (Ithaca, NY: Cornell University Press, 2006): 38.

87. Saguchi, "Kokumin Kenkōhoken to Iryō no Shakaika," 6.

88. Sugaya, *Nihon Iryō Seisakushi*, 201.

89. The political power of dentists was weaker than that of medical doctors. Dentists were not stipulated in the Medical Rules and Regulations (Isei) of 1874, because dentistry was considered to be part of medical science. Einosuke Obata successfully lobbied the government to create the dental license examination. But the number of dentists increased more slowly than the number of medical doctors. The Japan Dental Association was established in 1926, but it usually acted with the JMA. For more about the development of dental science and professionals, see Ishii Takuo, Nishimaki Akihiko, Shibutani Kō, *Standādo Shikaigakushi* (A standard history of dental science) (Tokyo: Gakkenshoin, 2009).

90. Sugaya, *Nihon Iryō Seisakushi*, 200; Kōseishō Gojūnenshi Henshū Iinkai, *Kōseishō Gojūnenshi*, 552–53.

91. Shimazaki Kenji, *Nihon no Iryō: Seido to Seisaku* (Medical care in Japan: Institutions and policy) (Tokyo: Tokyo Daigaku Shuppankai, 2011), 50.

92. As quoted in Sugaya, *Nihon Iryō Seisakushi*, 266.

93. Nihon Ishikai Sōritsu Gojusshūnen Kinen Jigyō Suishin Iinkai, *Nihon Ishikai Sōritsu Kinenshi: Sengo Gojūnen no Ayumi* (Anniversary of the founding of the Japan Medical Association: Fifty years of progress after World War II) (Tokyo: Nihon Ishikai, 1997), 548.

94. Sōmae Kiyosada, "Jimintōseikenka niokeru Iryōseisaku: Hoshuseitō no Shakaiseisaku to Riekidantai" (Medical policy of the Liberal Democratic Party: Social policy of the Conservative Party and interest groups), *Nenji Seijigaku* 63, no. 1 (June 2012): 132.

95. Kōseishō Gojūnenshi Henshū Iinkai, *Kōseishō Gojūnenshi*, 430. See also Akagi Kazuko, "Iyakubungyō to Futatsu no Seisakumokuhyō: Iyaku Bungyō no Shinten no Yōin" (The separation of prescription and dispensing of medicines and two policies: Factors in the development of the separation of prescription and dispensing in Japan [Iyakubyngyo]), *Shakai Yakugaku* 32, no. 2 (2013): 33–42.

96. Kitajima Taichi, *Kitajima Taichi Jiden* (Biography of Taichi Kitajima) (Tokyo: Kitajima Sensei Kinen Jigyōkai, 1955), 103–7.

97. As quoted in Kawakami, *Gendai Nihon Iryōshi*, 452.

98. As quoted in Nomura, *Nihon Ishikai*, 45–46.

99. "Sejirōmu no Kanpeki Fujin: Kokumin Chōyōrei wo Kaisei Kyōka" (Perfect system for wartime labor: Reforming and improving the National Requisition Ordinance), *Asahi Shimbun*, December 16, 1941.

100. Kawakami, *Gendai Nihon Iryōshi*, 482.

101. Kawakami, *Gendai Nihon Iryōshi*, 482.

102. Nomura, *Iryō to Kokumin Seikatsu*, 46–47.

103. Kawakami, *Gendai Nihon Iryōshi*, 453. For the development of state-initiated mass organizations, see Gregory J. Kasza, *The Conscription Society: Administered Mass Organizations* (New Haven, CT: Yale University Press, 1995).

104. Nomura, *Iryō to Kokumin Seikatsu*, 98.

105. Nomura, *Iryō to Kokumin Seikatsu*, 91–92.

106. Quoted in Nomura, *Nihon Ishikai*, 52.

107. Kitajima, *Kitajima Taichi Jiden*, 113–14.

108. "Ishikai Shintaisei Kimaru: Seihu no Kenmin Seisaku ni Kyōryoku" (Change in the medical associations: To make them cooperate with the government), *Yomiuri Shimbun*, August 19, 1942.

109. Toshihiko Nakayama was appointed as the vice president.

110. Miwa Kazuo, *Mōi Takemi Tarō* (The fighting doctor, Takemi Tarō) (Tokyo: Tokuma Shoten, 1995), 171. The Japan Dental Association was also reorganized. See Kōseishō Imu Kyoku, *Isei Hyakunen* (One-hundred-year history of medicine) (Tokyo: Gyōsei, 1976), 309.

4. REFORMING HEALTH CARE WITH THE UNITED STATES

1. Harold S. Quigley, "Democracy Occupies Japan," *Virginia Quarterly Review* 23 (Spring 1947): 522. Although General MacArthur was supposed to consult with the Far Eastern Commission and the Allied Council for Japan, which were created as policymaking and advisory organizations by the Allied nations, most of his consultations resulted in the organizations' rubber-stamping his decisions, or else he just ignored them. See Toshio Tatara, "1,400 Years of Japanese Social Work: From Its Origins through the Allied Occupation, 552–1952" (PhD diss., Bryn Mawr College, 1975), 288, 372.

2. For a more detailed description of how GHQ and US domestic politics affected the development of health insurance policy and health care administration in postwar Japan, see Takakazu Yamagishi, *War and Health Insurance Policy in Japan and the United States: World War II to Postwar Reconstruction* (Baltimore: Johns Hopkins University Press, 2011), chap. 6; and Adam D. Sheingate and Takakazu Yamagishi, "Occupation Politics: American Interests and the Struggle over Health Insurance in Postwar Japan," *Social Science History* 30, no. 1 (Spring 2006): 137–64.

3. Kobayashi Keiji, "Tsunetō Kyo no Shōchō Tennōseiron to Minshushugiron" (Kyo Tsunetō's theory of the symbolic-emperor system and democracy), *Osaka Shiritsu Daigakushi Kiyō* 11 (2018): 22. Kanamori entered the Ministry of Finance in 1912 after graduating from Tokyo Imperial University and served as the head of the Cabinet Legislation Bureau during the Keisuke Okada administration. Kanamori resigned the position after he was attacked by the military and the right-wing political forces who saw the emperor as a living god; Kanamori's idea was close to the theory of the emperor as an organ of the State (*tennō kikan setsu*).

4. For details of the process the United States went through in adopting its plan of indirect governance, see Iokibe Makoto, *Beikoku no Nihon Senyō Seisaku: Sengo Nihon no Sekkeizu*, Jō (US occupation policy toward Japan: A plan for postwar Japan, vol. 1) (Tokyo: Chūō Kōronsha, 1985).

5. At the rank of senior bureaucrats, 145 members were purged. A total of 830 out of 42,251 bureaucrats were purged. Hans H. Baerwald, *The Purge of Japanese Leaders Under the Occupation* (Berkeley: University of California Press, 1959), 82.

6. T. J. Pempel, "The Baby Target: 'Reform' of the Japanese Bureaucracy," in *Democratizing Japan: The Allied Occupation*, ed. Robert E. Ward and Yoshikazu Sakamoto (Honolulu: University of Hawaii Press, 1987), 179.

7. As for GHQ's reforms of civil service system, see Byung Chul Koh, *Japan's Administrative Elite* (Berkeley: University of California Press, 1989), 32–66.

8. Eiji Takemae, *Inside GHQ: The Allied Occupation of Japan and Its Legacy* (New York: Continuum, 2002), 225–27. The terms *GHQ* and *SCAP* are interchangeable in the Japanese context, although the title *SCAP* pertained to MacArthur himself.

9. The PHW lasted until June 1951, when it was reduced to a division of the Medical Section.

10. Theodore Cohen, *Remaking Japan: The American Occupation as New Deal* (London: Collier Macmillan, 1987).

11. The State-War-Navy Coordinating Committee (SWNCC), an interdepartmental body responsible for postwar planning, was the main actor in the United States. Soon after Japan accepted the Potsdam Declaration, the committee finalized its draft of its "US Initial Post-Surrender Policy for Japan" (SWNCC-150). John W. Dower, *Embracing Defeat: Japan in the Wake of World War II* (New York: W. W. Norton, 1999), 72; Takemae, *Inside GHQ*, 225–28.

12. Tatara, "1,400 Years of Japanese Social Work," 283.

13. Sugiyama Akiko, *Senryōki no Iryōkaikaku* (Medical reform during the US occupation) (Tokyo: Keisō Shobō, 1995), 44.

14. Kōseishō Gojūnenshi Henshū Iinkai, *Kōseishō Gojūnenshi, Kijutsu Hen* (Fifty-year history of the Ministry of Health and Welfare description volume) (Tokyo: Chūō Hōki Shuppan, 1988), 579. This repatriation operation included those nationals of other countries who chose to stay or were forced to stay in Japan during the war.

15. Kōseishō Gojūnenshi Henshū Iinkai, *Kōseishō Gojūnenshi*, 810–11; Sugiyama, *Senryōki no Iryōkaikaku*, 98.

16. Kōseishō Gojūnenshi Henshū Iinkai, *Kōseishō Gojūnenshi*, 590–91. To understand what GHQ did from the perspective of Sams, see Crawford Sams, *Medic: The Mission of an American Military Doctor in Occupied Japan and Wartorn Korea* (New York: Routledge, 1998).

17. Kōseishō Gojūnenshi Henshū Iinkai, *Kōseishō Gojūnenshi*, 588–89. There are two kinds of administrative officers. Officers of one type are trained in general administration. Those of the other type, technical administrative officers, have degrees in their special policy areas.

18. Jitsunari Fumihiko, "Wagakuni no Koshūeiseigaku Kyōiku no Rekishieki Gaikan to Kadai" (Historical overview of the subjects of public health education in Japan), *Igakukyōiku* 43, no. 3 (June 2012): 158.

19. For information on Sams, see Troy J. Sacquesty, "A Civil Affairs Pioneer: Brigadier General Crawford Sams, US Army Medical Corps," Office of the Command Historian, https://arsof-history.org/articles/v6n1_crawford_sams_page_1.html, accessed July 23, 2021.

20. Sugiyama, *Senryōki no Iryōkaikaku*, 50.

21. Sams, *Medic*, 264.

22. SCAP PHW, "Membership of Advisory Commission on Labor," December 30, 1945, RG 331, Records of Allies Operational and Occupational Headquarters, World War II, 1907–1966, box 9382, file 8, National Archives at College Park (NACP); Takemae Eiji, "GHQ Rōdō Ka no Hito to Seisaku: GHQ Rōdō Ka no Gunzō" (Personnel and policy in the GHQ Labor Section: Overview of the GHQ Labor Section), *Nihon Rōdō Kyōkai Zasshi* 24, no. 9 (1982): 68–69. Before joining the federal government, Stanchfield served as the chief of the Research, Statistics and Planning Section of the Michigan Unemployment Compensation Commission.

23. Cohen, *Remaking Japan*; Dower, *Embracing Defeat*, 220.

24. SCAP PHW, "Report on the Japanese Social Insurance Programs by the Labor Advisory Committee," 5, May (no exact date) 1946, RG 331, Records of Allies Operational and Occupational Headquarters, World War II, 1907–1966, box Com 2–Japan, NACP.

25. SCAP PHW, "Report on the Japanese Social Insurance Programs by the Labor Advisory Committee," 5.

26. SCAP PHW, "Advisory Commission on Labor First Interim Report," 2, April 5, 1946, RG 331, Records of Allies Operational and Occupational Headquarters, World War II, 1907–1966, box 9382, file 8, NACP.

27. SCAP PHW, "Report on the Japanese Social Insurance Programs by the Labor Advisory Committee," 15.

28. SCAP PHW, "Report on the Japanese Social Insurance Programs by the Labor Advisory Committee," 15.

29. Yoneyuki Sugita, "The Beveridge Report and Japan," *Social Work in Public Health* 29, no. 2 (2014): 159.

30. SCAP PHW, "Memorandum for Record: Candidates for Civilian Positions in Social Security and Insurance Division," January 21, 1947, RG 331, Records of Allies Operational and Occupational Headquarters, World War II, 1907–1966, box 9382, file 8, NACP.

31. Forest Harness, "Letter to the Honorable John Taber, United States House of Representatives," September 9, 1947, RG 331, Records of Allies Operational and Occupational Headquarters, World War II, 1907–1966, box 9383, file 8, NACP; Monte M. Poen, *Harry S. Truman versus the Medical Lobby: The Genesis of Medicare* (Columbia: University of Missouri Press, 1979), 42–43.

32. SCAP PHW, "Memorandum for Record: Air Priority for Social Security Mission," August 14, 1947, RG 5, MacArthur Memorial Loose Papers, Public Health and Social Security mission, Q–RA Rainbow Division, 1945–1951, microfilm 64, MacArthur Memorial, Norfolk, Virginia.

33. William Wandel, "Letter to I. S. Falk," June 14, 1947, RG 331, Records of Allies Operational and Occupational Headquarters, World War II, 1907–1966, box 9382, file 8, NACP.

34. Sugiyama, *Senryōki no Iryōkaikaku*, 100.

35. This committee was led by Tokujirō Kanamori. This report also included the establishment of Unemployment Insurance.

36. Kōseishō Gojūnenshi Henshū Iinkai, *Kōseishō Gojūnenshi*, 811; Yoshihara Kenji and Wada Masaru, *Nihon Iryōhoken Seidoshi* (The health insurance system of Japan) (Tokyo: Tōyō Keizai Shuppansha, 1999), 132. The Society-Managed Health Insurance program within the HI was excluded from this proposal, although dependents of SMHI beneficiaries were included.

37. Shakaihoshō Kenkyūjo, ed., *Nihon Shakaihoshō Zenshi Shiryō: Shakaihoken* (Early history of Japanese social security: Social insurance) (Tokyo: Shiseidō, 1981), 163–67.

38. Tatara, "1,400 Years of Japanese Social Work," 336.

39. Saguchi Takashi, "Bebarijji Hōkokusho to Wagakuni Shakaihoshō Keikaku: Nihon Shakaihokenshi no Issetsu" (Plan relating to Japanese social security and the Beveridge Report: A history of Japanese social insurance), *Waseda Shōgaku* 143 (January 1960): 72.

40. Suetaka Makoto, "Shakaihoshō Seido no Nihonteki Seikaku" (Japanese characteristics of the social security system), *Rōdō Hyōron* 5, no. 1 (1950): 3. See also Saguchi, "Bebarijji Hōkokusho to Wagakuni Shakaihoshō Keikaku," 62.

41. Saguchi, "Bebarijji Hōkokusho to Wagakuni Shakaihoshō Keikaku," 71.

42. Deborah J. Milly, *Poverty, Equality, and Growth: The Politics of Economic Need in Postwar Japan* (Cambridge, MA: Harvard University Asia Center, 1999), 101.

43. "Saitei Seikatsu wo Mamoru Shakaihoshō Seido" (Social security system to protect minimum level of life), *Asahi Shimbun*, October 12, 1946, as quoted in Saguchi, "Bebarijji Hōkokusho to Wagakuni Shakaihoshō Keikaku," 665. See also Sugiyama, *Senryōki no Iryōkaikaku*, 100.

44. Soeda Yoshiya, *Seikatsuhogoseido no Shakaishi* (A history of public assistance in Japan) (Tokyo: University of Tokyo Press, 1995), 87; Milly, *Poverty, Equality, and Growth*, 103.

45. Forest Harness, "Telegram to General Douglas MacArthur," August 20, 1947, RG 331, Records of Allies Operational and Occupational Headquarters, World War II, 1907–1966, box 9383, file 8, NACP.

46. War Department, "Radio Message to SCAP: Social Security Mission." August 30, 1947, RG 331, Records of Allies Operational and Occupational Headquarters, World War II, 1907–1966, box 2140, file 15, NACP.

47. George F. Lull, "Letter to Crawford F. Sams," April 6, 1948, RG 331, Records of Allies Operational and Occupational Headquarters, World War II, 1907–1966, box 9382, file 7, NACP. Before his tenure as the president, Lull was deputy surgeon general of the US Army.

48. George W. Coon, "Letter to General Douglas MacArthur," September 30, 1947, RG 5, MacArthur Memorial Loose Papers, Public Health and Social Security Mission, Q–RA Rainbow Division, 1945–1951, microfilm 64, MacArthur Memorial, Norfolk, Virginia.

49. Douglas MacArthur, "Letter to Dr. Charles Farrell," September 7, 1947, RG 5, MacArthur Memorial Loose Papers, Public Health and Social Security Mission, Q–RA Rainbow Division, 1945–1951, microfilm 64, MacArthur Memorial, Norfolk, Virginia.

50. "MacArthur Reports Socialized Medicine Is Not Planned by US for Japan," *Journal of the American Medical Association* 135, no. 2 (1947): 101.

51. Douglas MacArthur, "Letter to Forest Harness," December 24, 1947, RG 5, MacArthur Memorial Loose Papers, Public Health and Social Security mission, Q–RA Rainbow Division, 1945–1951, microfilm 64, MacArthur Memorial, Norfolk, Virginia.

52. Sugiyama, *Senryōki no Iryōkaikaku*, 101–4.

53. Crawford F. Sams, "Letter to George Lull, 18 May 1948," May 18, 1948, RG 331, Records of Allies Operational and Occupational Headquarters, World War II, 1907–1966, box 9382, file 7, NACP.

54. SCAP PHW, "Social Security Mission Report," RG 331, Records of Allies Operational and Occupational Headquarters, World War II, 1907–1966, box 9382, file 10, NACP.

55. American Medical Association, "Report of the Mission of the American Medical Association," (no exact date) 1948, RG 331, Records of Allies Operational and Occupational Headquarters, World War II, 1907–1966, box 9383, file 1, NACP.

56. Tatara, "1,400 Years of Japanese Social Work," 349.

57. Kōseishō Gojūnenshi Henshū Iinkai, *Kōseishō Gojūnenshi*, 498.

58. Kawakami Takeshi, *Gendai Nihon Iryōshi* (History of modern Japanese health care) (Tokyo: Keisō Shobō, 1965), 498; Sugiyama, *Senryōki no Iryōkaikaku*, 197; Dower, *Embracing Defeat*, 540–41.

59. Kōseishō Gojūnenshi Henshū Iinkai, *Kōseishō Gojūnenshi: Kijutsu Hen*, 598.

60. Kawakami, *Gendai Nihon Iryōshi*, 501; Takashi Saguchi, *Kokumin Kenkō Hoken: Keisei to Tenkai* (The formation and development of the National Health Insurance Act) (Tokyo: Kōseikan, 1995), 77–79; Yoshihara and Wada, *Nihon Iryōhoken Seidoshi*, 81; Saguchi, *Kokumin Kenkō Hoken*, 79.

61. Kojima Yonekichi, "Kokumin Kenkō Hoken Hō no Kaisei ni Taisuru Hihan" (Criticism of the National Health Insurance Act Amendment), *Shakaihoken Jōhō* 2, no. 10 (1948): 4.

62. Kōseishō Gojūnenshi Henshū Iinkai, *Kōseishō Gojūnenshi*, 598–99.

63. Kōseishō Gojūnenshi Henshū Iinkai, *Kōseishō Gojūnenshi*, 831–32; Saguchi, *Kokumin Kenkō Hoken*, 86; Yoshihara and Wada, *Nihon Iryōhoken Seidoshi*, 129.

64. Sugita Yoneyuki, "Universal Health Insurance: The Unfinished Reform of Japan's Healthcare System," in *Democracy in Occupied Japan: The US Occupation and Japanese Politics and Society*, ed. Mark E. Capiro and Yoneyuki Sugita (New York: Routledge, 2007), 163.

65. Kōseishō Gojūnenshi Henshū Iinkai, *Kōseishō Gojūnenshi*, 810–14, 826–28.

66. Yoshihara and Wada, *Nihon Iryōhoken Seidoshi*, 125; Yūki Yasuhiro, *Iryō no Nedan: Shinryōhōshū to Politics* (The price of medicine: Politics and the fee schedule) (Tokyo: Iwanami Shoten, 2006), 18–19.

67. Nihon Ishikai Sōritsu Gojusshūnen Kinen Jigyō Suishin Iinkai, *Nihon Ishikai Sōritsu Kinenshi*, 8–10. At the same time, the Japan Medical Corporation was also dissolved.

68. As quoted in Nihon Ishikai Sōritsu Gojusshūnen Kinen Jigyō Suishin Iinkai, *Nihon Ishikai Sōritsu Kinenshi*, 9.

69. Nihon Ishikai Sōritsu Gojusshūnen Kinen Jigyō Suishin Iinkai, *Nihon Ishikai Sōritsu Kinenshi*, 10.

70. William E. Steslicke, "The Political Life of the Japan Medical Association," *Journal of Asian Studies* 31 (1972): 849.

71. Arioka Jirō, *Sengo Iryō no Gojūnen: Iryōhokenseido no Butaiura* (Fifty years of postwar medical care: Behind the scenes in the health insurance system) (Tokyo: Nihon Iji Shinpōsha, 1997), 37. When Sams criticized German-style medicine and suggested introducing US-style medicine, Tamiya publicly opposed the suggestion by pointing out the German tradition had produced excellent medical research and recommending that this tradition should be modified but not done away with. Suzuki Yasutaka, "Tamiya Sensei ni Tsukaete" (Serving under Dr. Tamiya), in *Tamiya Takeo Sensei wo Shinobu* (Remembering Dr. Tamiya Takeo), ed. Takemi Tarō (Tokyo: Medical Culture, 1964), 190–91.

72. Nihon Ishikai Sōritsu Gojusshūnen Kinen Jigyō Suishin Iinkai, *Nihon Ishikai Sōritsu Kinenshi*, 20–21.

73. Takemi Tarō, *Jitsuroku Nihon Ishikai* (The true story of the Japan Medical Association) (Tokyo: Asahi Shuppan, 1983), 33. Takemi Tarō was then the vice president and resigned along with Tamiya. There were other serious challenges from Sams that were not directly related to the JMA. For example, Sams introduced the US-style internship into Japanese medical education. Sam unsuccessfully tried to make Japanese medical education the same as US medical education, which required four years of undergraduate education and four years of medical school (including the internship). The Japanese medical degree is awarded to those who complete six years of education in a medical school. Sugaya, *Nihon Iryō Seisakushi*, 494–97; Sey Nishimura, "Hachinensei Ishi Yōsei Kyōiku: GHQ Samusu Junshō no Teian" (Promoting health in Japan under the American Occupation, 1945–1952: The design of the eight-year medical education program), *Igakukyōiku* 44, no. 6 (December 2013).

74. Kōseishō Gojūnenshi Henshū Iinkai, *Kōseishō Gojūnenshi*, 669. The association was renamed the Japanese Nursing Association in June 1951.

75. Steslicke, "Political Life of the Japan Medical Association," 851.

76. Yoshihara and Masaru, *Nihon Iryō Hoken Seidoshi*, 132–34; Nakata Yoshio, "Shakai Hoshō Seido Shingikai no Secchi ni Tsuite" (Thoughts on the Advisory Council on Social Security), *Shakaihoken Johō* 3, no. 1 (January 1949): 7.

77. Yoshihara and Masaru, *Nihon Iryō Hoken Seidoshi*, 133.

78. Yoshihara and Masaru, *Nihon Iryō Hoken Seidoshi*, 134.

79. Suetaka, "Shakaihoshōseido no Nihonteki Seikaku," 2.

80. Kōseishō Gojūnenshi Henshū Iinkai, *Kōseishō Gojūnenshi*, 837; Sugita, "Universal Health Insurance," 164.

81. As quoted in Sugita, "Universal Health Insurance," 163.

82. Quoted in Yoshihara and Wada, *Nihon Iryōhoken Seidoshi*, 137.

83. Tokuo Kojima, "Shakaihoshōseido Shingikai ga Umarerumade" (The formation process of the Advisory Council on the Social Security System), *Shakaihoken Shunpō* 267 (November 1950): 6.

84. Yoshihara and Wada, *Nihon Iryōhoken Seidoshi*, 137.

85. Kojima Tokuo, "1951nen eno Kitai (My hope for 1951)," *Shakaihoken Shunpō* 271 (January 1951): 6.

5. ACHIEVING UNIVERSAL HEALTH INSURANCE

1. Paul A. David, "Clio and the Economics of QWERTY," *American Economic Review* 75, no. 2 (1985): 332–37.

2. Peter A. Hall and Rosemary Taylor, "Political Science and the Three New Institutionalisms," *Political Studies* 44, no. 5 (December 1996): 939. See also Peter A. Hall, "Policy Paradigm, Social Learning, and the State," *Comparative Politics* 25, no. 3 (April 1993): 275–96.

3. Paul Pierson, "Not Just What but When: Timing and Sequence in Political Process," *Studies in American Political Development* 14, no. 1 (Spring 2000): 72–92.

4. For the detailed transformation of conservative parties, see Kenzō Uchida, "Japan's Postwar Conservative Parties," in *Democratizing Japan: The Allied Occupation*, ed. Robert E. Ward and Yoshikazu Sakamoto (Honolulu: University of Hawaii Press, 1987).

5. This party's name was initially translated as the Social Democratic Party of Japan. But as the left wing gained in power, its English name became the Socialist Party of Japan. Then, in 1991, the party went back to being called the Social Democratic Party of Japan, as socialist forces declined all over the world. To avoid confusion, in this book I translate this party's name consistently as the Socialist Party of Japan.

6. Matsumura joined the merged LDP. Yoshida joined in 1957.

7. Chalmers Johnson, *MITI and the Japanese Miracle: The Growth of Industrial Policy, 1925–1975* (Stanford, CA: Stanford University Press, 1982), 200.

8. Yoshihara Kenji and Wada Masaru, *Nihon Iryōhoken Seidoshi* (History of Japanese health insurance) (Tokyo: Tōyō Keizai Shuppansha, 1999), 140.

9. Nomura Taku, *Nihon Ishikai* (The Japan Medical Association) (Tokyo: Keisō Shobō, 1976), 56.

10. Takemi Tarō, ed., *Tamiya Sensei wo Shinobu* (In memory of Professor Tamiya) (Tokyo: Medicaru Karuchua, 1964), 273.

11. Under GHQ's direction, medical vocational schools were either promoted to becoming medical universities or abolished. Ikegami Naoki, *Nihon no Iryō to Kaigo* (Japan's health and long-term care system) (Tokyo: Nihon Keizai Shimbun Shuppansha, 2017), 16.

12. Arioka Jirō, *Sengo Iryō no Gojūnen: Iryōhokenseido no Butaiura* (Fifty years of postwar medical care: Behind the scenes in the health insurance system) (Tokyo: Nihon Iji Shinpōsha, 1997), 19.

13. Takahashi Akira, "Shakaihoshō eno Kadai" (The problem of social security), *Shakaihoken Jihō* 22, no. 5 (1948): 1.

14. Arioka, *Sengo Iryō no Gojūnen*, 19.

15. Yoshihara and Wada, *Nihon Iryōhoken Seidoshi*, 125.

16. Yūki Yasuhiro, *Fukushishakai ni Okeru Iryō to Seiji: Shinryōhōshū wo Meguru Kankeidantai no Ugoki* (Medicine and politics in the welfare society: Activities of interest groups regarding the fee schedule) (Tokyo: Honnoizumisha, 2004), 40.

17. Yasuda Iwao, "Shakaihoshō heno Hansei" (Reflections on the social security system), *Shakaihoshō Shunpō*, no. 235 (1950): 4.

18. Yoshihara and Wada, *Nihon Iryōhoken Seidoshi*, 238; Arioka, *Sengo Iryō no Gojūnen*, 49.

19. Nomura, *Nihon Ishikai*, 56–57.

20. Arioka, *Sengo Iryō no Gojūnen*, 54.

21. Arioka, *Sengo Iryō no Gojūnen*, 559–60.

22. Nihon Ishikai Sōritsu Gojusshūnen Kinen Jigyō Suishin Iinkai, *Nihon Ishikai Sōritsu Kinenshi*, 33. Kanto/Koshin'etsu includes Chiba, Gunma, Ibaraki, Kanagawa, Nagano, Niigata, Tochigi, Tokyo, and Yamanashi Prefectures. It is one of eight regions in Japan.

23. Arioka, *Sengo Iryō no Gojūnen*, 54–58.

24. Arioka, *Sengo Iryō no Gojūnen*, 60–61.

25. Arioka, *Sengo Iryō no Gojūnen*, 67–68.

26. Arioka, *Sengo Iryō no Gojūnen*, 67.

27. Takemi Tarō, *Chōshinki* (Diary of listening to the heart) (Tokyo: Jitsugyo no Nihon Sha, 1978), 224–25; Takemi, *Jitsuroku Nihon Ishikai*, 36–37.

28. Arioka, *Sengo Iryō no Gojūnen*, 82.

29. Arioka, *Sengo Iryō no Gojūnen*, 74.

30. For more about situating what happened the 1950s in the development of health insurance policy, see Takakazu Yamagishi, "Health Insurance Politics of Japan in the 1940s and the 1950s: The Japan Medical Association and Policy Development," *Journal of International and Advanced Japanese Studies* 9 (March 2017): 193–204.

31. Arioka, *Sengo Iryō no Gojūnen*, 36. Like doctors, dentists did not charge much for diagnosis but made money mostly from charging for materials, especially gold, used to fill teeth.

32. Arioka, *Sengo Iryō no Gojūnen*, 33.

33. "Dairokkai Rinji Iyakuseido Chōsakai: Ishikai no Shuchō tsuini Yaburu" (The 6th Provisional Research Council on the Pharmaceutical System: Blocking the JMA's demands), *Shakaihoken Shunpō*, no. 278 (March 1951): 15–16.

34. Yoshida Hideo, "Rinji Shinryōhōshū Iyakuseido Iryōseido Chōsakai no Inshō to Sono Hihan (Jō): Tokuni Chūritsuiin no Tachiba kara" (An impression and criticism of the Extraordinary Investigating Committee on the Fee Schedule and Pharmaceutical System, part 1: The perspective of a neutral committee member), *Shakaihoken Shunpō*, no. 280 (April 1951): 7.

35. William E. Steslicke, "The Political Life of the Japan Medical Association," *Journal of Asian Studies* 31, no. 4 (August 1972): 850.

36. Arioka, *Sengo Iryō no Gojūnen*, 82. The amendment was introduced by Dr. Ōishi Buichi and others.

37. Steslicke, "Political Life of the Japan Medical Association," 850.

38. Takemi, *Chōshinki*, 141.

39. Nihon Ishikai Sōritsu Gojusshūnen Kinen Jigyō Suishin Iinkai, *Nihon Ishikai Sōritsu Kinenshi*, 47.

40. Kimura Chūjirō, "Sakaihoshō eno Jōnestu" (Passion for social security), *Shakaihoken Shunpō*, no. 415 (January 1955): 4.

41. Ikura Yasumasa, *Shindan Takemi Tarō* (Evaluating Takemi Tarō) (Tokyo: Sōshisha, 1979), 53.

42. Kawakami Takeshi, *Gendai Nihon Iryōshi* (History of modern Japanese health care) (Tokyo: Keisō Shobō, 1965), 285–86. The group was popularly called "the seven-member committee," but it did not have an official name.

43. Nihon Ishikai Sōritsu Gojusshūnen Kinen Jigyō Suishin Iinkai, *Nihon Ishikai Sōritsu Kinenshi*, 46.

44. Nihon Ishikai Sōritsu Gojusshūnen Kinen Jigyō Suishin Iinkai, *Nihon Ishikai Sōritsu Kinenshi*, 47.

45. "Toishikai de Hoken'i Sōjitai wo Ketsui" (The Tokyo Medical Association decides to resign from health insurance practice), *Shakaihoken Shunpō*, no. 402 (1954): 15.

46. Arioka, *Sengo Iryō no Gojūnen*, 86–87.

47. Arioka, *Sengo Iryō no Gojūnen*, 89, 121.

48. Takemi, *Jitsuroku Nihon Ishikai*, 58.

49. Takemi, *Jitsuroku Nihon Ishikai*.

50. Obata Isei, "Shinnen Shokan" (New Year's greeting), *Shakaihoken Shunpō*, no. 451 (January1956): 5.

51. Arioka, *Sengo Iryō no Gojūnen*, 121.

52. As quoted in Arioka, *Sengo Iryō no Gojūnen*, 90.

53. Arioka, *Sengo Iryō no Gojūnen*, 122–23.

54. Arioka, *Sengo Iryō no Gojūnen*, 122.

55. Arioka, *Sengo Iryō no Gojūnen*, 123.

56. Arioka, *Sengo Iryō no Gojūnen*, 123.

57. Hido Shuichi, "Itansha Takemi Tarō" (A heretic, Tarō Takemi), *Chūōkōron* 79, no. 7 (July 1964): 247.

58. Sugimura Hisahide, *Fūun wo Yobu Otoko* (A dangerous man) (Tokyo: Jiji Tsūshinsha, 1977), 102.

59. Tanaka Shigeru, *Takemi Tarō wo Okoraseta Otoko: Inaka Ishikaichō Funtōki* (The man who made Tarō Takemi angry: Diary of the hard struggle of a small-town medical association president) (Tokyo: Mirai Shuppan 1984), 39.

60. Sugimura, *Fūun wo Yobu Otoko*, 111.

61. Takemi, *Chōshinki*, 106.

62. Sugimura, *Fūun wo Yobu Otoko*, 111.

63. Hido, "Itansha Takemi Tarō," 252.

64. Miwa Kazuo, *Mōi Takemi Tarō* (The fighting doctor, Tarō Takemi) (Tokyo: Tokuma Shoten, 1995), 114.

65. Miwa, *Mōi Takemi Tarō*, 119.

66. Miwa, *Mōi Takemi Tarō*, 119–20.

67. Miwa, *Mōi Takemi Tarō*, 252.

68. Hido, "Itansha Takemi Tarō," 252.

69. Sugimura, *Fūun wo Yobu Otoko*, 115.

70. Takemi Tarō, *Senzen Senchū Sengo* (Prewar, wartime, postwar) (Tokyo: Kōdansha, 1982), 194, 218; Miwa, *Mōi Takemi Tarō*, 150.

71. Miwa, *Mōi Takemi Tarō*, 150; Sugimura, *Fūun wo Yobu Otoko*, 119.

72. Takemi, *Jitsuroku Nihon Ishikai*, 30; Miwa, *Mōi Takemi Tarō*, 159. Sasa and Takemi had a chance to work together on ideas for reorganizing the JMA when GHQ requested them to transform it along the lines of the American Medical Association. Takemi Tarō, *Jitsuroku Nihon Ishikai*, 31.

73. Hamada Masato, *Kuromaku Kenkyū* 3 (Study of backroom bosses, vol. 3) (Tokyo: Shinkokuminsha, 1979), 26.

74. President Obata was removed from office in March by an extraordinary House of Delegates meeting. The no-confidence vote was 82–51. For details, see Nihon Ishikai Sōritsu Gojusshūnen Kinen Jigyō Suishin Iinkai, *Nihon Ishikai Sōritsu Kinenshi*, 56.

75. Nihon Ishikai Sōritsu Gojusshūnen Kinen Jigyō Suishin Iinkai, *Nihon Ishikai Sōritsu Kinenshi*, 56.

76. Arioka, *Sengo Iryō no Gojūnen*, 89–90.

77. "Nichii Shinyakuin Rinji Daigiinkai de Kimaru: Kaichō ni Takemi Tarō shi" (The new JMA executives were chosen in the extraordinary House of Delegates meeting: Takemi Tarō is the president), *Shakaihoken Shunpō*, no. 498 (April 1957): 20.

78. "Nichii Shinyakuin Rinji Daigiinkai de Kimaru."

79. Tanaka, *Takemi Tarō wo Okoraseta Otoko*, 4.

80. For details on Takemi's background, see Takakazu Yamagishi, "A Short Biography of Takemi Tarō, the President of the Japan Medical Association," *Journal of the Nanzan Academic Society Social Sciences* 1 (January 2011): 49–56.

81. Hido, "Itansha Takemi Tarō," 254.

82. As quoted in Miwa, *Mōi Takemi Tarō*, 196.

83. William E. Steslicke, *Doctors in Politics: The Political Life of the Japan Medical Association* (New York: Columbia University Press, 1973), 46.

84. Mizuno Hajime, *Daremo Kakanakatta Nihon Ishikai* (The unknown JMA) (Tokyo: Sōshisha, 2003), 64.

85. For Takemi's thoughts on the government's role, see Takemi, *Jitsuroku Nihon Ishikai*.

86. "Rinji Daigiinkai ni okeru Takemi Kaichō no Shūnin Aisatsu" (President Takemi's greeting at the extraordinary House of Delegates meeting), *Nihon Ishikai Zasshi* 37, no. 9 (May 1957): 579.

87. Takemi Tarō, *Suntetsu Igen* (Warnings from a doctor) (Tokyo: Nihonijishinposha, 1972), 5.

88. Takemi Tarō, "Shakai Iryō no Mono to Kokoro" (Material and immaterial matters in social medicine), *Shakaihoken Shunpō*, no. 343 (January 1953): 6.

89. Tanaka, *Takemi Tarō wo Okoraseta Otoko*, 14.

90. Nomura, *Nihon Ishikai*, 59.

91. Takemi, *Suntetsu Igen*, 117–18. Also see Nihon Ishikai Sōritsu Gojusshūnen Kinen Jigyō Suishin Iinkai, *Nihon Ishikai Sōritsu Kinenshi*, 57.

92. Arioka, *Sengo Iryō no Gojūnen*, 131.

93. John Campbell and Naoki Ikegami point out that there were LDP politicians who acted in the interests of the JMA in exchange for the JMA's mobilizing to help these politicians in their elections. Politicians who exchange institutional favors for election support are called *zokugiin* (tribal Diet members). According to Campbell and Ikegami, the health care policy area tended to be more affected by *zokugiin* than any other policy area. Ikegami Naoki and John Campbell, *Nihon no Iryō: Tōsei to Baransu Kankaku* (Health care in Japan: Control and sense of balance) (Tokyo: Chūkō Shinsho, 1996), 24.

94. Takemi, *Jitsuroku Nihon Ishikai*, 62.

95. Arioka, *Sengo Iryō no Gojūnen*, 135.

96. "Rinji Daigiinkai ni okeru Takemi Kaichō no Shūnin Aisatsu," 579.

97. Takemi, *Jitsuroku Nihon Ishikai*, 59.

98. Quoted in Arioka, *Sengo Iryō no Gojūnen*, 140.

99. Arioka, *Sengo Iryō no Gojūnen*, 148.

100. Takemi, *Suntetsu Igen*, 163.

101. Miwa, *Mōi Takemi Tarō*, 200–203.

102. Takemi, *Jitsuroku Nihon Ishikai*, 59.

103. "Nichibyō wa Nichii to Iken Tairitsu" (The JHA's opinion that differs from the JMA's), *Shakaihoken Shunpō*, no. 517 (November 1957): 17.

104. Kanzaki San'eki, "Watashi no Koseishōan ni Taisuru Kangaekata" (My thoughts on the MHW's proposal), *Shakaihoken Shunpō*, no. 518 (November 1957): 4.

105. "Chūōiryōkyōgikai Mata Konran" (The Central Social Insurance Medical Council in confusion again), *Shakaihoken Shunpō*, no. 518 (November 1957): 18.

106. "Shinryō Hōshū Shingi wo yosoni Kanzaki Mondai Shinkokuka" (Deepening Kanzaki problem in place of fee-schedule discussion), *Shakaihoken Shunpō*, no. 518 (November 1957): 16.

107. As quoted in Miwa, *Mōi Takemi Tarō*, 208.

108. "Iryōkyōgikai eno Hansei" (A reflection on the Central Social Insurance Medical Council), *Shakaihoken Shunpō*, no. 576 (June 1959): 3.

109. Nihon Ishikai Sōritsu Gojusshūnen Kinen Jigyō Suishin Iinkai, *Nihon Ishikai Sōritsu Kinenshi*, 60.

110. The fee schedule gives each medical procedure and drug a number of points. The cost of each is calculated by multiplying by ten yen.

111. Takemi, *Jitsuroku Nihon Ishikai*, 67.

112. Arioka, *Sengo Iryō no Gojūnen*, 156–57.

113. As quoted in Arioka, *Sengo Iryō no Gojūnen*, 157.

114. Miwa, *Mōi Takemi Tarō*, 212–14.

115. Miwa, *Mōi Takemi Tarō*, 213; Arioka, *Sengo Iryō no Gojūnen*, 156.

116. For ways interest groups retain their members, see Mancur Olson, *The Logic of Collective Action: Public Goods and the Theory of Groups* (Cambridge, MA: Harvard University Press, 1971.

117. Arioka, *Sengo Iryō no Gojūnen*, 72–73.

118. Miwa, *Mōi Takemi Tarō*, 204.

119. Takemi, *Chōshinki*, 109.

120. Takemi, *Jitsuroku Nihon Ishikai*, 123.

121. As quoted in Arioka, *Sengo Iryō no Gojūnen*, 147.

6. CONSOLIDATING UNIVERSAL HEALTH INSURANCE

1. Kent E. Calder, *Crisis and Compensation: Public Policy and Political Stability in Japan, 1949–1986* (Princeton, NJ: Princeton University Press, 1988), 366–67.

2. This was named after a universally known myth in which Amaterasu-ōmikami, the Shintō sun spirit, hid in a cave (*iwato*). It meant that the economic boom was the largest since the god hid in the cave.

3. This was named after the Shintō spirit, who created the islands of Japan.

4. For party politics and economic growth, see J. A. A. Stockwin, *Governing Japan: Divided Politics in a Major Economy*, 3rd ed. (Oxford: Blackwell, 1999), 54–69; T. J. Pempel, *Policy and Politics in Japan: Creative Conservativism* (Philadelphia: Temple University Press, 1982), 46–75.

5. Paul Pierson, "The New Politics of the Welfare State," *World Politics* 48, no. 2 (January 1996): 144.

6. For policy changes during the occupation, see John W. Dower, *Embracing Defeat: Japan in the Wake of World War II* (New York: W. W. Norton, 1999).

7. Yamamoto Masayoshi, "Kokumin Kenkō Hoken Tenbō" (The prospects for the NHI program), *Shakaihoken Shunpō*, no. 236 (January 1950): 8.

8. As quoted in Arioka Jirō, *Sengo Iryō no Gojūnen: Iryōhoken Seido no Butaiura* (Fifty years of postwar medical care: Behind the scenes in the health insurance system) (Tokyo: Nihon Iji Shinpōsha, 1997), 105.

9. As quoted in Arioka, *Sengo Iryō no Gojūnen*, 93.

10. Sugaya Akira, *Nihon Iryō Seisakushi* (History of Japanese medical policy) (Tokyo: Nihon Hyōronsha, 1977), 293.

11. Sugaya, *Nihon Iryō Seisakushi*, 297. The Japan Socialist Party, albeit with a slightly different version, was on the side of the latter group.

12. Arioka, *Sengo Iryō no Gojūnen*, 101.

13. As quoted in Sugaya, *Nihon Iryō Seisakushi*, 293. See also Nihon Ishikai Sōritsu Gojusshūnen Kinen Jigyō Suishin Iinkai, *Nihon Ishikai Sōritsu Kinenshi: Sengo Gojūnen no Ayumi* (Anniversary of the founding of the Japan Medical Association: Fifty years of progress after World War II) (Tokyo: Nihon Ishikai, 1997), 52.

14. Arioka, *Sengo Iryō no Gojūnen*, 94.

15. William E. Steslicke, "The Political Life of the Japan Medical Association," *Journal of Asian Studies* 31, no. 4 (August 1972): 851–52.

16. As quoted in Arioka, *Sengo Iryō no Gojūnen*, 95.

17. Arioka, *Sengo Iryō no Gojūnen*, 109.

18. Arioka, *Sengo Iryō no Gojūnen*, 109.

19. Takemi Tarō, *Suntetsu Igen* (Warnings from a doctor) (Tokyo: Nihonijishinpōsha, 1972), 131.

20. Yamazaki Iwao, "Higan wo Nozomu Toshi ni" (To make this year be fruitful), *Shakaihoken Shunpō*, no. 487 (January 1957): 7.

21. Arioka, *Sengo Iryō no Gojūnen*, 109. See also Yamazaki Iwao, "Keiei no Kanpeki na Kokuho wo" (Seeking perfect management of the National Health Insurance Program), *Shakaihoken Shunpō*, no. 451 (January 1956): 9. Election of city mayors was introduced after the war. Before that time, they were chosen by the central government.

22. Yasuda Iwao, "Teishotoku Kaisō no Iryōmondai" (Medical problems of the low-income class), *Shakaihoken Shunpo*, no. 487 (January 1957): 4.

23. Arioka, *Sengo Iryō no Gojūnen*, 109–10.

24. Nihon Ishikai Sōritsu Gojusshūnen Kinen Jigyō Suishin Iinkai, *Nihon Ishikai Sōritsu Kinenshi*, 62–63. In ordinance-designated cities, such as Tokyo, Osaka, and Nagoya, wards had responsibility for implementing the NHI.

25. Kojima Tokuo, "Kokuho ni okeru Hihokensha Soshiki no Kessei" (To form an organization of insured persons), *Shakaihoken Shunpō*, no. 523 (January 1958): 17.

26. Two actors can introduce bills in the Diet: the executive branch and Diet members. The former process is called *naikaku rippō* and the latter, *giin rippō*. Most laws result from the former process. But Diet members occasionally introduce bills when requested by a specific industry, region, or other interest group.

27. As quoted in Arioka, *Sengo Iryō no Gojūnen*, 70.

28. Arioka, *Sengo Iryō no Gojūnen*, 169–72.

29. Nihon Ishikai Sōritsu Gojusshūnen Kinen Jigyō Suishin Iinkai, *Nihon Ishikai Sōritsu Kinenshi*, 54.

30. Takemi, *Suntetsu Igen*, 201.

31. William E. Steslicke, *Doctors in Politics: The Political Life of the Japan Medical Association* (New York: Columbia University Press, 1973), 75.

32. Steslicke, *Doctors in Politics*, 73.

33. As quoted in Takemi Tarō, *Jitsuroku Nihon Ishikai* (The true story of the Japan Medical Association) (Tokyo: Asahi Shuppan, 1983), 96.

34. Nihon Ishikai Sōritsu Gojusshūnen Kinen Jigyō Suishin Iinkai, *Nihon Ishikai Sōritsu Kinenshi*, 69.

35. Steslicke, *Doctors in Politics*, 69.

36. Arioka, *Sengo Iryō no Gojūnen*, 52.

37. As quoted in Arioka, *Sengo Iryō no Gojūnen*, 211.

38. As quoted in Arioka, *Sengo Iryō no Gojūnen*, 213.

39. Arioka, *Sengo Iryō no Gojūnen*, 183.

40. Arioka, *Sengo Iryō no Gojūnen*, 182–84.

41. Iyasu Tadashi, *Aru Hoshu Seijika: Furui Yoshimi no Kiseki* (A conservative politician: Personal history of Yoshimi Furui) (Tokyo: Ochanomizu Shobō, 1987).

42. Sugaya, *Nihon Iryō Seisakushi*, 291; Arioka, *Sengo Iryō no Gojūnen*, 184–85.

43. Sugaya, *Nihon Iryō Seisakushi*, 310.

44. "Nichii Byōin Kanrisha Bumon wo Shinsetsu" (The JMA created the Subcommittee of Hospital Administrators), *Shakaihoken Shunpō*, no. 573 (May 1959): 17.

45. Arioka, *Sengo Iryō no Gojūnen*, 188–90.

46. Sugaya, *Nihon Iryō Seisakushi*, 300.

47. Arioka, *Sengo Iryō no Gojūnen*, 120.

48. "Gonin'i Tōshin wa Fugōri" (Five-Member Committee Report is irrational), *Shakaihoken Shunpō*, no. 569 (April 1959): 23.

49. Yoshida Hideo, "Iryōhoshōiinkai no Tōshin (Report of the Medical Security Advisory Committee)," *Shakaihoken Shunpō*, no. 570 (April 1959): 4.

50. Kondō Bunji, "Kurōto no Mita Saishūhōkoku" (The final report from the viewpoint of a professional), *Shakaihoken Shunpō*, no. 576 (June 1959): 4.

51. Nihon Ishikai Sōritsu Gojusshūnen Kinen Jigyō Suishin Iinkai, *Nihon Ishikai Sōritsu Kinenshi*, 72.

52. Nihon Ishikai Sōritsu Gojusshūnen Kinen Jigyō Suishin Iinkai, *Nihon Ishikai Sōritsu Kinenshi*, 72.

53. Takemi, *Jitsuroku Nihon Ishikai*, 98.

54. Hido Shuichi, "Itansha Takemi Tarō" (A heretic, Tarō Takemi), *Chūōkōron* 79, no. 7 (July 1964): 254.

55. Arioka, *Sengo Iryō no Gojūnen*, 194–95.

56. Nihon Ishikai Sōritsu Gojusshūnen Kinen Jigyō Suishin Iinkai, *Nihon Ishikai Sōritsu Kinenshi*, 74.

57. Arioka, *Sengo Iryō no Gojūnen*, 201–2; Miwa Kazuo, *Mōi Takemi Tarō* (The fighting doctor, Tarō Takemi) (Tokyo: Tokuma Shoten, 1995), 250.

58. Takemi, *Jitsuroku Nihon Ishikai*, 102.

59. Iwai Hirokata, "Takemi Taisei no 25nen to Korekara no Iryō" (Twenty years of the Takemi regime and the future of medicine), in *Takemi Tarō no Hito to Gakumon* (Tarō Takemi as a person and academician), ed. Takemi Kinen Seizonkagaku Kenkyūkikin Takemi Tarō Kinen Ronbun Henshūiinkai (Tokyo: Maruzen, 1989), 373.

60. Takata Kioaki, *Nadao Hirokichi* (Hiroshima: Chūgoku Shinbunsha, 1991), 103.

61. Hido, "Itansha Takemi Tarō," 255.

62. Miwa, *Mōi Takemi Tarō*, 252.

63. Miwa, *Mōi Takemi Tarō*, 137.

64. Takemi, *Jitsuroku Nihon Ishikai*, 119; Sugimura Hisahide, *Fūun wo Yobu Otoko* (A dangerous man) (Tokyo: Jiji Tsūshinsha, 1977), 128.

65. Steslicke, "Political Life of the Japan Medical Association," 853.

66. Miwa, *Mōi Takemi Tarō*, 219.

67. Arioka, *Sengo Iryō no Gojūnen*, 174.

68. Arioka, *Sengo Iryō no Gojūnen*, 196, 199.

69. Nihon Ishikai Sōritsu Gojusshūnen Kinen Jigyō Suishin Iinkai, *Nihon Ishikai Sōritsu Kinenshi*, 23.

70. Nomura Taku, *Nihon Ishikai* (The Japan Medical Association) (Tokyo: Keisō Shobō, 1976), 61.

71. Arioka, *Sengo Iryō no Gojūnen*, 220.

72. As quoted in Arioka, *Sengo Iryō no Gojūnen*, 199.

73. Arioka, *Sengo Iryō no Gojūnen*, 199; Nihon Ishikai Sōritsu Gojusshūnen Kinen Jigyō Suishin Iinkai, *Nihon Ishikai Sōritsu Kinenshi*, 76.

74. Nihon Ishikai Sōritsu Gojusshūnen Kinen Jigyō Suishin Iinkai, *Nihon Ishikai Sōritsu Kinenshi*, 81; Arioka, *Sengo Iryō no Gojūnen*, 223–24.

75. Arioka, *Sengo Iryō no Gojūnen*, 217.

76. Taniguchi Yasaburō, "Shakaihoshō no Kankoku" (Recommendations for the social security system), *Shakaihoken Shunpō*, no. 271 (January 1951): 4.

77. Nihon Ishikai Sōritsu Gojusshūnen Kinen Jigyō Suishin Iinkai, *Nihon Ishikai Sōritsu Kinenshi*, 82; Arioka, *Sengo Iryō no Gojūnen*, 197.

78. Takata, *Nadao Hirokichi*, 104.

79. Yūki Yasuhiro, *Fukushishakai ni okeru Iryō to Seiji: Shinryōhōshū wo meguru Kankeidantai no Ugoki* (Medicine and politics in the welfare society: Activities of interest groups regarding the fee schedule) (Tokyo: Honnoizumisha, 2004).

80. Sugaya, *Nihon Iryō Seisakushi*, 301.

81. Tomonō Taketo, "Shakaihoshō Tōgō no Kinkyūsei" (An urgent need for social security integration), *Shakaihoken Shunpō*, no. 276 (February 1951): 4.

82. Steslicke, "Political Life of the Japan Medical Association," 853.

83. Arioka, *Sengo Iryō no Gojūnen*, 210.

84. Arioka, *Sengo Iryō no Gojūnen*, 225.

85. Yoshihara Kenji and Wada Masaru, *Nihon Iryō Hoken Seidoshi* (History of Japanese Health Insurance) (Tokyo: Tōyō Keizai Shinpōsha, 1999), 193.

86. Yoshihara and Wada, *Nihon Iryō Hoken Seidoshi*, 193.

87. Yoshihara and Wada, *Nihon Iryō Hoken Seidoshi*, 195.

88. Yoshihara and Wada, *Nihon Iryō Hoken Seidoshi*, 199–201.

7. MAKING UNIVERSAL HEALTH INSURANCE SURVIVE

1. The Ministry of Finance, "Japanese Public Finance Fact Sheet," https://www.mof .go.jp/english/budget/budget/fy2017/04.pdf, accessed January 9, 2019.

2. Paul Pierson, "The New Politics of the Welfare State," *World Politics* 48, no. 2 (January 1996): 143–44.

3. Pierson, "The New Politics of the Welfare State," 147.

4. Yūki Yasuhiro, *Iryō no Nedan: Shinryōhōshū to Politics* (The price of medicine: Politics and the fee schedule) (Tokyo: Iwanami Shoten, 2006), 22.

5. Takemi Tarō, *Jitsuroku Nihon Ishikai* (The true story of the Japan Medical Association) (Tokyo: Asahi Shuppan, 1983), 183–84.

6. Yūki Eiichi, *Futari no don Takemi Tarō Tanaka Kakuei to tomoni tatakatte* (Memoir of fighting with two bosses: Tarō Takemi and Kakuei Tanaka) (Tokyo: Keizai Ōraisha, 1985), 67–68; Yūki, *Iryō no Nedan*, 88–90.

7. Sugimura Hisahide, *Fūun wo Yobu Otoko* (A dangerous man) (Tokyo: Jiji Tsūshinsha, 1977), 96–97.

8. Takemi, *Jitsuroku Nihon Ishikai*, 183.

9. Takemi Tarō, *Ishindenshin* (Heart-to-heart communication about sincere medicine) (Tokyo: Jitsugyononihonsha, 1976), 55.

10. Takemi, *Jitsuroku Nihon Ishikai*, 192.

11. William E. Steslicke, *Doctors in Politics: The Political Life of the Japan Medical Association* (New York: Columbia University Press, 1973), 67.

12. Miwa Kazuo, *Mōi Takemi Tarō* (The fighting doctor, Tarō Takemi) (Tokyo: Tokuma Shoten, 1995), 214.

13. Arioka Jirō, *Sengo Iryō no Gojūnen: Iryōhokenseido no Butaiura* (Fifty years of postwar medical care: Behind the scenes of the health insurance system) (Tokyo: Nihon Iji Shinpōsha, 1997), 229.

14. Yūki, *Futari no Don Takemi Tarō Tanaka Kakuei to Tomoni Tatakatte*, 76–78.

15. Miwa, *Mōi Takemi Tarō*, 241.

16. Ikura Yasumasa, *Shindan Takemi Tarō* (Evaluating Tarō Takemi) (Tokyo: Sōshisha, 1979), 47.

17. Yūki, *Futari no Don Takemi Tarō*, 72.

18. Nomura Taku, *Nihon Ishikai* (The Japan Medical Association) (Tokyo: Keisō Shobō, 1976), 70–71.

19. Yūki, *Iryō no Nedan*, 90–91.

20. Yoshihara and Wada, *Nihon Iryōhoken Seidoshi*, 231.

21. Yoshihara and Wada, *Nihon Iryōhoken Seidoshi*, 232; Saguchi Takashi, Mori Mikio, Miura Fumio, *Rōjin ha Doko de Shinuka: Rōjinfukushi no Kadai* (Where the elderly die: Problems of welfare for the elderly) (Tokyo: Shiseido, 1970), 156. For the rise and fall of non-LDP governors and mayors, see Ichirō Okada, *Kakushin Jichitai: Nekkyō to Zasetsu ni Nani wo Manabuka* (Progressive municipalities: Lessons from the enthusiasm and setback) (Tokyo: Chūōkōron, 2016).

22. Kōseishō Gojūnenshi Henshū Iinkai, *Kōseishō Gojūnenshi*, 1360.

23. John Creighton Campbell, *How Policies Change: The Japanese Government and the Aging Society* (Princeton, NJ: Princeton University Press, 1992), 207.

24. Margarita Esteves-Abe, "Negotiating Welfare Reforms: Actors and Institutions in the Japanese Welfare State," in *Restructuring the Welfare State: Political Institutions and Policy Change*, ed. Bo Rothstein and Sven Steinmo (New York: Palgrave/Macmillan, 2002), 164.

25. Saguchi, Mori, and Miura, *Rōjin ha Doko de Shinuka*, 147–49.

26. Yoshihara and Wada, *Nihon Iryōhoken Seidoshi*, 232–35.

27. Shinkawa Toshimitsu, *Nihongata Fukushi no Seijikeizaigaku* (Political economy of Japanese-style welfare) (Tokyo: San'ichi Shobō, 1993), 107–9.

28. Kōseishō Gojūnenshi Henshū Iinkai, *Kōseishō Gojūnenshi*, 1363.

29. Margarita Esteves-Abe, *Welfare and Capitalism in Postwar Japan* (New York: Cambridge University Press, 2008), 165.

30. Yoshihara and Wada, *Nihon Iryōhoken Seidoshi*, 292.

31. Shinkawa, *Nihongata Fukushi no Seijikeizaigaku*, 131–32.

32. Arioka, *Sengo Iryō no Gojūnen*, 82.

33. "Nichibyō Tachiba wo Futatabi Senmei" (The Japan Hospital Association made its position clear), *Shakaihoken Shunpō*, no. 518 (November 1957): 17.

34. Takemi Tarō, *Chōshinki* (Diary of listening to the heart) (Tokyo: Jitsugyo no Nihon Sha, 1978), 233.

35. Arioka, *Sengo Iryō no Gojūnen*, 82.

36. Hamada Masato, *Kuromaku Kenkyū 3* (Study of backroom bosses, vol. 3) (Tokyo: Sinkokuminsha, 1979), 33, 87.

37. Takemi, *Jitsuroku Nihon Ishikai*, 203; Mizuno Hajime, *Daremo Kakanakatta Nihon Ishikai* (The unknown JMA) (Tokyo: Sōshisha, 2003), 88.

38. Miwa, *Mōi Takemi Tarō*, 338.

39. Miwa, *Mōi Takemi Tarō*, 338.

40. Iwai Hirokata, "Takemi Taisei no 25nen to Korekara no Iryō" (Twenty years of the Takemi regime and the future of medicine), in Takemi Kinen Seizonkagaku Kenkyūkikin Takemi Tarō Kinen Ronbun Henshūiinkai, *Takemi Tarō no Hito to Gakumon* (Takemi as a person and academician) (Tokyo: Maruzen, 1989), 374.

41. Miwa, *Mōi Takemi Tarō*, 331.

42. Miwa, *Mōi Takemi Tarō*, 337.

43. Yūki, *Futari no Don Takemi Tarō Tanaka Kakuei to Tomoni Tatakatte*, 81. There were four prefectures that decided not to follow the JMA's direction.

44. Yūki, *Futari no Don Takemi Tarō Tanaka Kakuei to Tomoni Tatakatte*, 81.

45. Yūki, *Futari no Don Takemi Tarō Tanaka Kakuei to Tomoni Tatakatte*, 61, 81.

46. Ministry of Health, Labor, and Welfare, "Ishi, Shikaishi, Yakuzaishi Tōkei" (Statistics of doctors, dentists, and pharmacists), https://www.mhlw.go.jp/toukei/list/33-20.html, accessed March 4, 2020.

47. Miwa, *Mōi Takemi Tarō*, 363–64.

48. Takemi, *Ishindenshin*, 22–23.

49. Reagan used this phrase as a campaign slogan. He also used it in his first inauguration address. UC Santa Barbara, American Presidency Project, "Inaugural Address," January 20, 1981, https://www.presidency.ucsb.edu/documents/inaugural-address-11, accessed December 31, 2019.

50. This was included in Thatcher's speech at the Conservative Party Conference in October 1975. Margaret Thatcher Foundation, "Speech to Conservative Party Conference," https://www.margaretthatcher.org/document/102777, accessed December 31, 2019.

51. Shinkawa, *Nihongata Fukushi no Seijikeizaigaku*, 158.

52. Shinkawa, *Nihongata Fukushi no Seijikeizaigaku*, 158.

53. Gerald L. Curtis, *The Japanese Way of Politics* (New York: Columbia University Press, 1988), 76–77.

54. "Iryōseisaku Hisutorī Zadankairoku" (Record of discussion meeting of medical policy history), *Iryō to Shakai* 27, no. 3 (2017): 300.

55. Yoshihara and Wada, *Nihon Iryōhoken Seidoshi*, 313.

56. Shinkawa, *Nihongata Fukushi no Seijikeizaigaku*, 183.

57. Mizuno, *Daremo Kakaranakatta Nihon Ishikai*, 146.

58. Yoshimura Jin, "Iryōhi wo Meguru Jōsei to Taiō ni Kansuru Watashi no Kangaekata" (The problem of medical costs and my ideas for a solution), *Shakaihoken Shunpō*, no. 1424 (March 1983): 12–14.

59. Yoshimura, "Iryōhi wo Meguru Jōsei to Taiō ni Kansuru Watashi no Kangaekata," 12.

60. Ikegami Naoki and John Campbell, *Nihon no Iryō: Tōsei to Baransu Kankaku* (Health care in Japan: Control and sense of balance) (Tokyo: Chūkō Shinsho, 1996), 138.

61. "Iryōseisaku Hisutorī Zadankairoku," 305.

62. "Iryōseisaku Hisutorī Zadankairoku," 300.

63. Pierson, "New Politics of the Welfare State," 147.

64. "Iryōseisaku Hisutorī Zadankairoku," 338.

65. Pierson, "New Politics of the Welfare State," 147.

66. Steslicke, *Doctors in Politics*, 11–12.

67. Mizuno, *Daremo Kakanakatta Nihon Ishikai*, 144.

68. Mizuno, *Daremo Kakanakatta Nihon Ishikai*, 144–45.

69. Mizuno, *Daremo Kakanakatta Nihon Ishikai*, 152.

70. Mizuno, *Daremo Kakanakatta Nihon Ishikai*, 163–68.

71. Mizuno, *Daremo Kakanakatta Nihon Ishikai*, 153–58.

72. Arioka, *Sengo Iryō no Gojūnen*, 397.

8. JAPANESE HEALTH CARE IN THE GLOBALIZATION ERA

1. Eric Schickler, *Disjointed Pluralism: Institutional Innovation and the Development of the US Congress* (Princeton, NJ: Princeton University Press, 2001).

2. Frances McCall Rosenbluth and Michael F. Thies, *Japan Transformed: Political Change and Economic Restructuring* (Princeton, NJ: Princeton University Press, 2010), 147; Jeff Kingston, "Demographic Dilemmas, Women and Immigration," in *Critical Issues in Contemporary Japan*, ed. Jeff Kingston (London: Routledge, 2014), 192–93.

3. Ōmori Wataru, Yamasaki Shirō, Katori Teruyiki, Inagawa Takenobu, et al., *Kaigo Hoken Seidoshi: Kihon Kōsō kara Hō Sekō made* (The history of the Long-Term Care Act: From the initial plan to policy implementation) (Tokyo: Tōyō Keizai Shinpōsha, 2019), 29; Ikegami Naoki, *Nihon no Iryō to Kaigo* (Japan's health and long-term care system) (Tokyo: Nihon Keizai Shimbun Shuppansha, 2017), 118.

4. The six other parties were the Japan New Party (Nihon Shintō), the New Party Sakigake (Shintō Sakigake), the Japan Renewal Party (Shinseitō), the Japan Socialist Party (Nihonshakaitō), New Komeito (Shin Kōmeitō), and the Socialist Democratic Federation (Shakaiminshurengō).

5. The Ministry of Foreign Affairs, "Dai 129kai Kokkai ni okeru Hosokawa Naikaku Sōridaijin Shisei Houshin Enzetsu" (Administrative policy speech of Prime Minister Hosokawa in the 129th Diet), https://www.mofa.go.jp/mofaj/gaiko/bluebook/1995_1/h07-shiryou-1-1.htm#a1, accessed January 10, 2020.

6. Yoshihara Kenji and Wada Masaru, *Nihon Iryō Hoken Seidoshi* (History of Japanese health insurance) (Tokyo: Tōyō Keizai Shinpōsha, 1999), 471. For details of the social security reforms, see Mari Ōsawa, *Social Security in Contemporary Japan* (New York: Routledge, 2011).

7. Ōmori et al., *Kaigo Hoken Seidoshi*, 87.

8. The Advisory Council on Social Security, "Shakaihoshō no Saikōchiku (Kankoku): Anshin shite Kuraseru 21 Seiki no Shakai wo Mezashite" (Recommendations for reconstruction of the social security system: A twentieth-first century society where needs are met), http://www.ipss.go.jp/publication/j/shiryou/no.13/data/shiryou/souron/21.pdf, accessed October 16, 2019.

9. Yoshihara and Wada, *Nihon Iryōhoken Seidoshi*, 490; Ōmori Wataru et al., *Kaigo Hoken Seidoshi*, 49.

10. Yoshihara and Wada, *Nihon Iryōhoken Seidoshi*, 472.

11. "Kaigo Hoken Monogatari (Dai 39 Wa): 'Kaigo no Shakaika and Ichimannin Shimin Iinkai' Tōjō" (The history of long-term care: The beginning of socialized long-term care and the 10,000 Citizens Committee), *Kaigohoken Jōhō* (June 2007): 62–65.

12. Ōmori Wataru et al., *Kaigo Hoken Seidoshi*, 400–34.

13. Ryū Masato, "1980nendai Ikō no Iryōkyōkyū Seidokaikaku no Tenkai: Seisaku Gakushūron no Shiten kara" (The development of the medical-provider system after the 1980s: From a policy-learning perspective)," *Nenpō Seijigaku* 66, no. 1 (June 2015): 229.

14. National Diet Library, "Administrative Speech and General Policy Speech," http://kokkai.ndl.go.jp/SENTAKU/syugiin/139/0001/13912130001006a.html, accessed October 11, 2019.

15. Yoshihara and Wada, *Nihon Iryōhoken Seidoshi*, 474, 482.

16. Yoshihara and Wada, *Nihon Iryōhoken Seidoshi*, 466.

17. Yoshihara and Wada, *Nihon Iryōhoken Seidoshi*, 508.

18. The Ministry of Health, Labor, and Welfare, "Kōseirōdōshō no Hajimari" (The establishment of the Ministry of Health, Labor, and Welfare), https://www.mhlw.go.jp/kouseiroudoushou/shigoto/dl/p03.pdf, accessed November 5, 2019.

19. Koizumi served as the minister of health and welfare three times. The first and second times were under the Takeshita and Uno administrations in 1988 and 1989. Koizumi was appointed again by Hashimoto Ryutarō in November 1996.

20. The head of the LDP is decided by the votes of the Diet members, registered party members, the members of the Liberal National Congress (Jiyū Kokumin Kaigi), and members of the People's Political Association (Kokumin Seiji Kyōkai).

21. He ran in the upper house election in 2004 as an active cabinet member and won.

22. For the Koizumi administration reforms and their policymaking process, see Aurelia George Mulgan, *Japan's Failed Revolution: Koizumi and the Politics of Economic Reform* (Canberra: Asia Pacific Press, 2002).

23. Yu Uchiyama, *Koizumi and Japanese Politics: Reform Strategies and Leadership Style* (New York: Routledge, 2010), 57–58.

24. Mizuno Hajime, *Daremo Kakanakatta Nihon Ishikai* (The Unknown JMA) (Tokyo: Sōshisha, 2003), 211.

25. Yūki Yasuhiro, *Iryō no Nedan: Shinryōhōshū to Politics* (The price of medicine: Politics and the fee schedule) (Tokyo: Iwanami Shoten, 2006), 108.

26. Niki Ryū, "Ko Uematsu Haruo Moto Nihonishikaichō ga Shudō shita 2004nen no Kongōshinryō Zenmen Kaikin Soshi no Rekishiteki Igi" (The significance of the movement led by the late JMA president Uematsu Haruo opposing the removal of the ban on mixed treatments), *Bunkaren Jōhō*, no. 483 (June 2018): 16–23.

27. Yoshioka Seiko, "Kōki Kōreisha Iryōseido wo Meguru Keii to Minaoshi no Dōkō (The formative and implementation process of the Advanced Elderly Medical Service System)," *Rippō to Chōsa*, no. 288 (January 2009): 81.

28. Kobayashi Shigetaka and Nishikawa Yoshiaki, "Kōki Kōreisha Iryōseido no Konran wo Megutte: Kojin to Setai no Shiten kara Kenshō" (Confusion in the new health-care

system for elderly people in Japan: Examining the issue from a personal and household perspective), *Nagoya Bunri Daigaku Kiyō* 9 (2009): 18.

29. Niki Ryū, "Koizumi/Abe Seiken no Iryōkaikaku: Shinjiyūshugitekikaikaku no Tōjō to Zasetsu" (Medical reforms in the Koizumi and Abe administrations: The rise and fall of neoliberal reform), *Shakaiseisaku* 1, no. 2 (April 2009): 15.

30. Niki, "Koizumi/Abe Seiken no Iryōkaikaku," 14.

31. See, e.g., "Nara no Ninpu ga Shibō, Jūkyū no Byōin ga Tensō Kyohi, Rokujikan Hōchi" (A pregnant woman died, nineteen hospitals rejected the patient, she was left alone for six hours), *Asahi Shimbun* (October 17, 2006), http://www.asahi.com/special /obstetrician/OSK200610170023.html, accessed January 13, 2020.

32. Naoki Ikegami, ed., *Universal Health Coverage for Inclusive and Sustainable Development: Lessons from Japan* (Washington, DC: World Bank Group, 2014), 24.

33. The New Frontier Party dissolved in 1997. Some former New Frontier Party Diet members joined the DPJ in 1998.

34. Niki Ryū, "Nihon no Seikenkōtai to Minshutō no Iryōseisaku" (The change of government in Japan and the DPJ's medical policy), *Nihon Iji Shinpō*, no. 4480 (March 6, 2010): 105–9.

35. Democratic Party of Japan, "Minshutō no Seiken Seisaku Manifesto 2009" (The DPJ's Policy Plan Manifesto 2009), http://archive.dpj.or.jp/special/manifesto2009/pdf /manifesto_2009.pdf, accessed January 31, 2020.

36. "Kōki Kōreisha Iryō no Hokenryō Shisan: Jittai wa Kōsotoku Setai hodo Futan Karuku" (Estimate of the premium for the Advanced Elderly Medical Service System: Rich families have less burden), *Tokyo Shimbun*, July 6, 2008.

37. "Kokiiryō Saiteihoshōnenkin Tanaage: Minshutō Shakaihoshō de Jōho" (Putting the issue of the Advanced Elderly Medical Service System and the minimum guaranteed pension into cold storage: The DPJ compromised in the area of social security), *Asahi Shimbun*, June 12, 2012, http://www.asahi.com/special/minshu/TKY201206110607.html, accessed January 25, 2020.

38. As quoted in Niki, "Koizumi/Abe Seiken no Iryōkaikaku," 16.

39. Niki, "Koizumi/Abe Seiken no Iryōkaikaku," 16.

40. "Tōkei Fusei: Seiken Taiō 'Futekisetsu' 61% Asahi Shimbun Yoronchōsa" (Statistical cheating: The government's response was "inappropriate" according to 61% in *Asahi Shimbun* poll), *Asahi Shimbun*, February 18, 2019, https://digital.asahi.com/articles /ASM2L3K6WM2LUZPS001.html, accessed January 31, 2020.

41. Mizuno, *Daremo Kakanakatta Nihon Ishikai*, 190.

42. Mizuno, *Daremo Kakanakatta Nihon Ishikai*, 190.

43. As quoted in Mizuno, *Daremo Kakanakatta Nihon Ishikai*, 194.

44. Mizuno, *Daremo Kakanakatta Nihon Ishikai*, 194.

45. Mizuno, *Daremo Kakanakatta Nihon Ishikai*, 195–96.

46. Japan Medical Association Research Institute, "About the JMARI," http://www .jmari.med.or.jp/english/about_E.html, accessed October 23, 2019.

47. Mizuno, *Daremo Kakanakatta Nihon Ishikai*, 196–99.

48. Japan Medical Association, "Tusboi Kaichō '2015nen Iryō no Gurando Dezain' wo Kataru" (President Tsuboi talks about the "Grand Design of Medicine for 2015"), *Nichii News*, no. 936 (September 2000), http://www.med.or.jp/nichinews/n120905a.html, accessed October 23, 2019.

49. Tsuboi Eitaka, *Waga Iryōka Kumei Ron* (The theory behind my medical revolution) (Tokyo: Tōyō Keizai Shinpōsha, 2001).

50. Mizuno, *Daremo Kakanakatta Nihon Ishikai*, 208.

51. Japan Medical Association, "Tusboi Kaichō '2015nen Iryō no Gurando Dezain' wo Kataru."

52. Mizuno, *Daremo Kakanakatta Nihon Ishikai*, 206–7.

53. Mizuno, *Daremo Kakanakatta Nihon Ishikai*, 211–12.

54. Japan Medical Association, "Tsuboi Kaichō Yonsen Hatasu," *Nichii News*, no. 974 (April 2002), http://www.med.or.jp/nichinews/n140405a.html, accessed June 9, 2020.

55. OECD, "Gender equality: Women make up most of the health sector workers but they are under-represented in high-skilled jobs," https://www.oecd.org/gender/data /women-make-up-most-of-the-health-sector-workers-but-they-are-under-represented -in-high-skilled-jobs.htm, accessed June 9, 2020.

56. Yūki, *Iryō no Nedan*, 122–23.

57. Yūki, *Iryō no Nedan*, 162–67.

58. Japan Medical Association, "Iryō ni okeru Kisei Seido Kaikaku ni taisuru Nihonishikai no Kenkai: TPP Kōshō Sanka Hyōmei ni Kanren shite" (The JMA's opinion on regulatory reform of medical care: Regarding participation in the TPP negotiations), November 30, 2011, http://dl.med.or.jp/dl–med/nichikara/tpp/TPP_20111130_word.pdf, accessed January 30, 2020.

59. Yokota Kumiko, "Ishikai wa Aturyokudantai dewanaku 'Inochi to Kenkō wo Azukaru Dantai, Kaichō ga Hanron" (The Japan Medical Association is not a lobbying group but an organization that is responsible for people's health and lives), *Diamond Online* (January 31, 2019), https://diamond.jp/articles/-/192422, accessed October 12, 2019.

60. Japan Medical Association Research Institute, "Nihon no Iryō no Gurando Dezain: Gaiyō Ban" (Grand Design of Medicine of Japan for 2030: Summary version), http://dl.med.or.jp/dl–med/teireikaiken/20190327_1.pdf, accessed November 22, 2019.

61. In the upper house, 124 out of 248 members were elected. Fifty were elected to the House of Councillors' proportional district. The district is the whole nation. Each party makes a candidate list, and the party is given seats depending on the number of votes. Parties' lists usually feature representatives of supporter groups and well-known people, such as actors.

62. "San'insen Shūhyōteika, Ishikai ni Kikikan Shinryōhōshūkaitei he 'Eikyōryoku Sagaru" (The upper house election, decreasing power to gain votes, concern about reduced influence on the fee-negotiation process), *Tokyo Shimbun*, July 28, 2019, https:// www.tokyo-np.co.jp/article/19983, accessed October 12, 2019.

63. Johns Hopkins University, "Mortality Analysis," https://coronavirus.jhu.edu/data /mortality, accessed June 11, 2020.

64. "Shingata Korona Uirusu Kansenshō Taisaku Senmonka Kaigi no Kaisai nitsuite" (To hold the Novel Coronavirus Expert Panel), https://www.cas.go.jp/jp/influenza /senmonka_konkyo.pdf, accessed June 25, 2020.

65. Ryusei Takahashi, "It's Official: Tokyo Olympics Delayed until 2021 Due to Coronavirus," *Japan Times*, https://www.japantimes.co.jp/sports/2020/03/24/olympics/official -coronavirus-outbreak-fast-tracks-decision-postpone-tokyo-2020/#.XvQBjPJUvSI, accessed June 20, 2020.

66. Tomoya Saito, "The Secret of Japan's Success in Combating COVID-19," *Japan Times*, https://www.japantimes.co.jp/opinion/2020/06/02/commentary/japan-commentary /secret-japans-success-combating-covid-19/, accessed June 20, 2020.

67. "'Taigan no Kaji to . . .' Ikasarenakatta Kyōkun" (Somebody else's problem: Never learned from lessons in the past), *Asahi Shimbun*, June 23, 2020, https://digital.asahi.com /articles/ASN6Q7WBKN6MULBJ006.html, accessed June 25, 2020.

68. Konno Harutaka, "Shingata Korona Taiō: Kōrōshō no 53% ga 'Hiseiki Kōmuin' no Genjitsu" (Response to Novel Coronavirus: The reality is that 53% of the MHLW officials are irregular employees), *Yahoo Japan News*, https://news.yahoo.co.jp/byline /konnoharuki/20200227-00164904/, accessed June 25, 2020.

69. "Yokokura Kaichō 'Iryō Kikiteki Jōkyō Sengen' wo Happyō" (President Yokokura presented "the state of medical emergency"), *Nichii News* 1407, April 20, 2020, https://www.med.or.jp/nichiionline/paper/pdf/n1407.pdf, accessed April 25, 2020.

70. Tokyo Medical Association, "Tokyo Ishikai karano Iryo Kinkyū Jitai Sengen" (Declaration of the state of medical emergency from the Tokyo Medical Association), https://www.tokyo.med.or.jp/wp-content/uploads/press_conference/application/pdf/20200406-1.pdf, accessed April 15, 2020.

71. Koizumi Tomoyo, "Shiroi Kyotō no Nozomanu Senkyo," *NHK Seiji Magajin*, https://www.nhk.or.jp/politics/articles/feature/40579.html, accessed February 7, 2021.

72. Hasegawa Manabu, "Korona Jūdai Kyokumen de 'Onrrain Shinryō' ni Mōhantai: Nihon Ishikai no Zureta Ninshiki" (The fierce opposition to online diagnostics in a critical corona situation: The JMA's wrong understanding), *Gendai Bijinesu*, https://gendai.ismedia.jp/articles/-/71546, accessed June 25, 2020.

73. "The Greeting of the Japan Medical Association," Japan Medical Association, https://www.med.or.jp/jma/about/chairman.html, accessed February 8, 2021.

CONCLUSION

1. John C. Campbell and Naoki Ikegami, *The Art of Balance in Health Policy: Maintaining Japan's Low-Cost, Egalitarian System* (New York: Cambridge University Press, 1998).

2. Ogasawara Yasuhi, "Naze Jimintō Seijika wa Shitugen wo Kurikaesunoka? 'Kodomo wo Uman Yatsuga Warui' Hatsugen no Kongenteki Haikci" (Why do LDP politicians repeat their improper remarks? The fundamental background of the statement that 'Women who don't give birth are incompetent'), *HuffPost*, March 4, 2019, https://www.huffingtonpost.jp/entry/ogasawara0304_jp_5c7cb648e4b0e1f776537ddb, accessed December 2, 2019.

3. "'Josei wa kodomo wo Umu Kikai' Yanagisawa Kōrōshō Shōshika Meguri Hatsugen" ("Women are birth machines": The minister of health, labor, and welfare Yanagisawa's remarks on the declining birth rate), *Asahi Shimbun*, January 28, 2007, http://www.asahi.com/special/060926/OSK200701270070.html, accessed December 2, 2019.

4. "'Josei wa kodomo wo Umu Kikai' Yanagisawa Kōrōshō Shōshika Meguri Hatsugen."

5. Organisation for Economic Co-operation and Development, OECD.stat, "International Migration Database," https://stats.oecd.org/Index.aspx?DataSetCode=MIG, accessed January 15, 2020.

Index

Figures, notes, and tables are indicated by f, n, and t, respectively, following the page numbers.